Sept

Thinking of you both as we enjoy these
beautiful countrysides. London, Whales, &
Scotland will be remembered for a while.

Love. Mom & Dad

THE GUINNESS GUIDE TO

SAILING

THE GUINNESS GUIDE TO

SAILING

Peter Johnson

Editor: Alex Reid
Design and layout: Ian Wileman

©**Peter Johnson and Guinness Superlatives Ltd 1981**

Published in Great Britain by
Guinness Superlatives Ltd
2 Cecil Court, London Road
Enfield, Middlesex EN2 6DJ

'Guinness' is a registered trade mark of Guinness Superlatives Ltd

British Library Cataloguing in Publication Data:

Johnson, Peter
Guinness guide to sailing
1. Sailing
I. Title
797.1'24   GV811

ISBN 0–85112–216–7

Typeset, printed and bound in Great Britain by
Bemrose Specialist Print, Derby

Contents

Acknowledgements

Most of Part I was contributed by Chris Eyre who has for a number of years written about and also designed racing dinghies. He now sails an international canoe, the class being the oldest development one in the world. For board sailing, assistance was given by David Eberlin. Line drawings are all by Peter A. G. Milne, one of the foremost technical illustrators of sailing subjects.

All colour photographs, unless otherwise stated, are by Alastair Black: just a few come from elsewhere and are credited below. Black and white photographs are mainly by Chris Eyre, Colin Jarman, Barry Pickthall and the author. They are all credited below except for those taken by the author.

Australian Sailing 13, 33, 34, Beken of Cowes 11, Bob Bond 29, T. Bees 31, D. Butler 25, Champion Photos 22, Vic Croft 37, Frank Dye 20, Chris Eyre 16, 19, 21, 30, 43, 46, D. Forster 223(7), T. Gore 26, T. Hoare 19, Colin Jarman 87, 104, 116, 125, P. Kay 32, Ben Kocivar 38, William Payne 24, 27, 79 (lower), 91, Mike Peyton 146 (3, 4), Barry Pickthall 74, 82, 84, 85, 86, 88, 103, 106, 164, 192, 214(1), 216, Eileen Ramsay 45, Stanley Rosenfeld 41, Stowe 15, S. Tapp 21, H. Turner 41, Nicholas Wood 16.

Introduction

For thousands of years men and women had to sail if they wanted to cross the sea. Today nobody has to use wind to move across rivers, seas and oceans, but thousands are fascinated by this means of propulsion. They spend hours, days, or even many weeks, in sailing.

In the seventeenth century, the attractive pastime was discovered of sailing and sometimes racing, in what became known as a yacht and so crossing the water became not merely an unpleasant necessity. In the late twentieth century there is every variation of leisure sailing developed, but it conveniently splits into three main categories and this book is so divided.

Inshore racing comprises those courses which are completed in a few hours round marks within sight of the shore. The open sailing dinghy is the most popular vehicle for this. With a crew of two or three, it gives an exciting ride, planing because of its light weight. Modern devices like the trapeze give additional speed and appeal. Self bailers throw out the water, as fast as it comes in and a hundred other gadgets, changing inventively every year, enable sophisticated sailing to be brought from home and launched from a trailer.

In the inshore category too come open keel boats. The term is used for ballasted vessels which cannot capsize, but are not designed for extensive passages. All over the world there are such classes moored in an estuary or port, ready for their owners to go racing: particular classes of boat often last for many years. Close to the shore are found sailing trials and experiments and in particular these pages mention the attempts on the world sailing speed record. It is always a low speed in absolute terms, but the quest produces some shapes quite unlike those of other boats and tells much about the behaviour of craft in the interface (so scientists would have it) between air and water. The biggest inshore boats which are raced are 12-metre class yachts and these are built solely to compete in the America's Cup, which since 1851 has remained, despite numerous challenges and attempts, firmly in American hands. At the other end of the scale is the new game of board sailing, only known since 1967.

Quite different from all this activity is cruising under sail. The cruising yacht may be a week-end cottage afloat, or someone's dream of a voyage around the world. She is a holiday, an escape into complete relaxation, an intense hobby, a life of a different sort. Cruisers can be quite individual in shape and purpose, not beholden to any rating rule or racing restriction. Yet there are many skills and aspects common to all cruising people and these form the contents of the chapters of this most popular part of sailing. World wide charter has made cruising in previously exotic waters a possibility for many.

Offshore racing is the aggressive end of sailing yacht development. Only existing in its present form for about sixty years, it has progressed to the stage where yachts of between forty and seventy feet can actually race around the world, through several oceans including the Roaring Forties, with certainty. Ocean racing over such distances and across narrower seas has had a profound and beneficial effect on the design and construction of small craft under sail. Modern materials, especially plastics and alloys, have been important, but without the spur of racing they would never have been tried out in yachts. Ocean racing multihulls sail (or is it fly?) at amazing speed in the open ocean, sometimes manned by only one or two persons.

Most aspects of sailing are international. Classes and organizations, design and building methods are not confined to national characteristics. After all the environment at sea is the same whatever nationality is the boat. For the landsman the oceans separate the countries of the world, but to a seaman the water is a link between the nations.

Part One

Inshore racing and sailing

'A dinghy mast costs no more than a large cutter's cross tree and in the event of the mast falling down there is no danger to life and limb on a dinghy as there is with a larger vessel. Because of this great difference, the small boat designer is generally in advance of the designer of large vessels; not because his ideas are more original, but because he can carry them out so easily and cheaply....'

Uffa Fox in *Sailing, Seamanship and Yacht Construction* (1934)

I

Small boat sailing

Many sailors first experience yacht racing as a crew in a friend's dinghy, small catamaran or open keelboat; in the next few chapters we will look at this important section of the sport, its features, origins, development, boat types, construction, tuning and what it takes to be a winner.

The widely varying hull and rig forms used nowadays indicate small boat sailing's random origins and relatively uncontrolled development. Dinghy racing started up in different parts of the world in a similar way; in Britain, various yacht clubs developed their own dinghy designs using the simple concept of adding centre-board, rudder and sails to ordinary rowing dinghies; the very best of the early designs and one of the first purpose built craft was developed as a result of the West of England Conference in the early years of this century. In 1927 it was the first dinghy to be recognized by the Yacht Racing Association and subsequently was the first dinghy to be adopted by the International Yacht Racing Union (IYRU) when it was formed; we know its descendants today as International Fourteens. Forty years before the birth of the Fourteen, the Royal Canoe Club introduced sails on some of their craft; this was the origin of the International Canoe class, present day editions of which are the fastest single-handed dinghies in the world.

The Americans and the Australians developed theirs in a similar fashion, although the Australians treated racing as a pretty ruthless business even in the early days; this probably had a lot to do with their habit of gambling on anything that moves.

The twin hulled catamarans were introduced to modern sailing in the fifties as a direct derivation of the ancient craft that south sea islanders have used for water transport from

time immemorial. The catamaran designs of today are the fastest sailing craft of all; Tim Coleman's *Crossbow*, holder of the world sailing speed record is a catamaran with one of its hulls, the windward one, offset slightly behind the

Uffa Fox's design *Avenger*, **a radical Fourteen Foot International in 1928 is ancestor to today's planing dinghies**

other; the Tornado catamaran is the fastest of all the Olympic sailing classes.

Classes of small, open keelboats came about as a gradual evolution from sail driven fishing craft and the enormous, professionally crewed yachts of the nineteenth century which were owned by the nobility and treated by them in much the same manner as they treated their race horses. They usually did not even bother to leave the warmth of the club house or steam yacht from where they could watch and wager on the races in comfort. As the smaller boats developed, professional crews disappeared and the owners became the helmsmen. Most modern classes, with the exception of the Tempest which has a trapeze, were conceived as sedate racing types with fixed, weighted keels to make them inherently more stable than dinghies. The keen racing classes, however, do use the righting power of their crew weight as much as they are allowed by class rules; usually this amounts to sitting out with the aid of toe straps.

During the fifties the sport of small boat sailing exploded on an international scale and by the mid sixties possibly as many as a million

Modern Fourteen Foot International: note there is no decking at all

people throughout the world were racing every weekend. Responsibility for this period of rapid growth can be claimed by the original sponsors of the various classes, initially yachting magazines and subsequently, in some instances, the national press. Such notable boats as the Snipe, Cadet, GP14 and Heron fall into the first category, the Enterprise and the Mirror into the latter. In addition, there were several excellent classes that blossomed with only a little encouragement from yachting authorities and the media including the 505, Fireball, 420 and OK.

Although some people learn their sailing in small boats with the intention of graduating to offshore racing or offshore cruising, the vast majority are satisfied with the variety and enjoyment offered by dinghies, catamarans and open keelboats; there are designs to suit beginner or expert, child or adult, lightweight or heavyweight, poor or wealthy, weightlifter or acrobat, Sunday cruiser or hot rod racer.

What are the advantages of small craft over their bigger offshore relatives? The most

Early Australian Eighteen Foot Skiff

obvious one is the big saving in costs; whilst sailing cannot, by any stretch of the imagination, be considered a cheap sport, dinghies are relatively inexpensive in purchase price, running expenses, maintenance, parking and transportation. It is only when one considers some of the Olympic classes that any overlap occurs between small craft prices and those of the smallest offshore keelboats.

Other plusses of small boat racing include the fact that the sensation of speed and excitement exceeds anything an offshore craft can offer; it is genuinely less dangerous if attended by the normal rescue facilities; it takes place normally over a predictable time period so you know when to arrange to meet friends in the bar, you may get wet and cold doing it but hot showers and dry clothes are always close at hand. Add to these the ease of launching, hauling out and transportation and one has an impressive array of reasons for taking up small craft racing and staying committed to it for good.

Racing is organized by all sailing clubs every summer week-end and by many in the

Modern Eighteen Foot Skiff

winter as well; normally speaking, a separate race is run for any class that turns out consistently in large enough numbers. Most follow a policy of allowing new classes to race initially in mixed class handicap races until they generate a sufficient following to gain club class status. Conversely, a club class will be demoted to handicap races if turnouts drop below an acceptable level. In an attempt to maintain the strength of recognized classes, clubs often restrict the size of handicap fleets and pressure new members to buy one of a small number of alternative types.

All classes of any importance have fixture lists of open events, held usually by clubs which have a fleet of the same class. Racing crews, with an eye towards winning a championship, expend a tremendous amount of effort and time attending national and international events in order to learn from expert opposition and to gauge their own standards against it. Championships, particularly international ones, are usually a lot of fun for the participants, combining best quality racing with a hectic social programme.

13

2

Sailing dinghies

The right choice of dinghy depends upon all sorts of criteria and ultimately, what you want out of the sport. Balancing the competitive environment offered by one class against your needs in the areas of boat behaviour and performance can be one of the main alternatives. For instance, the standard of competition in the UK Enterprise fleet is very high but you may not be keen on the boat's relatively sluggish behaviour and its lack of physical and technical challenge. Therefore, in spite of the lack of a similar depth of quality competition in the Hornet class, you might choose it for its lively performance.

Another very important influence on choice is whether you can find a local club which, at best, has an active fleet of your favoured class or, at worst, will allow it to compete in mixed class handicap races. You can buy a 'one-design' where all the boats in the class are as near identical as possible or you might decide on one of the international or national restricted classes where you can decide on hull shape, layout and sail plan within limitations, laid down by class rules. But be warned, many so called one-design classes have tolerances on hull shape and freedoms in layout and rig that make the choice of builder, mast maker and sailmaker critical when attempting to assemble a winning boat.

In order to avoid describing every one of the numerous dinghy classes that can be found in small or even reasonably large numbers in one country alone, only those classes with international distribution or those that epitomize the ultimate in design theory and performance are included in this book.

'Easy to sail' and children's classes

Everyone has to start somewhere and there are some particularly good beginner's boats available: the unknowledgeable can be caught out by a slick advertising line, so it is best to take expert advice or stick to tried and tested designs.

Optimist
LENGTH 7ft 7in (2·31m).
HULL 77lb (35kg).
SAIL AREA Main 35ft² (3·25m²).

This is the very best boat for a small child, providing single-handed sailing with stability and good performance in spite of its tiny length and sail area. It is not uncommon to see large fleets of these helmed by children between the age of six and twelve. Around 100 000 of them are spread to all the continents of the world; their main strongholds in spite of having originated in the USA are to be found in Northern and Western Europe, particularly Scandinavia.

The top racing versions of the Optimist are remarkably sophisticated, using advanced construction techniques and rigs. Many are still made of plywood although there are now ultra-strong glass/foam sandwich editions available. To get the very best out of this sailing matchbox, considerable skill in the setting of the sail is needed because of the sprit-sail rig. In rough water the diminutive experts have to keep them at a steady angle of heel on all legs of a course, in order to reduce wetted area to a minimum. The only exception to this rule is downwind in heavy weather when they are held upright in order to promote a respectable, though rather bumbling planing performance.

Topper
LENGTH 11ft 2in (3·4m).
HULL 135lb (61·2kg).
SAIL AREA Main 56ft² (5·2m²).

The Topper is a neat and simple single-hander from the drawing board of Ian Proctor and produced, unusually for dinghies, in vacuum formed polypropylene. This is cheaper than glass-fibre so long as the fabulous expense of the highly specialized moulds is amortized on large scale production.

Much against expectations, the Topper has attracted some remarkably good helmsmen, most notable of these being John Caig, ex World Fireball Champion, who overcomes the disadvantage of his greater weight with his skill. The Topper does not really perform at its best with a crew weight of more than 140lb.

Cadet
LENGTH 10ft 7in (3·2m).
HULL 120lb (54·4kg).
SAIL AREA Main and jib 50ft² (4·65m²) plus spinnaker 49ft² (4·55m²).
This is the original junior racer for two youngsters; the class rules decree that only those of less than 18 years of age can race. She was designed in 1947 by Jack Holt for *Yachting World*, the magazine that spawned so many successful classes, with the idea of providing the complete learner's boat. It has main, jib and spinnaker and is no pushover to sail in a really heavy wind.

The class has produced some remarkable helmsmen, not least of all Rodney Pattisson, Olympic Gold Medallist in Flying Dutchmen. Even though it has passed its zenith in terms of popularity, the Cadet still retains an important position in international racing; large, active fleets can still be found in the UK, Northern Europe, Australia, South Africa and behind the Iron Curtain.

Modern racing Cadets are often still built by amateurs in marine ply, but commercial production is now mainly in glass fibre. Generous volumes of built-in buoyancy make the boat float high when capsized and come up virtually dry when righted. A slight disadvantage of this is that the boat has a tendency to turn turtle if the crew do not act quickly to prevent it, but since it can be recovered fairly easily from the inverted position, this should not be considered a great hazard.

Mirror dinghy
LENGTH 10ft 10in (3·3m).
HULL 135lb (61·2kg).
SAIL AREA Main and jib 69ft² (6·4m²) plus spinnaker 65ft² (6·0m²).
This is a classic, designed by Jack Holt in 1963. Despite its ugly appearance, it has a respectable performance and tolerates the fumblings of a beginner with the patience of a saint.

The Mirror is built in wood, usually by amateur builders from kits. The method of construction originally developed by International Moth builders, is dubbed the 'stitch and tape'

Optimist: the child's single-hander

The hull is made in two parts, deck and shell which are bonded together using a woven strip of copper and polypropylene; this is melted by passing an electrical current through it. The boat is crowned by an ultrasimple, unstayed mast with a sleeve-luff sail.

Originally developed to be built in Israel for export to the American market, over 20 000 have been sold since it was first introduced in 1976 and it continues to expand at the rate of 3 000 a year. The largest fleets are found in the UK and other countries of Northern Europe, but they can also be seen in virtually every continent of the world.

method; it involves the joining of pre-cut hull panels and bow and stern transoms with copper wire; the insides of the seams are then taped with glass fibre, the external protrusions of the copper stitches are trimmed flush and the outsides of the seams are similarly taped.

Three sails, main, jib and spinnaker, are set on its gunter rig; the advantage of this is that both mast and gaff can be stowed comfortably inside the boat, making transportation and storage that much easier.

Rejecting the possibility of becoming an officially recognized class of the International Yacht Racing Union, the Mirror continues to be administered by its original sponsors the London *Daily Mirror*. In spite or perhaps because of this, the Mirror is probably one of the most international of all dinghy classes with a total of 65 000 distributed in virtually every country of the western world. However, because of its rather sedate nature, keen racing fleets are really only found in about a dozen countries, the main one being the UK, but with important concentrations in Australia, South Africa and countries in Northern Europe.

Left: Cadet at Cadet Week, Burnham-on-Crouch
Below: International Europe—ideal for youths but possible for old 'uns who can still get under the boom

Racing dinghies for youths

There are several classes which are particularly suitable for teenagers, young adults and fit lightweights of any age. Some of them are designated by the International Yacht Racing Union for youth championships.

Europe
LENGTH 11ft (3·35m).
HULL 139lb (63kg).
SAIL AREA Main 80ft² (7·4m²).

The single-handed Europe was designed originally in the early sixties as one of many designs competing under the rules of the International Moth Class (see specialized dinghies). Designed by Alois Roland, a Belgian, it was sailed by his son Joel, who won the World Moth Championships in 1963. The success of any design in a development class, such as the Moth, is inevitably only a passing phase and by 1964 the brilliant Swiss Dunand and Frenchman Fauroux had eclipsed the Europe's performance with their designs. However, so many Europes were sailing by that time in France and Belgium, that they decided to form their own one design class. Since then, the boat has spread throughout Europe and subsequently, to other

continents. Nowadays, it can be found in Australasia and North America.

The Europe, as its pedigree might suggest, is a beautifully mannered boat with superb rough water characteristics; its single sail is set on an unstayed mast, normally of alloy. The boom is extraordinarily long, 9ft on a boat of only 11ft length overall. This teaches the helmsman to sail very upright on a reach to avoid catching the outer end of the boom in the water which, when it happens, often leads to a capsize.

The Europe performs best with a crew weight of between 100lb and 140lb; it does not suit a larger person or anyone who is not extremely supple as the boom is set only one foot above the deck.

Some of the Europe's more experienced sailors, particularly the French, are extraordinary characters; one Saint Jean, often stands on his head on the side deck whilst sailing to windward!

420

LENGTH 13ft 9in (4·2m).
HULL 220lb (99·8kg).
SAIL AREA Main and jib 110ft² (10·2m²) plus spinnaker 90ft² (8·36m²).

The 420 is designated by the IYRU as the double-hander for international youth competition. It is a good boat with very predictable behaviour and a quite startling performance in heavy winds. It is built in glass fibre to very strict one-design rules which not only control hull and rig shapes but also which fittings are allowed. As a result of this, the price of the 420

is kept down to a level which parents can afford.

Designed by Christian Maury, it is not surprising to find that the class is very popular in France, its country of origin. Healthy fleets also exist in other parts of Western Europe, North America, Australia and Israel. The 420 has been displaced a couple of times by the Laser II for use in World Youth Championships as a result of some pretty aggressive but generous marketing tactics by the Laser builders. The fact that thousands of parents have bought the 420 for their teenage children to compete in, has caused the latest in a series of major conflicts between the sailing public and the governing body of the sport, the International Yacht Racing Union. Other 'causes célèbres' have been the choice of sailboard class for the Olympics, an argument which is still raging, and the selection of the Contender as an Olympic class and then not subsequently honouring this decision.

Laser II

LENGTH 14ft 5in (4·39m).
HULL 150lb (68kg).
SAIL AREA Main and jib 124ft² (11·52m²) plus spinnaker 115ft² (10·68m²).

The Laser II is Performance Sailcraft's second attempt to introduce a two man equivalent of the highly successful single-handed Laser (see below). It follows its namesake very closely in terms of hull shape, but has a jib and trapeze

Below: 420s revel in gusty conditions
Right: Laser II

in addition. Its low aspect rig helps to give it a fine turn of speed on a reach and run in a breeze but does nothing to help its windward performance.

The desperation of a large international business which is trying everything to find a new product with which to keep production lines busy, when sales of their original one are slowing down, is a sight to behold; it has resulted in the Laser makers adopting a very aggressive marketing policy for the Laser II, which is, in reality, a boat that would have little chance of establishing itself on its qualities alone.

The general purpose classes

There are several popular dinghies that can be described as both family day cruisers and out and out racing dinghies; because of their adaptability, they justify some attention.

Wayfarer
LENGTH 15ft 10in (4·8m).
HULL 373lb (169kg).
SAIL AREA Main and jib 141ft² (13·1m²) plus spinnaker 145ft² (13·5m²).

This is a solid reliable sea-going dinghy, designed deliberately as a cruising boat by Ian Proctor. It is probably the safest dinghy afloat as was amply demonstrated in the past by the epic single-handed voyages across the tempestuous North Sea and other stretches of open water by the adventurer Frank Dye.

One of the most famous Wayfarers of all. Frank Dye's boat lying to a sea anchor, mast lowered in an Atlantic gale, when on passage to Iceland

In contrast with its cruiser image, the Wayfarer is also raced very keenly by a considerable number of helmsmen, generally of more mature years than those who race the high performance classes. Racing fleets can be found in several countries and the boat is particularly popular with sailing schools.

Although it was originally designed for wood construction, most new Wayfarers are made in glass fibre. Only the pundits of Wayfarer racing and the traditionalists continue to buy the wooden version and, even then, there is no clear justification for believing that wood is faster than glass.

Albacore
LENGTH 15ft (4·6m).
HULL 260lb (118kg).
SAIL AREA Main and jib 125ft² (11·6m²).

The Albacore is one of the last designs of the late Uffa Fox and is one of his best efforts. Even though it was designed in 1954, it still fulfils the role of an ideal general purpose family dinghy as does the Wayfarer. Racing fleets can be found in the UK, Ireland and North America and sail numbers are now approaching 7000. The boat is used extensively by British Services' clubs because of its strength and because it requires little in the way of special technique to control it.

Enterprise
LENGTH 13ft 3in (4m).
HULL 250lb (113kg).
SAIL AREA Main and jib 113ft² (10·5m²) plus spinnaker in some countries only.

Jack Holt designed the Enterprise for the *News Chronicle*, a London newspaper, (now extinct) in 1955; they believed, quite correctly, that dinghy sailing could become a major participant sport with a little help from the media. Jack was asked for a boat with a relatively simple rig, which would require no special techniques to sail it but would still have a good turn of speed and thus be suited both for family cruising and serious racing. In addition, it had to be suitable for oars and a small outboard motor. He produced the very best compromise possible and the Enterprise became the most successful seller in the UK during the late fifties and early sixties. More than 20 000 have now been built and they can be seen in Canada, Australia, the Caribbean, South Africa and India as well as the British Isles.

The Enterprise has a double chined, rather dumpy hull shape crowned with a generous area

in its pale blue mainsail and jib. An optional spinnaker is also allowed by a few national associations. The lack of a trapeze makes for hard work holding the boat upright in heavy weather and its hull shape and long main boom encourage it to play sudden and quite unpredictable tricks offwind in similar conditions. By modern standards, the Enterprise is neither the ideal beginner's boat nor club racer but its strength in pure numbers and speed in light weather mean that it will continue to flourish, particularly on inland waters, for many years to come.

Although they are built in glass fibre, the very best racing versions continue to be built in ply. Nowadays the epoxy saturation process of building wooden boats is rapidly becoming the only accepted way of putting together a fast boat that is super strong, light and stays that way for a good few years. There are sufficient

Above: Albacore class
Below: Enterprise

latitudes in hull measurement rules to produce quite significant changes in shape and the specialist builders exploit these to the ultimate.

The typical Enterprise owner is a family man who belongs to a lake or river based sailing club but top racing crews are usually fit, earnest young men who have the strength and stamina to sail these boats in heavy weather.

Snipe

LENGTH 15ft 6in (4·7m).
HULL 381lb (172·8kg).
SAIL AREA Main and jib 128ft² (11·9m²).

The Snipe is the veteran one design dinghy. It was drawn up by Bill Crosby, the editor of *Rudder*, an American publication, (now extinct) in 1931. By modern standards it is slow for its size and very, very heavy. However, this does not prevent thousands of owners from racing Snipes very keenly at national and international level. The largest fleets are found in North and South America and in some parts of Northern Europe.

Single-handers

Some people prefer to sail on their own. It has advantages: no crew to find, cart around and argue with—it is just one man against the field and when you win or do well, your own individual achievement. The single-handed classes offer a wide variety of athletic and technical challenges from the relatively simple Laser or OK to the ultra testing, International Canoe, Moth or Contender.

Laser

LENGTH 13ft 10in (4·2m).
HULL 130lb (60kg).
SAIL AREA Main 76ft² (7·06m²).

The Laser has been the phenomenon of the dinghy scene during the seventies; in 1981 it was still by far the fastest growing class in the world with sail numbers passing the one hundred thousand mark only eleven years after it was designed by Bruce Kirby, the well known International Fourteen sailor. It can be found in virtually every country of the world, even behind the Iron Curtain. It provides the very best competition in large numbers that can be found in any class; the World Championship fleet has to be restricted to 400 boats, divided into four fleets.

It is an ultra simple boat with a single, sleeve luff sail set on an unstayed mast and is

The Snipe: a still popular fifty year old design started by an American yachting magazine

the nearest one can get to the reality of a true one-design, all boats being manufactured in moulds taken from the one original shape and sails and spars supplied strictly by the one builder, Performance Sailcraft. Even the fittings are controlled by class rules. The result is that Lasers are very close to the same speed as each other and they hold their second hand value.

It is potentially a quick boat in moderate and strong winds but, lacking a trapeze and having a small overall beam, it requires a heavy helmsman to sail it to its optimum in these conditions. Also, the helmsman's ability to keep the boat steady is taxed severely, when sailing off-wind in rough water. This is because it lacks directional stability as a result of its flat under-water shape. If you want the closest racing this is the class to choose.

Sunfish

LENGTH 13ft 10in (4·2m).
HULL 126lb (57kg).
SAIL AREA Main 86 ft² (8m²).

During the fifties the American small boat scene was beset by a plethora of 'board boats'; one of these was the Sunfish, not markedly superior

With numbers in excess of 180 000, the Sunfish is the world's numerically largest class

to many of its rivals, but destined with the benefit of aggressive promotion, to become numerically the largest class of sailing boat in the world. With numbers now in excess of 180 000 no other design comes anywhere near it and possibly none will ever overtake it.

The sailing performance and handling quality of the Sunfish are not brilliant; its low profile lateen rig, just like Arabic Dhows use, is not an efficient plan for sailing to windward and its flat and somewhat fat, underwater shape does not help it in rough water. But, put against these reservations its kindly manners towards beginners and lightweights, its cartopability and its extraordinary strength in numbers in the USA and the Caribbean and one is left with some respect for the boat and quite a lot for the champions of the class.

International Moth

LENGTH 11ft (3·35m).
HULL No minimum weight.
SAIL AREA Main 85ft² (7·9m²).

This is numerically the largest and most internationally spread development class; designers are allowed to draw up a hull shape, layout and sail plan which will beat the rest. As a result of the open rules which only restrict maximum hull length and beam and luff length and sail area, the Moth is by far the most advanced single-hander, vying with the Australian Skiff classes for title of 'most developed dinghy class'.

Over the years there have been two fundamental lines of development: one, the flat scow shapes of Australia and the other, the fine skiff shapes of America and Europe. The two race very closely in moderate winds but the skiffs generally outsail the scows in light airs and vice versa in heavy conditions. The advent of Mervyn Cook's flat, wedge shaped Magnum designs has helped the British hold on to the World Championship title for a few years now, much to the embarrassment of the Australians who always considered themselves to be the kings of Mothing.

With a hull weight of around 50lb and wings to bring the total beam to 7ft 4in, the

International Moth—Magnum 5, the latest in a string of World beating Moths from Mervyn Cook's board

Moth is the most exacting challenge to a helmsman's skill, balance and agility. It is certainly the most difficult singlehander to control, quite a lot more tricky than the International Canoe. The Moth has an absolutely electrifying performance for its size and will often humiliate sailors of much larger, high performance dinghies.

The Moth owner is usually young and slightly crazy, his or her antics on shore as well as afloat are legendary. They are fun loving eccentrics. Sailing an international event in a Moth is one long laugh.

Solo

LENGTH 12ft 5in (3·8m).
HULL 200lb (90·7kg).
SAIL AREA 90ft² (8·36m²).

Designed in 1955 by Jack Holt, over 3000 Solos are now raced in the UK, Holland and Australia. It has a double chine hull shape with a low aspect ratio and a fully battened main sail, which gives it a respectable but unspectacular

The Jack Holt designed Solo

performance; it is a boat that suits the less athletic.

Solos are built in wood and glass fibre; most recently glass/foam sandwich construction has been allowed and all the indications are that this will prove to be a source of strong, competitive hulls for the future.

OK

LENGTH 13ft 1½in (4m).
HULL 158½lb (72kg).
SAIL AREA 89ft² (8·3m²).

The OK was conceived as a cheap trainer for future Finn sailors. It was designed by Knud Olsen in 1957 and promoted by Axel Damgard and triple Olympic gold medallist Paul Elvstrom. The class grew rapidly with their efforts and spread first to north and east Europe and then to Australasia and the Far East.

As a trainer, the OK has fulfilled its intended role admirably with its single sail set on an unstayed mast which requires all the same kind of tuning as the Finn. However, the boat has sufficient popularity in its own right to be taken as a grown up racing class. The OK is

The single-handed OK dinghy

not especially responsive nor does it have a spectacular performance, but it does provide good close racing for its disciples.

Finn

LENGTH 14ft 9in (4·5m).
HULL 319lb (144·7kg).
SAIL AREA Main 110ft² (10·2m²).

The Finn was first selected as the Olympic single-hander in 1952 and, in spite of regular attempts over the years to replace it with a more modern boat, strength of political representation within the International Yacht Racing Union is likely to preserve this status in the foreseeable future. Its lack of performance and challenge to a helmsman's agility and speed of reaction makes it far from the ideal Olympic dinghy.

With a large mainsail of 110ft² (10·2m²), a narrow beam of only 4ft 10in and no trapeze, the Finn has always been considered to be a boat for the heavyweight with strength and stamina. This was certainly true in the early days, but the development of finely tuned mast and sail combinations since the late sixties has

brought the minimum practical helm weight down to 160lb. In fact, you do not have to be much heavier to sail a Finn than a Laser.

As a result of its sophisticated rig, the Finn points higher than virtually any other dinghy and is a real joy to sail. The real problem comes when, at the end of a hard day's racing, you try to pull your Finn up the slipway on its trolley; the all up weight of 350lb means that it is no single-hander to cope with ashore.

Contender

LENGTH 16ft (4·9m).
HULL 228lb (103·4kg).
SAIL AREA Main 112ft² (10·4m²).

This is a clever design, a smaller version of the Flying Dutchman hull shape with only one sail and a trapeze for the helmsman. It was designed by Bob Miller, an Australian, in 1968 in response to the IYRU's professed wish to find a replacement for the Finn as the Olympic single-hander. The Contender won the trials against several other good designs and was instantly granted international status but was never subsequently given a spot in the Olympics.

The Contender is a quick, responsive craft with a similar all round performance to the second rank two man trapeze boats like the 470 and Fireball. In rough conditions, the boat really flies but its flat shape and hard turn to the round bilges causes it to play some unpredictable tricks on a fast reach or run.

It is the ideal class, along with the even faster International Canoe, for Laser sailors to move on to. Good fleets of them can be found in Australasia, the UK, Holland and the USA.

International Canoe

LENGTH 17ft (5·2m).
HULL 138lb (63kg).
SAIL AREA Main and jib 107ft² (10m²).

This is truly the ultimate single-handed monohull with a performance close to the 505 and several per cent quicker than the Contender. Its long, lean shape coupled with its highly developed two sail rig make for its quite startling speed—it is really a catamaran with only one hull. To hold the Canoe up, the helmsman sits out on the end of a sliding seat; he would have to be ten feet tall to create the same leverage with a trapeze. Swooping along above the waves, riding the Canoe is the nearest one can

Top right: Three times world champion, Dave Pitman in action on his all wood Contender
Bottom right: International Canoe

get to flying like a gull. Looking at the Canoe one might assume that it is very difficult to sail, but most competent helmsmen find that they can cope with it after only a brief introduction.

The hull shape of the International Canoe is one-design but the deck layout is free and the rig is variable within specified maximum limits of mast height and sail area. Hulls are built in cold moulded wood or glass/foam sandwich and both seem to compete very much on level terms. The trend in rigs has been towards reducing total weight by using carefully braced lightweight masts and fewer battens.

Fleets of Canoes are localized at present in the south and east of England, Northern Germany, the Sounds of Sweden and the coast of North East USA. Small numbers are also present in other countries and the class is growing in popularity more quickly now than at any time in its history. During the past few years champions from many other classes have joined the Canoes; one is likely to cross tacks with world, European and national champions of Contenders, Moths, Toys and Hornets at every open meeting.

Two man, high performance classes

The boats described in this section are the most important of the fast centre-board types, from the Olympic Flying Dutchman, which behaves almost like a high speed keelboat, down to the Cherub, a very fast, lightweight twelve footer which requires the utmost agility from its crew.

Flying Dutchman

LENGTH 19ft 10in (6·05m).
HULL 365lb (165·6kg).
SAIL AREA Main and jib 200ft² (18·6m²) plus spinnaker 190ft² (17·6m²).

In the early fifties, the International Yacht Racing Union decided that there was a need for a high performance, two-man boat in the Olympics and they invited designers to submit prototypes for selection trials. The winner of these trials, by the narrowest of margins over the Coronet which was later modified to become the 505, was the Flying Dutchman designed by Van Essen. It has been sailed in every Olympic games since then.

Superficially one might assume that Olympic status would stimulate the popularity of a class but, in reality, it has restricted the Dutchman's growth. The reasons for this are simple;

the search for technical advances which will improve performance has meant that a boat capable of competing in top competition is extremely expensive, often incorporating exotic materials and hand made fittings. The class is seen as a select club for experts only; you only buy one if you are incredibly rich or very ambitious with an Olympic medal as your goal. In reality, the fact that last year's boat and last month's sails are never good enough means that you can buy a really good second hand Dutchman very cheaply; the only trouble is that with the exception of Germany you will have to travel a long way to find a good fleet of them to race with.

The Flying Dutchman is fast, extremely stable but too big to give the real feel of dinghy sailing. At 19ft 10in in length, it is the largest of all the international dinghy classes.

505

LENGTH 16ft 6in (5·03m).
HULL 280lb (127kg).
SAIL AREA Main and jib 146ft² (13·6m²) plus spinnaker 250ft² (23·2m²).

Although it is neither as numerous as the 470, nor blessed with the Olympic status of the Flying Dutchman, the 505 is without a doubt the premier international two-man trapeze dinghy in the western world. Designed by John Westell at the request of the French Caneton Class Association in 1954, its popularity has extended far and wide. From the early days when the French fleet was the most important and French crews were always in contention for international honours, the balance of power shifted firmly during the sixties in the direction of the UK, which now has the largest fleet and many of the best crews. Other strong nations include Sweden, the USA and Australia. Such notables as 'Gentleman' Jim Hardy, Steve Benjamin, Paul Elvstrom, Richard Creagh-Osborne, Harold Cudmore, David Pitman and a number of Olympic and International Champions in other classes have all raced in 505s at some stage of their careers.

The 'Five-Oh' is a brute of a boat with an ultimate performance in the same league as the Flying Dutchman, it takes skill and strength to get the best out of one in any kind of wind strength. Its round bilged hull shape tolerates a fairly wide range of crew weights without any clear deterioration in overall performance, but the ideal combination is a helmsman of between 130 and 150lb and a crew of 170 and 190lb with a height in excess of 6ft.

The modern top flight 505 is a beautifully engineered machine and the very best version is built in Britain by Parker in glass fibre. Composite construction—glass hull and wooden decks—is very popular and there are still some beautifully built wooden versions made but these do not seem to have any advantage in terms of boat speed.

International Fourteen

LENGTH 14ft (4·27m).
HULL 225lb (102kg).
SAIL AREA Main and jib 190ft² (17·65m²) plus spinnaker 190ft² (17·65m²).

The Fourteen is a rapid, high performance dinghy which severely tests the skill and strength of those who sail them. With crew on trapeze and a generous sail area, it really flies offwind but, because of its relatively short length by comparison with many other fast dinghies, it is difficult to sail fast to windward in strong winds.

The International Fourteen was the first dinghy class to be given 'International' status by the International Yacht Racing Union in 1927. Governed by measurement rules which allow considerable freedom in hull shape and sail plan, the Fourteens have contributed much to the advancement of sail boat theory over the years since then. Many famous designers, including Uffa Fox, Ian Proctor and Bruce Kirby, 'cut their teeth' in this competitive environment. The modern version is only a very distant relative of its ancestors and with the possible exceptions of the Australian Skiff classes and the International Moths it must be considered to be the ultimate example of dinghy hull thinking.

Within the confines of generally accepted trends, there are still significant variations in underwater shape amongst the top racing boats; there is one school of thought that preaches minimum keel curvature (rocker) and even distribution of displacement (underwater volume) from bow to stern. This is said to increase the maximum displacement speed achievable. There is another school of thought that only goes part of the way towards accepting this philosophy, arguing that finer ends and a deeper rocker reduce wetted surface, thus increasing light weather performance, and making the boat lose less speed when tacking. Proponents of the 'flat' school include Bruce Kirby with his recent Mk VII which resembles a Laser with high topside, and Charlie Bullock whose weird Opus designs with distorted chines have the least rocker of any modern competitive shapes. Both of these designs have won major international prizes but exponents of the compromise philosophy have done equally well in recent years with Phil Morrison's 'Snoggledog' winning the UK Open Championships for three years in succession and Bruce Kirby's much earlier Mk V, designed originally in 1969, taking the World Championships in 1979.

In the absence of any revolutionary design theories at present, it would seem that hull development has reached a plateau; choosing one shape rather than another will give you a slight edge in one type of wind and water conditions but no appreciable overall advantage across the whole range of weathers. The propositions that minimum hull weight should be reduced to 200lb and that the helmsman, as well as his crew, should be permitted to trapeze are presently under consideration. If these become law in 1984, there may well be a flurry of new designs drawn up to suit.

The large sail area and the trapeze carried by the Fourteen make it difficult to persuade a light alloy mast to stand up properly. Current practice is to use a fairly flexible section rigged with fixed spreaders and upper jumper stays.

More than 1100 Fourteens have been built over 50 years but the number currently racing has never been greater with 600 in fleets in the UK, USA, Canada and most recently, Japan.

An International Fourteen Footer at speed

470

LENGTH 15ft 5in (4·7m).

HULL 264lb (120kg).

SAIL AREA Main and jib 135ft² (12·5m²) plus spinnaker 140ft² (13m²).

The battle for international popularity, official recognition and finally, selection as an Olympic class between the 470 of French origin and the Fireball of British design was one of the great bureaucratic conflicts of the sailing world during the late sixties and the early seventies. The 470 was finally chosen as the Olympic class in 1972 and as a result, many cynics expected its popularity to suffer. They believed that club helmsmen would now look upon the class as an 'experts only' club and that the price of a competitive boat would rocket as attention was focussed on the development of more sophisticated hull construction, rigs and equipment.

Fortunately for the 470, two features have helped it partially avoid these pitfalls; first, it

470—seen here under excellent control in a full gale

had already reached a high level of popularity as a 'common man's' two up trapeze dinghy before Olympic status was thrust upon it and second, the class rules stipulate that only standard glass fibre materials can be used in its hull. Over 30 000 470s have been launched so far and its popularity goes from strength to strength in countries where it has been long established. Not unexpectedly, the largest fleets are to be found in France and mainland Europe with other important concentrations in Japan and the USA.

The 470, designed by André Cornu in 1963 for production in glass fibre, is beautifully mannered with a quite exceptional behaviour and performance in heavy winds and rough water. Its performance compares very closely with the Fireball, although its round bilge shape gives it the edge in light airs. The technique of planing a 470 to windward, pointing low, going faster and minimizing leeway plays a crucial part in winning races in this class. This practice

has now been copied by many other high performance classes.

As with other one design classes that allow minor tolerances in hull shape and construction, the 470 is affected by the 'fashionable' builder syndrome. One year Vanguard in the USA, Nautivela in Italy and Pajot Fontaine in France are favoured but the next time a championship might be won by a British Parker or French Lanaverre boat. If this happens the experts will be frantically changing boats to keep up with the new champions. The same thing happens with sail and mast makers. This occurs because the skill differential between crews can be tested, only if other variables affecting boat speed are systematically eliminated.

Hornet
LENGTH 16ft (4·88m).
HULL 285lb (129kg).
SAIL AREA Main and jib 143ft² (13·3m²) plus spinnaker 130ft² (12·1m²).

The Hornet was designed by Jack Holt in 1952 and is considered by many, even thirty years later, to be his finest creation. It is without a doubt the most sensitive and willing performer of all the larger two-man dinghies. Its straight hard chine hull shape gives it outstanding speed

Hornet class

on a close reach in heavy winds; indeed, there are no words sufficient to describe its beautiful manners in these conditions.

Sadly, in face of competition from the Fireball and the 470, it has never achieved the world wide popularity it so richly deserves. Nevertheless, good fleets can be found in Holland and Australia as well as the UK.

The layout and rig of the Hornet have gone through a gentle evolution over the years which has resulted most notably in the replacement of the crew's sliding seat with a trapeze, the jib with a genoa and the development of an enlarged mainsail and spinnaker.

The typical Hornet sailor is a bit of a cowboy, a practical joker, and the biggest joke he likes to play is to show Fireball sailors how it should be done in rough water. Olympic medallists, Reg White and Keith Musto began their sailing careers in the Hornet.

Fireball
LENGTH 16ft 2in (4·9m).
HULL 175lb (79·4kg)
SAIL AREA Main and jib 123ft² (11·4m²) plus spinnaker 140ft² (13m²).

At birth, designer Peter Milne's Fireball was hailed as something quite revolutionary; on reflection twenty years later, the only feature that remains remarkable is the boat's hull shape. When looked at in section, it has a flat floor joined to two side panels which, in turn, are attached to shallow topsides. Seen from the side, the Fireball has a flat keel line from the centreboard case to the stern and its bow curves upward to leave its slanted bow transom well above water level. In very strong winds the boat is really fast off wind. However, in rough water, when its bluff bow shape slows it down, it is easily outsailed by the more conventional, high performance dinghies to windward. In light winds this hull shape gives the boat absolutely no feel; it is rather like trying to carry out brain surgery with boxing gloves on your hands.

The fact that the 'Ball' is very simple to construct at home, helped it gain world-wide popularity. More recently, however, the top racing versions have been constructed in a female mould using the West epoxy system of joining the panels and it is now a pretty difficult proposition for an amateur to build a competitive boat from the official plans. In addition, the professionally made hulls exploit the tolerances that are allowed in hull shape, centreboard case plan and deck layout to produce a fundamentally faster boat than one strictly to the original plans. Thus from the early days when the Fireball was a cheap high performance racer, the best boat now costs more than the best 505 and, given the choice I would take the latter for its extra speed at sea.

Cherub class

Cherub

LENGTH 12ft (3·6m).
HULL 150lb (68kg).
SAIL AREA Main and jib 115ft² (10·7m²) plus spinnaker 140ft² (13m²).

The Cherub was conceived by John Spencer, a New Zealander, in 1953 as a restricted class which would allow hull and rig development whilst maintaining the basic form. It is without

a single doubt the finest small two-man racing dinghy with international distribution. With crew on trapeze and a large spinnaker set on a long pole, it provides the greatest test of skill and agility of any of the high performance two-man dinghies, only being outgunned by the Twelve Foot Skiff which remains a type indigenous to Australia and New Zealand. Numbers of these superb craft are now approaching 3000 with main fleets in New Zealand, Australia and the UK.

Class rules allow that the hull of a Cherub may be constructed from a wide variety of materials and this has resulted in competitive versions being made in glass/foam sandwich or marine ply using the West system. Top designers in the class include Ian Murray of Australia who has held the World Eighteen Foot Skiff Championship many times.

Lunatic fringe boats

There are some types of dinghy that make the blood of even the most seasoned of racing helmsmen run hot and most of these can be found in Australia and New Zealand where the waters are warm enough to make the occasional swim a pleasant interlude rather than the precursor to an attack of pneumonia. They are just that bit 'hairier' than the International Fourteen, Moth or Canoe primarily because of their enormous sail areas. Most notable of these are the Skiff development classes in Twelve, Fourteen, Sixteen and Eighteen Foot Divisions.

Twelve Foot Skiff

The Twelve is probably the craziest of all dinghy types with hull weights below 100lb and unrestricted sail areas of up to 600ft² all controlled by two men, both on trapeze. Because of the vast sail areas carried, hull shapes tend to be fairly stable with the ability to sail very rapidly at varying angles of heel. The Cherub sometimes claims to be the fastest twelve foot dinghy in the world but in up to twenty knots of breeze, the Twelve Foot Skiff will eat it 'bones and all' and beyond that wind strength the Skiff will change down to a smaller rig and remain a faster bet with the extra power of its second trapeze to take it to windward and larger spinnaker to take it downwind.

The Twelve Foot Skiff

Eighteen Foot Skiff

The Eighteen Foot Skiff is the fastest all round racing dinghy in the world and is raced primarily in Sydney Harbour by semi-professional crews. Without any restrictions on sail plan, the light weather rigs of these boats have a massive area approaching 2000ft² (186m²) including spinnaker. In the early days during the twenties and thirties, as many as ten crewmen were needed as ballast in strong winds, but the modern projectile with a hull weight of less than 150lb, is controlled by just three men. Everyone including the helmsman rides trapezes from the outer edge of alloy wings which are attached to and form an integral part of the gunwale structure.

Because of their expense and specialization, the Eighteen is found only in small numbers but fleets do exist in other parts of Australia apart from Sydney and also in New Zealand, USA, and a few in Europe.

Modern hull designs have straight entries and parallel lines throughout the afterbody. When combined with the buoyant sections required to support the enormous press of sail, the resulting shapes are very easily kept in a straight line and tolerate a certain amount of heeling angle without developing weather or lee helm or losing very much speed.

Eighteen racing in Sydney Harbour is a popular spectator sport with ferry loads of fans and bookies chasing the fleet from mark to mark. The tremendous expense of campaigning one with its fragile hull, constructed in highly expensive materials and three rigs of different sizes to suit various wind strengths, makes the carrying of large advertisements on the sails in return for sponsorship an essential part of skiff racing. In all other racing classes throughout the world such advertising is prohibited.

The unique Australian Eighteen Foot Skiff

3

Speed on two hulls

Based on ancient Pacific Islands craft, catamarans have become popular throughout the world since their introduction to the sport in the early fifties. The most popular of these have hull shapes which make centre-boards unnecessary and are thus ideal for launching from an exposed beach. The speed around the course of the better catamarans is fantastic—considerably faster than any other type of racing sailcraft including keel boats and high performance dinghies.

Hobie Cats

LENGTH 14ft (4·3m)   16ft (4·8m)
HULL 240lb (109kg)   340lb (154kg)
SAIL AREA 118ft² (10·6m²)   218ft² (19·6m²)

Hobies are the most popular catamaran designs in the world. There are three types varying in overall length; the Fourteen, the Sixteen and the Eighteen. The original was the single-handed Hobie Fourteen which Hobie Alter, an American, designed in 1968. He followed this with the two-man Sixteen in 1970 which took off so quickly that it has since outgrown its smaller predecessor in numbers. There are now 55 000 of them and 36 000 Fourteens.

Hobie uses asymmetrical, 'banana' hull shapes to develop hydrodynamic lift; ideally they should be sailed with their windward hulls flying just clear of the surface so that they do not counteract the lift generated by the fully immersed leeward float. In high winds with crew on trapeze they go like a train but the strange hull shape and lack of centre-boards makes them a little sluggish by comparison with the more conventional catamarans in light winds.

The Hobie Eighteen class was launched in 1977 and has already sold five thousand boats. All three classes have their popularity centred on the USA but have a strong following in Australia as well.

Dart

LENGTH 18ft (5·5m)
HULL 295lb (134kg).
SAIL AREA Main and jib 173ft² (16·1m²).

Designed by Rodney Marsh of 'C' Class and Olympic Tornado catamaran fame, the Dart is the most sophisticated of the catamaran classes without a centre-board. Because the Tornado has become prohibitively expensive as a result of its Olympic status, the Dart is intended to fulfil the role of an everyman's high performance catamaran. It does this admirably and its international popularity is growing at a spectacular pace. It is not surprising to find that the largest fleets of Darts are in those countries where the Hobie has not had a great success. Catamaran for catamaran, the Dart is a better interpretation of the beach catamaran concept than the Hobie.

Unicorn

LENGTH 18ft (5·5m).
HULL 200lb (90·7kg).
SAIL AREA Main 150ft² (13·9m²).

This single-handed catamaran was originally designed by John Mazotti in 1966 to be built from two flat sheets of ply for each hull, glassed flat over the back part of the keel and then once set, pulled up into a fine bow shape. Since then they have inevitably been built in glass and even cold moulded veneer but many new boats are still built by amateurs using the original method.

The Unicorn measures within the International 'A' Class rule which is the IYRU's restricted single-handed catamaran class. So the Unicorn not only races as a one-design with fleets in the UK and other European countries, (Canada, Zimbabwe and South Africa) but also as a highly competitive contender for World 'A' class honours. Other 'A' Class designs which compete in the IYRU's international events include the highly successful Rhapsody from Australia and the Wing A from Germany.

Condor

LENGTH 16ft 4in (5m).
HULL 225lb (102 kg).
SAIL AREA Main and jib 185ft² (17·2m²).

This is a conventional catamaran with outstanding rough-water behaviour. Smaller in length than the Dart, its performance is almost exactly the same. With nearly 1000 Condors sailing in the UK, Australasia, Northern Europe and North America, its fine qualities are nevertheless relatively unrecognized when compared with the popularity of the Hobie and Dart beach catamarans.

Left: Unicorn catamaran

Below: Condor catamaran

Tornado

LENGTH 20ft (6·1m).
HULL 279 lb (126·5 kg).
SAIL AREA Main and jib 235ft² (21·8m²).

This is the Olympic catamaran class and probably the fastest sailing boat with significant international distribution. It is a very expensive machine and the intention to win an Olympic medal is the only justification for buying one in preference to the Dart or Hobie Eighteen. The fine, easily driven hulls are directly descended from the best 'C' Class catamaran shapes. These are designed to cut through rough water rather than fly over the top in the way that dinghies do. One of the secrets of winning Tornado races is to push the boat so fast that the leeward hull is nearly driven under; the key is to avoid taking it too far.

Patient Lady V, **C class catamaran and winner of the Little America's Cup in 1980**

'C' Class

LENGTH (including rudders) 25ft (7·6m).

HULL No minimum.

SAIL AREA (including spars) 300ft² (27·9m²).

The 'C' Class is governed by open design rules within which designers attempt to create the fastest craft. There are rules for a larger 'D' Class but the 'C' can claim to be the ultimate in sail boat development; it has spawned virtually every worthwhile one-design catamaran class apart from the Hobies. The only worthwhile racing that is still done in 'C's is match racing for the Little America's Cup which is challenged for in exactly the same way as the 12-metre event. America has held the cup for some years against repeated assaults by the Australians, Swedes and Italians.

The latest designs have the narrowest hulls imaginable with a minute cross sectional area to bring resistance to forward motion to an absolute minimum. Set slightly behind the centre of buoyancy is the most extraordinary semi-rigid aerofoil rig incorporating flaps to create increased aerodynamic pressure by the venturi effect of forcing air through a tapered slot just as happens with jib and main on a normal rig but here practised with considerably greater precision.

The Americans have attempted to foster a one-design 'C' catamaran called the Coyote but as yet this has no international significance and is competing for popularity with the two-trapeze Super Catamaran 20 which claims with every justification to be the fastest production catamaran in the world.

4

The classic keelboat

The open keelboat is the purest form of fixed keel racing boat, an uncompromising formula for day racing round the buoys in a seaway. Some keelboats are as strenuous to sail as high performance dinghies. In the particular case of the Olympic Soling, it provides the most gruelling physical exercise to be found in any class.

The largest keelboat still in general use is the 12-metre which is described in Chapter 7. All have ballasted keels which make them inherently more stable than dinghies and, to a greater or lesser extent, self righting in the case of a capsize. (The term keelboat is not usually used to refer to a habitable cruiser even though it has a keel.)

Flying Fifteen

LENGTH 20ft (6·1m).
HULL 725lb (329kg)
SAIL AREA Main and jib 150ft² (13·9m²) plus spinnaker 150ft² (13·9m²)

The Flying Fifteen is a rare masterpiece from the drawing board of Uffa Fox. He designed it in 1947 but it has yet to be bettered as the perfect crossover from dinghies to keelboats. It planes readily on a reach and is easily handled by a lightweight crew who sit the boat out in conventional dinghy fashion. The Flying Fifteen is a popular class in the UK and Australasia; there are smaller fleets in the USA and South Africa.

Tempest

LENGTH 22ft (6·7m).
HULL (including keel) 1020lb (463kg).
SAIL AREA Main and genoa 247ft² (22·9m²) plus spinnaker 225ft² (20·9m²)

The Tempest is the only international keelboat which is equipped with a trapeze; in fact, it behaves very much as one would expect a very stable high performance dinghy to. It was designed by Ian Proctor in response to a request by the IYRU to find a modern replacement for the Star as the Olympic two-man keelboat. It was used in the 1972 and 1976 Olympic Games but has since been dropped.

The original concept was to be able to raise the keel for launching and transportation so that only the bulb at the bottom was protruding from the hull; however, in order to obtain maximum performance the keel must be locked rigidly into the keelbox and therefore no top class Tempest uses this option, preferring to launch and trail the boat on a high standing trailer with the keel fully lowered. It is said that its large sail area, coupled with the hull's relatively low weight without the keel, make the engineering of a rigid rig to hull to keel structure difficult and for this reason, an old Tempest will probably not be as fast as a new one due to resultant structural deterioration. So, if you buy one, check the triangulation of shrouds and the bracing of the keel box very carefully before putting your money down.

Star

LENGTH 22ft 8½in (6·9m).
HULL 1480lb (671·3kg).
SAIL AREA Main and jib 280ft² (26m²)

Designed in 1911 and 1480lb in weight, the Star is nevertheless the most sensitive and difficult keelboat of all to sail—a real challenge to a top class crew. For many years, toe straps were not allowed so the crew rode the weather rail cossack style in order to get their weight as far to windward as possible. Nowadays the crew can use conventional toe straps in considerably greater comfort to help their valiant attempts to counterbalance the Star's enormous sail area. It has no spinnaker but who needs it with a mainsail as large as that of the Star.

Apart from a brief interlude during the seventies, the Star has been the two-man Olympic keelboat class since 1936.

Soling

LENGTH 26ft 9in (8·15m).

HULL 2280lb (1034kg).

SAIL AREA Main and jib 233ft² (21·6m²) plus spinnaker 255ft² (23·7m²)

In 1966 the IYRU announced that they were going to replace the Dragon as an Olympic class; in 1967 trials were held at Travemunde in North Germany, Britton Chance's design won by a narrow margin from the Echell's 22 but the selectors' eyes were caught by the smaller, but nearly as fast, Soling entered by Jan Linge.

From the sedate days of the trials when the crew sat on the side deck, the technique of sailing the Soling has developed rapidly, to the point at which the crew sits out so far on long toe straps that a hiking harness has to be worn.

Dragon

LENGTH 29ft 3in (8·9m).

HULL 3800lb (1724kg).

SAIL AREA Main and genoa 295ft² (27·4m²) plus spinnaker 330ft² (30·7m²).

Designed in 1927, the Dragon is a real ancient monument, yet the class is probably as popular today as it has ever been. It used to be an Olympic class but was superseded by the Soling in 1972 as the three-man keelboat. Since it lost its 'rich experts only' image, the class has revived with larger and larger fleets racing at club level in Germany and Australia; in other countries the existing fleets continue at their established levels.

Left: Flying Fifteen

Below: Star class: thrown out then restored to the Olympic Games

5

The stuff of winning

PUTTING TOGETHER A FAST BOAT

Despite the widely differing shapes and forms of small craft, there are many common elements that go towards making a boat fast in its own class.

The hull

The critical factors affecting hull performance are basic shape, strength, stiffness, weight and surface smoothness and each should be dealt with in turn:

Basic Shape

In a development class such as the Moth, Cherub or International Fourteen, different designs are allowed to race against each other on level terms. Each design will have marginal variations in performance according to wind and sea conditions and crew weight and it is up to the buyer to choose the most appropriate to suit his anticipated needs. In many so called one-design classes where it is intended that all hulls should be as near identical in shape to each other as possible, significantly faster boats are produced by builders who use the cumulative measurement tolerances allowed in class rules to make a somewhat different shape from that originally designed. If you do not have one of the best hull shapes available, you will make winning in top competition that much more difficult for yourself.

Skin Stiffness

A hull can appear to be a good fair shape without bumps or hollows when it is on dry land but if the skin is not stiff enough, the action of water pressure and the strains imposed on it by the rig, centre-board, rudder and crew will most certainly result in the hull altering shape when immersed. Unless these changes are deliberately induced to improve a hull's underwater shape, they will almost certainly slow you down. Before buying into a new class, check with the top owners to find out about the ideal skin stiffness; if they will not tell you or do not know, sneak into the dinghy park and check out the best boats by simply pushing in various places along the hull to see how much movement you get. Generally speaking, a hull skin should be absolutely rigid from the bow to 6 or 7 ft back; beyond this point the laminar flow of water over the hull surface starts to break down and slight imperfections in surface shape are less important although ideally the underwater shape should remain fair throughout the full length.

Structural Strength

A good hull should not twist or change its over-all shape significantly under load. The weight of the crew on a hull's gunwale, the ringing effect of a sliding seat or wings and even that of the centre-board and rudder, when pitted against the opposing force of the rig can cause a badly engineered hull to twist. Check that the centre-board case is properly braced, that the gunwales, wings or sliding seat are properly tied in with it and the rig structure. All the major opposing forces should thus be transferred into a rigid structure, and should not be able to move in relation to each other.

It is most important that the shroud and forestay bases and the mast foot are tied into this rigid structure, since a tiny movement of the stay bases towards each other or a slight downward shift of the mast step results in a quite dramatic reduction in rigging tension which in turn makes it far more difficult to make the rig stand up in the desired fashion.

Some of the lighter, high performance classes use a spaceframe structure of tubes and wires to balance the opposing forces but most still rely upon the rigidity provided by the hull's monocoque construction for strength. With this

Above: The skin of the hull must be stiff enough to take the pressure of water and pounding of the waves without distorting

Below: This International Canoe is demonstrating what happens if the shroud base and the mast base are not rigid; the mast is leaning forward forcing the bow down in the gusts

in mind it is worth checking regularly that there are no cracks in the joints at the edge of bulkheads and at particular stress points. Catamarans are an even more difficult structural problem but it is absolutely crucial to eliminate movement of one hull in relation to the other. The secret is in the strength of the joining beams and the way they are attached to the hulls.

Weight

Apart from the crew, the hull contributes the largest proportion of the total sailing weight of a small boat and as such should weigh as little as possible; most classes have a minimum allowable weight for the hull stripped of movable parts; a competitive boat will be within ounces of the minimum weight and will be carefully kept dry when not in the water so that the hull does not absorb moisture and get heavier. This process can occur very rapidly with a wooden craft which is protected only by conventional paints; two part polyurethane finishes are good but epoxy resin paints are the best possible protection against moisture absorption. Similarly, glassfibre can absorb a significant amount of water if the gel coat is damaged in any way; the moisture is drawn into the skin by capillary action and will cause irreparable damage if allowed to remain.

Weight distribution within the hull is considered by some top people to be critical and the majority would claim that a boat seems to perform better if weight is kept out of the ends of the hull and concentrated as centrally as possible. This is claimed to reduce the boat's tendency to pitch in rough water and to make the boat behave in a more lively manner. Strangely there are a few equally successful helmsmen who preach the absolute opposite; to support this a recent survey of the Flying Dutchman class showed that the fastest boats do not have the most centralized weight distribution.

The only thing that is absolutely indisputable is that a boat with a light overall weight when fully rigged will go faster, in all but the lightest of breezes, than a heavier one.

Incidentally, a gallon of water weighs 10lb so it is absolutely critical that your boat does not leak and that you keep an open cockpit, if your boat has one, dry whilst afloat.

Surface smoothness

As has been mentioned already a hull should have a generally fair shape; the actual smoothness of the finish is less important than the absence of lumps and hollows in the underwater shape. However, surface finish does have a small but important effect on performance although, once again there are two schools of theory; one which favours a silk smooth surface obtained by abrasing the surface with very fine grade wet and dry sandpaper or even wire wool; the other which favours the highly polished glossy finish which many now obtain by spraying the paint on in the same way as a car finish is applied.

The rig

So much for the hull; now for the power unit, the rig; the secret of a good rig is that it should deliver the maximum amount of power which can be managed and that it should be made as light as possible without sacrificing any of this power. There are no universal rules and you should check out the way the experts do it, noting what types of masts and sail they use.

Mast

Since the sixties, the vast majority of small craft masts have been made in high tensile aluminium alloy. Wood was used extensively before that but was found to be inferior in a number of very important aspects; weight for weight the metal mast was stronger, its bend characteristics were completely predictable and it recovered its shape, bend after bend without any appreciable loss of resilience.

At one time, masts with lots of bend were considered to be the ideal answer. It was claimed that the springy qualities of the mast temporarily stored and then released energy in waves and gusty winds. To a certain extent this was undoubtedly true but it was found impossible to avoid losing a significant part of the stored energy and in addition, it was virtually impossible to maintain an efficient aerodynamic shape in the sails with so much variation in bend from one moment to the next. Consequently, masts are usually set up to be pretty stiff these days with a certain amount of fore-and-aft bend being forced in by the kicking strap and mainsheet tension. This is effectively controlled by spreader systems, which rely on the torsional strength of the mast section and controllable mastgates at deck level.

Trapeze dinghies have to step heavier sections than other boats because of the compression forces imposed by the weight of the crew and the fact that the trapeze wire reduces the tension on the windward shroud which, in turn,

Rodney Pattisson's *Superdocious* **shows how a mast and mainsail should interact but even he had trouble making the front edge of the genoa stand up perfectly straight**

reduces the effectiveness of the fixed spreader system. Other standing rigging systems such as diamond wires, sometimes angled forwards above the hounds to support the topmast, 'Morrison wires' which join the end of the spreader to the mast at deck level and lowers are all used when appropriate to make the light weight sections stand up. A well rigged mast deflects sideways slightly above the hounds in heavy winds to free the leech of the mainsail when the boat would otherwise be overpowered.

The weight of the mast should be kept as light as possible since it can make a valuable contribution to keeping the all up weight of the boat to a minimum and its centre of gravity must be kept as low as possible in order to reduce the pitching and rolling effect that it creates in rough water.

Boom

The boom should be as light and stiff as possible so that the kicking strap and mainsheet tension is transferred directly to the mainsail leech; what it is made of, alloy or wood, is not important, but large diameter alloy tube is generally stiffer. A powerful, easily adjusted kicking strap arrangement is an essential part of the competitive rig. Equally, a good, adjustable foot outhaul

with an effective control of luff tension is the best way to control flow in the mainsail.

Mainsail

The shape, smoothness and ability to adjust in a controllable way, progressively flattening as wind strength increases, are the main criteria of a good mainsail. The maximum chord of the main under load should be from a third to half way aft from the mast. Controlling the sail shape, the depth of flow and the leech tension, is the most important aspect of making the boat fast in different wind and sea conditions. In the lightest of airs it should set quite flat with a slack kicking strap to induce a certain amount of twist in the top of the sail thus avoiding the breaking effect of a hooked leech and to allow for the large differences in wind speed between top and bottom. In moderate conditions the sail should set full with the leech tight and sheeted close to the centreline. As the wind increases, the sheeting angle should be increased and the sail progressively flattened by increasing luff and foot tension. In very heavy conditions the main should be allowed to twist a little when going upwind or on a close reach; this helps the boat to lift its bow and prevents being overpowered. Off wind in heavy conditions, reapply kicking strap tension to reduce twist but expect the sail to twist a certain amount in spite of this, so do not let the sheet out completely. In this weather, particularly in rough water or gusty winds, you are likely to break your mast if you allow the boom to push against the leeward shroud, as it will act as a pivot and the pressure on the outer end of the boom will cause the mast to 'pop' backwards low down—more light-weight masts are lost like this than any other way.

Foresails

Jibs and genoas require the same attention to shape and smoothness as mains although there is quite a difference in the shape from one class to another according to rules governing sail plan and sheeting arrangements. A large, overlapping genoa will have most of its chord curvature in the front fifty per cent with a relatively flat follow through and will be set pretty tight; a high aspect jib will have a large amount of flow throughout and will be sheeted close to the centreline at the foot. Both are allowed to twist to a degree which allows the wind to meet the front edge of the main at just the right angle. The exceptions to the rules are classes like the Enterprise where one is obliged to sheet the jib at a wide angle through a fairlead on the side-deck; this means that Enterprise jibs are con-siderably flatter than the close sheeted foresails on Fireballs, 505s and Solings.

Spinnakers

Apart from the single edged reaching spinnakers used by Australian Skiffs, the spinnaker is a double leading edge sail, it being possible to use either side at the front. In spite of it being an aerodynamic compromise, it does give consider-able extra speed when used correctly on any down-wind course from a beam reach to a dead run.

A good all round spinnaker should be able to spread its shoulders fairly flat at the top so that it is both close winded and presents a maxi-mum area to the wind.

New Materials

Both jibs and mains are now being made with cloth reinforced plastics; these exhibit better performance characteristics than the woven, filled Terylene or Dacron cloths but tend to deteriorate more rapidly in use. Over the next few years the Mylar or Melinex materials will be developed to overtake woven cloth on this score and there is no doubt that the days of woven sail cloths are numbered. The advantages of reinforced plastics are lower permeability, lower air friction and less distortion for a given weight thus allowing one to make a lighter more efficient sail. Ultimately, materials with no woven constituents at all will be developed and come into general use. The reduction in manu-facturing processes will reduce the cost of sails in real terms.

Lightweight plastic materials for spin-nakers will follow but at some distance in time because of the necessity to develop a plastic that will not deteriorate rapidly when folded repeat-edly.

Fins

The shape, stiffness and smoothness of rudders, centre-boards and keels are considered by many top racers to be more important than the same factors when applied to hulls. This has by no means been proved but one should not ignore the important contribution to performance that they can make. If class rules allow it, rudders and centre-boards should have aerofoil sections with rounded leading edges gently curved back to maximum thickness halfway back for centre-boards and a third for rudders and from there gradually tapered to a squared off trailing edge of no more than three millimetres in width.

To get the stiffness and finish combined with light weight, many boards are constructed in laminated softwood using epoxy glues which are then covered in glass or Kevlar mat. There are several specialist fin makers who charge exorbitant prices for this type of thing but really, if you have the patience, you can make a good job constructing one at home.

Sitting out aids

Every class of dinghy, catamaran and open keel-boat has a rule governing the method by which and the degree to which the crew's weight can be supported outboard in order to counteract the heeling effect of the wind in the sails.

Trapeze

The trapeze is the most common sitting out aid in high performance dinghies and catamarans. The crew wears a harness, which he hooks to a wire, attached to the mast above the hounds, and swings out to windward of the boat so that,

In rough water the crew raises his position slightly in order to avoid hitting the water and slowing the boat

when fully extended, his body will be horizontal and his feet his only contact with the hull. Most trapezes have an adjustable height control so that the crew can raise the hiking angle a little on a reach or in rough water to avoid slowing the boat's progress by dragging his or her body through the water. On catamarans there are normally toe loops on the gunwhale to give a firmer foot hold as their sudden acceleration and deceleration can cause some unwanted flying trapeze work by the crew.

Sliding Seat

This is an unusual but highly efficient hiking aid which is used by the International Canoe, various Australian classes and is an optional alternative to the trapeze on the Hornet. The seat is slid out from the side of the boat so that the crew may sit out on it. On the Canoe it is long enough for the helmsman to climb out so that his feet are a full 3ft from the gunwhale thus providing much greater leverage than is possible with a trapeze. The disadvantage of a normal sliding seat system is that its fore and aft position is fixed which means that crew

weight cannot be moved back on an offwind leg in order to discourage the bow from burying.

Wings

These are side decks extended far outboard of the real gunwale line using wooden or aluminium tube construction. The Moth class invented them but the most extraordinary examples of wings can be seen in the eighteen foot Skiff class where the helmsman and two-man crew trapeze from an outer structure.

Toe Straps

These are the most usual sitting out aid for helmsmen in all types of small craft and for crews of the more sedate types. With feet hooked under the straps the sailor can hang out over a gunwale using his or her weight to best advantage. Straps should be made of a material and rigged at a height inside the cockpit which is comfortable, so that the crew will be able to sit out hard for long periods without becoming worn out.

Tuning the instrument

No matter how well made your hull, rig and fins are, if they are not correctly positioned relative to each other, the boat will not perform well. If it does not point high to windward, the chances are the rig is positioned too far forward or the centre-board too far aft. If it points but goes very slowly to windward or, in extreme cases, flies uncontrollably into the wind when hit by a gust, the rig is too far aft or the centre-board is too far forward. If the boat goes slowly on the run the rig is probably too far aft again. Check the position and rake of the fastest boats' masts and their centre-board positions then experiment with minor adjustments to these to see if you can find the ideal position that suits the inevitable but usually slight differences between your boat and sails and theirs. You may even discover that little bit of extra speed which will make winning that bit easier.

THE FAST HELMSMAN AND CREW

Technique, strategic thinking, physical fitness and clothing are four identifiable factors that go towards making one helmsman or crewman better than the next.

Technique

There is a specific technique required to make each type of boat go quickly on every point of sailing—whole books have been written on the subject. The only way you will learn everything is by observing and questioning top helmsmen in your class. There are however, certain broadly similar methods for dinghies, others for catamarans and yet more for keelboats.

In general a dinghy is sailed with varying amounts of leeward heel in light winds to reduce wetted surface and bolt upright in heavy weather to keep the boat perfectly balanced. This is true for a beat or a reach but on a run, a dinghy will normally go quicker if it is heeled to windward with the boom stuck up in the air; do not try it in heavy winds as it will take the hint and capsize towards you. Catamarans are sailed as much as possible with one hull flying just clear of the water to reduce wetted surface but keelboats are generally sailed as upright as possible to maximize the lift provided by the keel and rudder.

Many high performance dinghies get to the windward mark quicker if they can be made to plane; this technique is extremely difficult to get just right. You have to point slightly lower to bring the boat up onto its bow wave and then keep it there; the danger is that you point too low and allow those who prefer to sail slower and higher to make better ground to windward. If you can do it right you will leave those who cannot for dead.

The most difficult point of sailing in catamarans is the dead run which has to be turned into a pair or more of broad reaches; in this way the wind can be accelerated across the sails, establishing the kind of laminar airflow that dinghies and keelboats can only achieve on a beat or a close reach. The speed of a catamaran reaching in this way is so much faster than that

Perfect balance and really flying

1

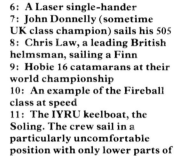

1: *Relax,* US 126, an Etchells 22 one-design keel boat
2: Tornado worlds. A flying trapeze on a flying hull
3: Toppers
4: 505 dinghies in a gate start at a world championship at Hayling Island
5: Mirror dinghies on a jolly reach. Only spinnakers among the sails are allowed to differ in colour
6: A Laser single-hander
7: John Donnelly (sometime UK class champion) sails his 505
8: Chris Law, a leading British helmsman, sailing a Finn
9: Hobie 16 catamarans at their world championship
10: An example of the Fireball class at speed
11: The IYRU keelboat, the Soling. The crew sail in a particularly uncomfortable position with only lower parts of the leg inboard
12: One of the long established Dragon class

2

3

4

6

5

7   8

9   10

11   12

possible if it runs directly before the wind, that it will arrive at the leeward mark far more quickly in spite of having covered as much as fifty per cent extra distance.

In keelboats, keeping the boat sufficiently upright so that its underwater shape is not too distorted and coaxing these normally heavy craft onto the plane are particular techniques that can win races.

Neat and efficient tacking, gybing, spinnaker handling and mark rounding are matters that must be perfected so that each manoeuvre costs little or no speed. Roll tacking of dinghies in light airs can actually increase speed but has now been outlawed by the International Yacht Racing Union if there is any suspicion that the boat comes out of the tack faster than it went into it.

Strategic thinking

The cardinal rules of race strategy are starting dead on the gun, keeping clear of wind interference caused by other boats and maintaining a position between those following you and the next mark.

You can either make a standing start by lying stationary on the line until the gun goes or you can make a flying start, which is more difficult as you have to arrive exactly at the right moment and there has to be room amongst all those making the standing start for you to get in.

Planning your course to take account of tidal systems and forecasted wind shifts is all

Always wear a life-jacket in a centreboarder

part of pre-race preparation along with setting up the boat just right for the weather conditions.

Physical fitness

A combination of some physical training and plenty of time afloat is the ideal way to tune the body and build up your stamina. Physical training can be achieved by running, swimming, circuit training or playing squash but the benefits of these should never be overestimated; there is no substitute for sailing if you want to strengthen the muscles you are going to use when you are racing.

Tiredness and exhaustion affect your powers of concentration and judgement in addition to reducing your ability to handle the boat correctly. So get fit if you want to win.

Clothing

If in doubt always opt for warmer clothing than you think you will need; better to be too hot in a wet suit than to be cold without. A wet suit is essential for dinghy and catamaran sailing or good thermal wear with waterproof overalls for keelboat sailing. The windage created by a man on trapeze should not be ignored and to minimize this, stretch fit overalls are now produced by several different manufacturers which can be worn over wet suits and life jackets.

On the subject of life jackets, never go afloat without one and always wear it if there is any kind of wind strength; serious accidents are rare in small boat sailing but when they do happen they can be fatal if sensible precautions are not taken.

6

More speed

Quite separate from other sections of sailing is the speed record sport; here boats are designed specifically to achieve the highest speed possible over a measured distance and because they are not required to be able to perform at all angles to the wind or to race around buoys, many are built and rigged so that they can only sail on one tack and then with only a minor variation in wind angle.

Attempts on world speed records have been centred very much around the RYA Annual Speed Trials at Weymouth, UK, since they were begun in 1972. More recently other events have been instigated in Hawaii and Holland. There are five official classes divided according to sail area used; they are the 10m² Class, the 'A' Class (10·1–13·94 m²), the 'B' Class (13·95–21·84m²), the 'C' Class (21·85–27·88m²) and the Unlimited Class for larger sail areas.

The fastest boat in the world so far and by a considerable margin is Tim Coleman's *Crossbow II*, a catamaran with the long, slim windward hull set slightly behind the other. It was designed by Rod MacAlpine-Downie of 'C' Class catamaran fame; she recorded 36·04 knots at Weymouth in October 1980.

Much to the embarrassment of competitors in the 'A', 'B' and 'C' Classes, their speeds are not as fast as the 10 Square Metre record which is held by Jaap Van Der Rest using a single-handed prototype sailboard designed by Garry Seaman of Tencate Sports. He set his record of 24·63 knots in Hawaii in July 1980 proving that big is not necessarily beautiful when you are searching for high speeds and making the 'A', 'B' and 'C' records, set by complex hydrofoil-borne catamarans, seem like poor value for expenditure.

Tim Coleman confidently predicted, after his 1980 record, that he could pass the 40 knot barrier with his existing equipment; how much farther this quest for the ultimate speed goes depends upon his continued sponsorship, but it will be no surprise if he builds another even faster machine before he finally gives it up.

Current world records

Class	Craft	Type and Designer	Speed (Knots)	Date
10m²	Tencate Board	Prototype by Garry Seaman	24·63	18. 7.80
A	Mayfly	Hydrofoil catamaran by Ben Wynne	23·04	3.10.77
B	Icarus	Hydrofoil Tornado by James Grogono	23·80	8.10.80
C	(nf)²	Hydrofoil catamaran by Prof. Bradfield	24·40	11.78
Unlimited	Crossbow II	Catamaran by Rod MacAlpine-Downie	36·04	17.11.80

1: *Crossbow II*, holder of the
world sailing speed record
2: *Crossbow* with a hull flying
3: *Slingshot*, a boat designed in
America to attempt the world
sailing speed record
4: *Icarus*, another contender
for sailing speed record
5: *Force 8*, one of the
contenders in a sailing record
speed week

4

5

7

Each end of the sailing world

The 12-metre class and the sailboard could hardly present a greater contrast. Twelve-metres used only for America's Cup, need large crews of 11 men and are designed to a rating rule created in 1907. If the boat is not racing, you can sit in the cockpit observing the relatively slow tacking, gybing and sail handling. There are few in commission in the world at any one time, less than ten usually, and then only in countries with long yachting traditions—the United States, England, France and Sweden. Stability comes mainly from a huge and expensive lead keel and the whole yacht with her sophisticated equipment and wardrobe of sails is expensive. It will cost at least a million dollars to build and campaign for a season. A 12 does not have an engine, so as an addition a sizeable tender becomes necessary to tow in harbour or calm at the end of a race.

What a contrast to the sailboard which was only invented in 1967 by Hoyle Schweitzer and James Drake in California. Previously, materials would hardly have allowed the craze to spread because the boards would have been too heavy. Simplicity is everything: there is no rudder, keel or seating and ashore it is carried under the arm or on the roof of a car (or on the deck of a cruising yacht). More contrasts with 12s—thousands in all countries sail them—alone, despite stunts with two or more and a few tandem boards. The only equipment is the board, one sail, one boom, a mast, a joint and a few control lines. Now, in the eighties we find just a little of this simplicity is eroded with special boards for racing as well as board clothing and other equipment.

The board and the board sailor

The sailboard consists of a thin flat polyurethane-filled plastic or wooden hull, with skeg and centre-board to prevent leeway and give directional control. Skegs are generally plastic and pushed through a hole in the board or screwed on, whereas centre-boards are either daggerboards or swivel centre-boards. The rig is attached to the board, at a point in front of the centre-board, via a universal joint. Rigging on a sailboard is provided by the sailor who holds a two-sided boom attached to the mast, with which the board is controlled. A sailboard has no rudder. This is the major difference between a conventional sailing craft which uses a rudder to divert the waterflow and so change direction, as opposed to the board which changes the position of the sail plan to steer. Potentially this method of steering is very efficient, providing instant response once mastered correctly. The universal joint also allows incredible speeds, such as the under 10m² world speed record held by a board. These speeds in excess of 24 knots are achieved by pulling the rig sideways, thereby creating lift on the board and sailor, so reducing displacement, making the hull skim over the water—a highly exhilarating experience.

Many who try board sailing give up at an early stage because it appears too tiring. This is due to spending the first few hours pulling the rig up, physically very demanding as the board sailor is continually lifting a large amount of water in the sail. Once the basics are learnt and falling off becomes a thing of the past, the forearms suffer due to having to grip the boom. The harness, which clips to the boom via a harness rope, alleviates this problem; a harness is similar to the trapeze harness on many high performance dinghies except that the hook is at chest level.

Physically a board requires the same degree of fitness as a Laser. It is demanding when sailed hard, but it is equally possible just to cruise. As such the sport is an easy and enjoyable method of keeping fit. Technique is more important than physical strength, as many girls have shown the men by beating them in straight

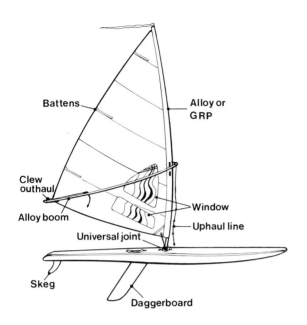

Battens

Alloy or
GRP

Clew
outhaul

Alloy boom

Window

Universal joint

Uphaul line

Skeg

Daggerboard

**The parts of a sailboard. Essentially different from a
sailing boat because of the jointed mast and lack of rudder**

races whatever the wind strength, during European championships.

The spectacular growth of board sailing over the last few years is partially due to the glamorous image, but ease of transport and price are also important factors. The sport is well organized with the UK Boardsailing Association (UKBSA) and IYRU internationally. The UKBSA has left many dinghy associations gaping, using a micro-computer, professional race officer and back-up team to give exceptional, well organized race meetings for over 200 boards. The racing is divided into two experience groups, each having a light, heavy and ladies fleet; the B fleet also have junior results. Board sailing has spread throughout the country in a controlled manner, especially where water authorities have opened suitable lakes, and there are now thousands of board sailors in the UK. Sailboard clubs have sprung up both inland and round the coast and established sailing clubs have also accepted the craft as a club fleet. Inland clubs are normally based on reservoirs or gravel pits, West Midlands (Birmingham) and Nottingham being two major centres. Schools and clubs are situated round most cities on small local lakes. the south coast also has concentrations of boards, especially at Hayling, Weymouth and Stokes Bay.

Boards are very easy to transport. A man or woman can handle them off a car roof with

ease allowing small groups of sailors to appear on a beach. Although this allows a great deal of freedom, it is also potentially dangerous and only the foolhardy sail without company. Once the basic manoeuvres are mastered board sailing is easy. Rather like riding a bicycle it suddenly clicks and off you go, then the remainder of the learning process is more gradual.

The school is the best way to learn board sailing in a few hours as it requires only a minimal outlay and gives the learner a chance to try the sport before spending too much. A school with either a qualified RYA instructor or windsurfer instructor should be chosen from the RYA's list. Learning is quicker and less heartbreaking under proper supervision.

Those who wish to learn the hard way, by trial and error, should bear several points in mind:
(a) choose a small sheltered stretch of water with no current and little wind.
(b) never try on your own.
(c) allow enough room to drift with the wind.
(d) dress properly.

Theory of board sailing

Directional control is achieved by moving the rig: backwards to luff up into the wind, forwards to bear away. The easiest way to understand how the rig movement affects board direction is to think of the body as the link between the rig and board. With the rig moved back there is more force to the rear, and the back leg effectively pushes the stern round so the board luffs. Conversely, with the rig forward the force pushes the bow round so the board bears away. After a short while these movements are natural and the sail's angle of attack can also be used for steering; for example, feathering the luff means only the back of the sail is pulling so luffing occurs, and letting the back of the sail lose wind causes the board to bear away.

Learning to sail consists of three steps:
(a) raising the rig
(b) sheeting in
(c) control and tacking.

Raising the rig

Hauling up the rig and sheeting in should be practised on shore, and then on the water. The board should then be put on the water with the rig at right angles to leeward. An assistant holding the board to steady it helps teach balance at this stage. Stand with the feet either side of

Left: A board, a sail. One of the original Hoyle Schweitzer Windsurfer class

Above: Board sailing in surf. Note the hinged mast

Below: Freestyle board sailing. This is the 'rail ride splits'

the mast and grasp the uphaul line. Lean out against the weight of water on the sail and as it starts to drain, stand upright working up the uphaul line. Generally, this is when most beginners pull too hard and fall over backwards when they do not allow for the lack of water in the sail; slowly and surely works best. After a short while this stage is mastered and you are standing holding the uphaul line with the sail flapping at right angles to the board.

Sheeting in

Sheeting in is fairly simple, the secret being to move slowly and surely. The majority of beginners do not set the sail correctly, with the luff not filling properly, resulting in the board luffing, tacking, and then a swim is involved. Hold on to the uphaul rope with the back hand, then cross the hand over and grip the boom. Push the rig forward and grab hold of the boom with the back hand; if the sail is pulling

properly you are now sailing and may need to correct the direction the board is going. The rig should be leaning forward and the whole sail pulling as in the photograph.

Control and tacking

Luffing is achieved by leaning the rig back, bearing away by leaning the rig forward. The next priority becomes turning around; often while learning, this is involuntary, when the sailor falls off and turns around manually. However, the correct method is to luff up to head to wind, step round the front of the mast and sail off on the opposite tack. An experienced boardsailor can tack faster than a dinghy. While learning to tack it is often easier to sail beyond head to wind, then let the sail flap and walk round the front slowly. Allow the rig to settle down (at right angles to the board) then sail off as normal, at your own pace.

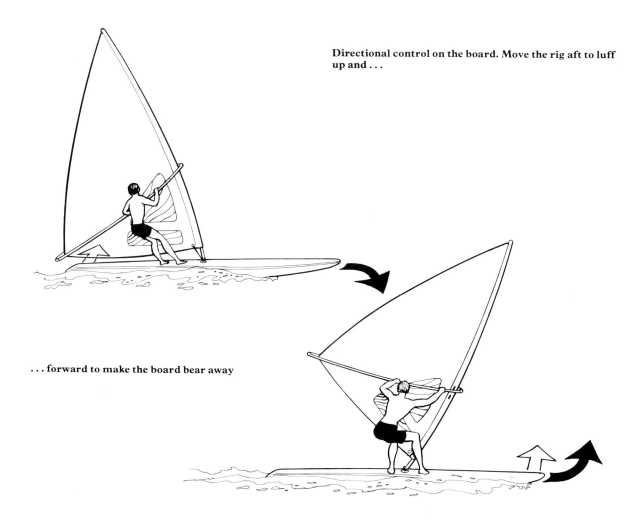

Directional control on the board. Move the rig aft to luff up and . . .

. . . forward to make the board bear away

Right: The board sailing rescue signal

Below: A 'head-dip' stunt in freestyle surfing

Above: Boards racing. A mixture of classes
Below: Board sailing in many classes grows apace
Right: Sailboards on a 'distance' race in the swells off Hawaii

A knowledge of rescue techniques will hopefully be unnecessary but is still essential. The rig should be rolled and if there are rescue craft around, wave one clenched fist slowly above the head. Self-rescue requires you to lie on the board and paddle back, or else sit on the front and paddle.

Beating comes after learning reaching, but running requires expertise and balance, due to having nothing to balance against. Gradually, expertise is built up in the stronger winds, when the sailor leans out further over the water, until the head skims the waves in really strong winds. The front leg should be kept straight to act as a brace against the wind force, while the back leg is bent to prevent catapulting over the front. Experienced sailors can handle conditions which prevent most dinghies going out. Having mastered the principles of boardsailing, keener sailors often move onto racing, freestyle or wavejumping.

Racing

Racing falls into two categories:
1. Open class, which allows all makes of board to race together.
2. One-design class racing, on a single type and make of board, normally with only standard equipment.

Board shape varies from a flat board with little rocker such as the Windsurfer or Sea Panther, to the newer 'V'd displacement boards. The displacement board has a 'V'd bow with plenty of rocker; as such they cut through the water more easily in light winds or chop, but are more unstable, especially downwind. Although the boards are being used in top class racing, they are not ideal for the beginner. The flatter boards, which nearly every manufacturer has in his range, are easier to sail on the sea and in strong winds and can also be used for freestyle, and class racing in many cases. Race results consistently show that it is the person, not the board, who reaches the top.

Sails come in various sizes and cuts, generally a board comes with a full-size racing sail, though some have the smaller all-weather sail. Racing sails are also available from specialist sail makers. Manufacturers can provide a storm sail for heavy weather and also a 'kids' rig' in some cases.

One-design class racing on a single type of board is on the increase. The two largest one-design classes in England are the Windsurfer and Sea Panther, with the Windglider (now an Olympic class) growing. Attendance at the national championships is around the 100 mark, while series races are often attended by 30 boards. The 1980 Windsurfer World's at Grand Bahama Island attracted 437 competitors from 37 countries. Racing at all board sailing meetings is under the IYRU rules, as in any dinghy class, with a few clarifications. For instance, a board is capsized when 'the mast is touching the water', the mast foot is used for defining when a luff is permitted, and a deliberate capsize in crowded situations is not allowed.

IBSA run a European and world championship at various venues throughout the world. The racing is held over several weight groups and the top few sailors of each country are automatically in the finals; otherwise there are qualifying rounds for the remaining places. Windgliders and Windsurfers are IYRU recognized classes.

A tandem board

Freestyle and wavejumping

Sailboarding has various fringe aspects such as wavejumping and freestyle. Freestyle is an ideal spectator sport which is increasing in popularity. The UKBSA organize a national championship at which competitors are allowed three minutes to compete a routine through several eliminating rounds to a final. The routine should be a smooth flowing compilation of tricks. Marks are given for originality, number of tricks and difficulty of tricks. The showmanship and flair involved in the presentation make the difference between first and second place. The routine normally starts with a rail ride, that is sailing the board on its edge. The main body of the routine includes such tricks as head dipping, duck tacking, back to sail and others. A spectacular exit off the board is the normal method of finishing the routine.

The board is either ejected out of the water or the sailor jumps off the board. Ejection is achieved by pushing the back or front of the board down and jumping off, thereby making the board jump out of the water. This is done when on the rail or with the board flat. The second finish involves the sailor leaving the board by a back-dive or somersault round the boom, finishing in the water.

Freestylists normally use a flat board because of stability and the mast foot should be securely jammed in. Learning tricks is a good way of passing the time in light winds and most sailors try a few tricks soon after starting sailing. Many tricks take only a few hours to master in their basic form and it is up to the individual to build on this and produce something different. New tricks are continuously being developed.

A most spectacular aspect of the sport is wavejumping, bringing a new generation of flat boards with footstraps and odd looking skegs. Wavejumping started in Hawaii, where in waves up to 20ft (6m) a few enthusiasts jumped their windsurfers off waves, normally ending up in the water afterwards. The Windsurfer Rockets and a good number of custom boards have since been developed specifically for wavejumping.

The wavejumping board has a smaller daggerboard further back than normal with twin skegs. Grip is provided by footstraps fixed at strategic points on the board. These stop the expert falling off and allow him to control the board in the air. Footstrap kits are available for most boards, and with a storm daggerboard wavejumping is feasible.

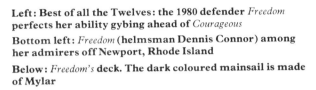

Left: Best of all the Twelves: the 1980 defender *Freedom* perfects her ability gybing ahead of *Courageous*

Bottom left: *Freedom* (helmsman Dennis Connor) among her admirers off Newport, Rhode Island

Below: *Freedom's* deck. The dark coloured mainsail is made of Mylar

Right: A 12-metres' pattern on the sea. The 1977 successful defender of America's Cup. *Courageous* **(helmsman Ted Turner)**

Below: It is lonely on the bow of a 12-metre when match racing

Below: Would-be challengers for America's Cup, *Sverige* **and** *France.* **Neither Sweden nor France has ever made the finals. Since 1967 it has always been Australia that has challenged**

Then to the largest

Boats designed and built to the 12-metre rule are the largest class to be raced inshore. Although there are rules insisting on a minimum area of watertight deck, the boats are open large keel boats and not designed for crossing open waters, but for sailing round closed courses within sight of the shore. This does not mean that they cannot stand heavy weather, or undertake sea passages from port to port for racing. Of course, when being moved from Europe or Australia to America for racing, they are carried on board ship.

Before 1940, 12-metres were one of several 'metre boat' classes (8s and 6s were the other common sizes) found in main yachting countries, but even then they were not numerous. The British Yacht Racing Association of 12-metre certificates for 1935 gives four boats to the 'old rule' and a further six boats new or building to the 'new rule'. Now in Britain, if one 12-metre yacht is built it is a major event and the same goes for France and Sweden and Australia. No 12s have been built since 1940 in any country other than these except the United States. The only reason for building a 12 is to challenge or defend for the America's Cup. For that reason the average number built every third year (the usual frequency of the event) is two, with perhaps a further one or two boats receiving major alterations to update them.* Altogether 13 new 12s were built in the USA between 1958 and 1980.

Twelves are not the biggest sailing yachts; IOR maxi boats are on average 15ft (4·6m) longer, but they are particularly expensive to run because of the intensive and competitive nature of an America's Cup campaign, whether contending for a place as a challenger or a defender. They are essentially 'wasteful', because ocean racers of this size can go on racing in different parts of the world and then cruising and chartering, but a 12-metre is just a racing boat and its value plummets, when the America's Cup season is over. The exception to this is the one winner, which is in demand as a key trial horse for the next defence in three years' time. True, some 12s have been converted to ocean racers and even cruisers, but this is exceptional and probably only because they were available at a very low price for the size of boat offered. One remembers *American*

---

* For the historical facts and the superlatives of America's Cup see *The Guinness Book of Yachting Facts and Feats*, Section 3, The America's Cup.

Eagle, sailed remarkably by Ted Turner in IOR events (1969 to 1975, by 1981 she was renamed *Warbaby* and still cruising) for some years and at one stage holder of the Fastnet race elapsed-time record and *Evaine*, a 1938 British 12, which cruised extensively including across the Atlantic after her racing days (which lasted to 1958) were over.

The America's Cup course is in the open sea off Newport, Rhode Island. Today an Olympic type course is used and the races are unusual in being match events. That is to say only two boats take part, the defender and the challenger. All other contenders have previously been disposed of in elimination races by both defenders and the several national challengers. The total nominal distance is about 24·3 miles (actually longer for tacking and tactical diversions). As an Olympic course has three windward legs, straight into the wind, the boats are designed to point close and powerfully. The boat ahead once going to windward should be able to cover her opponent thus making it extremely difficult to get through. The logic of this is to 'win the start' as well and the boats should be designed to excel in rapid pre-start movements.

Since 1958, when America's Cup racing transferred from older, larger classes to 12-metres, the successful American defenders have beaten six Australian boats and two British. Other British, French and Swedish boats have been eliminated in challengers trials. American boats contending for the defence are listed below. In each case the eventual defender is shown first (a first appearance in the list for the year indicates recent build).

1958 Columbia (beat Sceptre, Brit.)
     Easterner
     Vim (built 1937)
     Weatherly
1962 Weatherly (beat Gretel, Aus.)
     Nefertiti
     Easterner
     Columbia
1964 Constellation (beat Sovereign, Brit.)
     American Eagle
     Nefertiti
     Easterner
     Columbia
1967 Intrepid (beat Dame Pattie, Aus.)
     Constellation
     American Eagle
1970 Intrepid (beat Gretel II, Aus.)
     Valiant
     Heritage

1974 Courageous (beat Southern Cross, Aus.)
Intrepid
Mariner
Valiant
1977 Courageous (beat Australia, Aus.)
Independence
Enterprise
Intrepid
1980 Freedom (beat Australia, Aus.)
Clipper
Courageous
Enterprise

Why use the wasteful, impracticable 12-metre? Because she is expensive and exclusive. It is the holder of America's Cup, the New York Yacht Club, which decides. There is a deed of gift to the cup which lays down a minimum size for competitors and this was *reduced* in 1956 to let in the 12s. The NYYC could allow large IOR boats, but the IOR would probably be unable to withstand the assault of designers when used for an inshore contest, so the result is uncertain and the effect on the IOR with all its fleets probably dangerous. The 12-metre rule is restrictive and means closely matched designs. There is scope for designers but it is subtle. Dimensions are not very widely spaced and the defender in 1980, *Freedom*, designed by Sparkman and Stephens, was LOA 63ft 0in (19·2m), LWL 47ft 0in (14·3m) beam 12ft 5in (3·8m), draft 9ft (2·7m), displacement about 60 000lb (27·3 tonnes). Each design varies the main dimensions under a simple formula which contains length (L), sail area (SA), freeboard (F) and a dimension (d), which is the difference in length of a chain stretched around the section and a chain touching the section. The lighter the displacement of the boat, the more tucked up will be the section and the bigger will be (d).

$$\frac{L + 2d + \sqrt{SA} - F}{2·37} = 12 \text{ metres}$$

The formula is

So the designer can have more sail area but less length; or less displacement but then less sail area. But the figures cannot exceed 12 metres. There are also numerous restrictions on materials, dimensions such as height of mast and genoa/spinnaker and the underwater profile, so the small keels and spade rudders of ocean racing boats are not seen.

A modern 12-metre will be constructed in aluminium; before 1974 they had to be of traditional wood build. The rule allows only 11 crew in total and restricts the amount of open cockpit to 96·8ft² (9m²), so a typical 12 has a helmsman cockpit aft with a navigator (tactician) and mainsheet trimmer, then just forward the brawny members of the crew, the men who handle the genoa sheets and spinnaker sheets and gear, the grinders (on winches) and tailers (on the sheets being 'ground'). Near the foot of the mast there may be one or more small cockpits for the mast men who control halyards and other lines in that area. Two men will be available for the foredeck, one of these able to go right forward when gybing the spinnaker and another man may be below to handle sails and lines which come and go from there. Such arrangements will vary between and on boats as schemes and drills are developed. There are no lifelines along the edge, as in other sailing yachts, and no engine. Usually there is a steering wheel; there may be two abreast of each other so the helmsman can sit far to one side or the other. On some boats there may even be a tiller: this was favoured on the Swedish *Sverige*, contender in 1977 and 1980. The main winches have to be coffee grinders (see page 179).

The sight of a 12 in the distance is unmistakable, because of its rig. The rule prevents a mast head rig and the huge mainsail has an old-fashioned look about it, with a long main boom. The single mast is around 87ft (26·5m) high and will be tapered and refined so that loss of masts in the work up towards the America's Cup are not uncommon. Mast bend is induced for extra performance and further increases the engineering problems. Adjustable ram and deck level and adjustable, running backstays control and bend in the huge aluminium spar. In America, a Cup campaign almost always sees advances in sails. In the early sixties it was the incentive that brought American sailcloth of Dacron into a lead, never quite lost, and in 1980 the latest film synthetics such as Mylar and Kevlar were in use. The latter explains the pale brown colour of some panels in photographs of the 12s. Both materials decrease in porousness, stand up in their designed shape in a greater range of wind speeds and hold shape at a given wind speed and point of sailing with greater accuracy. Research into such sails spills out into yachting generally and many are the materials, designs of equipment and techniques that have been generated in 12-metres for sailing yachts in general. Perhaps the 12s are not wholly wasteful after all.

Planing in a 470 Olympic class dinghy

Part Two

Cruising under sail

'Remember and write it down "Cruising is not racing".
If your boat is a home and a companion, and at the same
time a genius that takes you from place to place and, what
is more, a good angel, revealing unexpected things, then
you must put away from yourself altogether the idea of
racing. The cruiser, the strong little, deep little boat, is
all I have called it. It is a complete satisfaction for man;
but if you let in racing you are letting in the serpent . . . .'

Hilaire Belloc in *The Cruise of the Nona* (1925)

8

Cruising people

A cruising boat is often regarded as a step up from the sailing dinghy. It is really more of a step sideways into a distinctive manner of spending time upon the water. Instead of going out for the afternoon in an athletic, or at least semi-athletic pursuit, the cruising sailor and his family live on the boat—and with it. As with the dinghy, it may be just for an afternoon, or it may be a week-end, or a week—or an extended summer holiday. Or they may live on the boat all the year round; and this again may be moored comfortably in a berth or travelling —under sail—continuously.

The variety of types of cruising boats is never ending. This is literally true, because every week somewhere in the world (especially the sailing areas of Europe, America and the Far East) a new production boat comes on the market. There are just a few persons left who can afford the time, effort and finance to have a boat specially designed and built, but most of us sail *production boats*. Such production boats can have plenty of custom touches and variations to suit individuals. It is not a result only of whims, but different owners have different uses for their boats. Others have firmly held ideas on what contributes to safety at sea, comfortable living and priorities afloat.

The rationality of all this variety will be examined, but apart from logic it is fun to see and sail past so many different sailing boats. There is at least one human and one commercial factor in all this. A sailing yacht is an 'extra', a grown-up toy that does not have to be cost effective, or even be built to government rules; so there is a strong 'fashion' element. It should look like what we want it to look like. For instance it may have an 'up-to-date' line, or imitate some boat that has just made a rugged girdling of the world. Compared with a car, the tooling up is slight. New models of boats can take just a few months from drawing board to sailing prototype; this in turn fits in with the

sailing boat market which is very small when compared with cars. So there are numerous classes, relatively small production runs and a great number of small or medium sized boat builders contributing. A boat built in a back yard may be indistinguishable from a production line version. Such a remark could never apply to a car. If comparison of cruising boat production is made, it would be better paralleled to house building: all shapes and sizes, accommodating varying numbers of people, countless builders from one-man outfits to large public companies. But the analogy must not go too far. It was Arthur Ransome who wrote in the opening pages of *Racundra's First Cruise*: 'Houses are but badly built boats so firmly aground that you cannot think of moving them. They are definitely inferior things, belonging to the vegetable not the animal world, rooted and stationary, incapable of gay transition. The desire to build a house is the tired wish of a man content thenceforward with a single anchorage. The desire to build a boat is the desire of youth, unwilling yet to accept the idea of a final resting place.'

Sail and power

Since the purpose of cruising is to move enjoyably across the water, why not do this under power? The answer is that many sailors do indeed cruise under power: indeed the word 'cruiser' alone tends to denote a power boat. Here our subject is cruising under sail and the author is frankly partisan when it comes to motive power for pleasure. There is still around an element of the old rivalry, where sailing men talk about 'stink boats'. Even sails of small area, though, need a minimum of physical effort and many is the sailor who has turned to power in later years rather than give up cruising on the water. One lifelong yachtsman described this change of necessity as the 'sailopause'. If you

Trailer-sailer cruiser being launched by a family for day sailing in sheltered waters

Below: Another design of cruising running sail

Right: A cruising chute: no number, no spinnaker boom

Bottom right: A self steering powered Auto-helm does all the work here

**The contrasts of sailing. Smooth, sparkling water at
Brightlingsea on the east coast of England.
Heavy seas and grey skies on a race off the west coast
of Ireland**

One form of auxiliary power. An outboard motor through a special well (on an Impala 28)

are fortunate and fit to be able to handle your sails, then you will still be ninety-seven per cent certain, among today's sailing cruisers, to have a motor. The sailing boat without one is exceptional, her owner almost eccentric. Boats under 24ft may not have an inboard installation, but they are likely to have a neat system for handling an outboard motor, for entering port and for when the wind fails.

Yet it is one of the pleasures of sailing that, shortly after clearing the harbour and having hoisted sail while the motor moves the boat along, it can then be switched off. Without losing speed, the noise and vibration cease and instead comes the swish of water along the topsides. A sort of silence follows except for sea and wind, though they can have their own considerable sound at times. To be fair to the excellent modern yacht engine, it is a reassuring aid at the end of a passage, as the pier heads of some tricky harbour, where the wind baffles, is entered. The sails are secured and the power element takes over to make for mooring buoy or quayside. Such a manoeuvre could well be impossible under sail.

One of the choices in a cruising yacht is the amount of emphasis on sail on the one hand and power on the other in a particular design.

The options will be looked at more closely. One aspect of this is that the cruising owner or crew would do well to have a knowledge of (boat) engines—something not necessary for the dinghy sailor. There is other knowledge he requires more than the man in the dinghy. Aspects of this include navigation (or at least pilotage), an understanding of weather, handling under sail and power in confined waters, the rules about collision at sea, what to do in strong winds and in fog, improvisation and repair without outside help. To this brief list can be added the operation of any instrumentation on board such as the simple echo sounder or the more demanding radio transmitter. On a cruiser there is a need for the seaman's arts, which one can just get away without knowing when one is day-sailing a dinghy. Though a dinghy sailor ought to know, for instance, basic knots, bends and hitches, he can manage without too close an acquaintance of these. But a cruising crew will sooner or later be in real trouble without being able to make a bowline, a clove hitch or surge or sweat a line on a cleat.

Who sails the cruising boat?

The cruising boat is the essential family aspect of sailing. Once again, yes, you can sail an ocean racer with the family (it would be very unlikely to be only family, although there have been several well known competitors, where a father has a squad of sons in their twenties!). Family ocean racers will need to be strong crew as well. Dinghies are for the family though some will stay on shore, if only to assist in pulling up the slipway. But it is the cruiser where complete family groups are seen on board and make the entire crew. Indeed the production boat is frequently designed around the family—father (navigation), mother (galley), younger members (swimming and parties)—to the best of the market research of the builder or the personal experience of the designer.

A couple owning a cruiser and without persistent family ties are unlikely to enlist a group of young men to sail her. To begin with, such a squad may soon get bored and for them a keenly raced ocean racer, as discussed in the next part of this book, is undoubtedly needed. The whole trend is to be comfortable, and for the boat to be easily handled with just a few skilled persons (depending on the size), the others being guests or novices. The flexibility of numbers is a cruising characteristic. One afternoon, out packed with friends: a few days

Left: Brown sails and blue water are what cruising men dream about. Here are topsails a bowsprit and dinghy in convenient davits on this gaff ketch

Below: Two ketches and a sloop, in a friendly cruiser race off Antigua

Bottom: Dufour 28, typical of scores of modern production boats

Right: Motor sailer. A trawler type built by Fairways Marine

Below: A typical sight in British waters. A cruiser expecting bad weather heavily reefed and with small jib (note there are no sail numbers, which are only required for racing)

Bottom right: *Iskra,* a small gaff sloop which has crossed the Atlantic several times. Here she is guided by self steering only

What the crew must avoid. Running ashore in a deep keel boat. In this case the sand was smooth and the bay protected and boat was hauled off when the tide rose and wind moderated

later away on passage with two couples on board. Thus the boat must be easy to handle and in the following pages this will come in for some emphasis. There is an important balance here in the development of the cruiser on the one hand and the ocean racer on the other. Speed (within the laid down limitations) is everything for the racer and handling for such a boat means quick handling. If it needs a crew of eight on a 35-footer, to gybe round marks and lower spinnakers in the middle of the night, this number on this length means discomfort and little room to move around below on a wet day in harbour. Speed in handling is secondary to convenience with small numbers. How tense and exhilarating is racing! How relaxed and satisfying is cruising!

It is not proposed at every stage to compare the cruising boat and the racing boat. The reader can do this for him or herself by considering the two relevant parts of this book. But the parallel development mentioned above is worth a few observations. Parallel is perhaps not too accurate, because the types are tending to diverge, particularly since 1970. In the eighties this separation can only become more complete. Many years ago ocean racers were only sea-worthy, well-sailed cruising boats with some extra sails, but that was more than forty years ago. The development of offshore racing boats, which is financed by owners and sponsors who are all out to win, will continue to be of great benefit to the users of cruising boats. The throw-off is continuous, but a typical example is the self-tailing winch, which only requires one person to operate it effectively. Improvements in metal masts and their fittings are invariably passed on to production yachts. (Let the racing men break them first and find the limiting con-ditions!) A typical piece of racing equipment that is not of use to the cruiser is the grooved forestay that is common on racers and in which the jib is hoisted. Such grooves and double grooves enable sails to be hoisted while others are in position and they are alleged to give a better airflow over the genoa or jib for performance. On a cruising boat they so far have no application. Hoisting one headsail over another is very hard work because of the friction between the two, and when a sail is lowered it blows all over the deck. The cruising yacht will have the sail with metal hanks on a forestay which are relatively easy to haul up and ensure that the sail is under close control when it comes down.

If a cruiser does have a headsail in a groove, it will be most likely as part of a furler sail. This rolls up as the wind strength increases and can be totally rolled for harbour stowage. Yet the racing boat will not be seen with such a labour saving device, for the sail can never set with the perfection demanded for competitive sailing. Certain old racing boats will make very happy cruising vessels, but not all. In racing circles there are attempts from time to time to make rules which result in a 'dual purpose boat' (ie racing and cruising). Such aims are difficult to achieve, as will be seen when measurement rules are discussed.

So the cruising owner does not worry about what the racing boat—or even the other cruising boat—is doing. The boat and the rig and the handling only have to suit his ideas and his family and his friends—for the purpose of sailing on the sea.

Start cruising

Owning the boat is one way to get cruising under sail. Inflation means the author will not mention prices in terms of currencies, but for a boat that makes satisfactory passages in the open sea, the investment is considerable. Yet when there is mention of the cruising yachtsman, it is sole ownership that many immediately think of. Ownership! You are undisputed master of your ship, go where you like—or not go at all. Add equipment, or scrap other gear. Invite your friends, or get away from them by sailing off. There is genuinely the pleasure of ownership, relaxing on board your mobile floating home.

Because the scale of outlay is so different as between a dinghy and a cruising boat, the word 'investment' is used. Maybe it is a kind of excuse for taking otherwise usefully earning capital and expending it on such a massive item. This item is frequently the family's biggest single piece of property, after its own house. At times it has been better to put the money into a boat, rather than a good share or unit trust. But the result depends on the boat and on the share with which it is compared. The facts about investment are these. In times of inflation a boat of quality and reputation will hold its monetary value, or even increase it. It must be known in terms of its builder and designer. It should be a seagoing boat, which makes it easier to sell outside the country in which it lies. For instance it can be bought on England's south coast and sailed direct to Germany. When computing some sort of financial return, the owner must have had good use. In other words, it is no good just buying a boat and leaving it for a few years, because there is no dividend in the form of enjoyment. In any case, best preservation of value is by careful use and maintenance; neither storage on the one hand, nor being flogged to pieces on the other. This is where the cruising boat comes in. It can be a useful cruiser to someone at two years old, or ten years old; whereas an old ocean racer is no longer the hot shot that it was rightly designed to be when it was new.

The classic case of the boat that is a good investment is the Swan. There are Swan 37s, 441s, 65s and other marks. They were mostly designed as racers, but of moderate type with excellent cruising accommodation. The builders Nautor of Finland have a well-deserved international reputation. Their value holds and holds. They are glass fibre which has a potentially longer life than wood or metal. It may be indefinite—no one yet knows since its first application for boats in 1949. On the other hand boats with freak, unusual or dated features are unlikely to be easy to sell. Nor is a boat necessarily readily negotiable. World-wide the market waxes and wanes. Then, the whole system is dependent on generally peaceful and reasonably prosperous conditions.

Ownership therefore has its hazards and its pleasures. Once you own a boat you begin to see her faults as well as her advantages and boat ownership appears to be for most a continuing process. Yacht brokers say that the average time a person owns one boat is three years. Then the owner is after something with 'improvements'. Maybe he also wants to secure a better investment. To financial people, switching investments has a familiar and proved basis.

Other than ownership

It is not necessary to own a boat to cruise her. There is partnership, charter, sailing a club boat, borrowing or crewing. The first is only an extension of ownership. It obviously splits the cost, but has the usual need to give as well as take. What is not so obvious is that in the case of boats, used mainly at week-ends, it is quite common that a single owner or family cannot manage to use the boat every summer week-end. Therefore one does not envisage the partnership, each with a hand on the wheel! Rather the boat has better utilization by alternating sets of people.

Borrowing a boat or sailing a club boat are variations on chartering. The first is free, the second implies a more permanent and less commercial system. The important thing here is to make sure that the user knows all the workings of plumbing, electrics and motor as well as deck gear. (Before pumping the fresh water, there are two hidden cocks to open and don't expect the water to come until after eight strokes.) Because of the expense and difficulties of ownership, there are hundreds of charter and club boats all over the world. At the time of writing it is increasingly popular to get one's sailing in this way. Club boats are run by service and company organizations for their employees, with subsidized payment and the chance of getting to know how to sail the same boat over week-ends and then coming back for more for a longer holiday.

Charter can include every size and type of boat. It can cover most parts of the world from local charter in the Solent or Long Island Sound to more popular sunspots. The charter areas which are best known are the Caribbean and the Mediterranean. The first was for Americans and the second begun by Europeans, but now, of course, both fly to both. Such chartering may be crewed or bareboat. A crewed boat may have an owner manager on board and, depending on the size of the boat, his wife or other hands. Bareboat means that the charterer takes the boat away on his own. Fees are not small for any charter boat and for large yachts will run into thousands of dollars per week, but how else do you buy yourself on board a boat, which is at least temporarily yours to go where you will? Charter possibilities are considered later.

The potential owner should consider chartering or using a club boat. It is a chance to try out one type of boat or another under 'service' conditions. Just going for an afternoon sail and using that as the basis for the decision to buy is not nearly as thorough as living with the boat for a week or so. Unforeseen snags or pleasant bonuses will be found when eating, sleeping, night sailing, anchoring and in light and heavy weather to make the charter fee a premium worth paying. There are numerous instances of persons chartering a design—even when they did not contemplate ownership—and soon after ordering one of the same or similar type, or from the same boat builder.

The principal types

Let us list the main types of boat for cruising under sail. Owners and families use their boats in a variety of ways, yet the needs can come back to three broad requirements:

(a) A boat suitable for week-end cruising.
(b) A boat that can be used for effective passage making.
(c) A boat that can provide accommodation on board, but which is not going to be used for serious sailing. She will be used for day trips and usually return to a marina berth each evening, or often stay there all day.

Many of us like to think that we need a boat for use (b), but because of work and family commitments we only achieve use (c), or at least use (a). On the other hand, it is not necessary to plan an ocean voyage to need the boat to be fit for use (b). A holiday cruise across the North Sea can run into conditions which demand a boat to be fit for the ocean.

If those are the broadly different needs of cruising boats, then the boats themselves can also be divided into the following types, certainly as production boats go (for there is inevitably the one-off that fits into none of these categories):

(a) Sailing cruising yachts, perhaps with a division into large and small at 32ft (9·75m).
(b) Motor sailers.
(c) Cruising sailing boats which can be trailed behind a car or Land Rover type vehicle.
(d) Sailing boats for fishing and beach. These cruise around and make day trips, but do not race. They may have a cabin or cuddy, but are not for passage making, or extended living on board, or for racing.
(e) Cruising multihull vessels.

Top right: Pegasus 800, a production coastal cruiser with performance

Bottom right: Shallow draft demonstrated by this cruising sloop

(f) Vintage boats. Reproductions of specific old designs or generally dated in style. There are also boats which are simply old, but these can as well fit into (a) above, since we have given no date.

Most of these types will fit the three principal needs. For instance any of the above except for (d) will be adaptable for week-end cruising. Any one could be used for day trips, but the distinction may well lie in the way the boat is equipped and maintained rather than the basic design. One can even say that a boat capable of being trailered could do any of the three requirements. Many a very small boat has crossed the Atlantic, even though most of us would prefer sailing yachts over 30ft. If you walk with me along the yacht harbour pontoon, we could glance at one boat and then another and say 'That looks really good for a long trip', or 'Shouldn't think that goes out much, all right for a short trip on a fine day though'. Most would seem right for a week-end. We would make such remarks as we looked at the *type* and *design*, but also as we noticed little clues and small fittings. Those little clues might be the way the rigging was maintained, the ruggedness of the spars (mast and boom), the way equipment is stowed on deck. Of course, the boat does not reach the state she is seen to be in by her own efforts! It entirely reflects the kind of sailing and yachting attitude of the owner. It shows what he or she does with whatever the basic boat might be.

The salient implications of each of the six kinds of cruising boat are worth listing.

Conventional sailing cruising yachts

These are the go-anywhere boats in which we imagine great voyages to be contemplated. They have the longest tradition of all sea-going yachts—longer than ocean racers, longer than racing dinghies. Their exploits are often little different to those of one hundred years ago. The best of them are the most seaworthy (though the word is understood in different ways), the less useful ones are a lot of hard work. Most owe much to development in offshore racing. Being all-weather vessels with a strong rig and deep keel, they are restricted in the harbours and berths in which they can go. Primitive and shallow harbours may be closed to them. In

Above: A Drascombe Scaffie, 15ft, 4·5m small cruiser with fixed keel and traditional rig. This style of beach and coastal boat has strong appeal, partly as a reaction to 'modern' types

Right: Mirage 2700, one of many standard GRP designs for the small cruiser market

Below: Drascombe Coaster (21ft 9in) built in Devon has GRP hull, wood spars and is for cruising off beach or in estuary. A large cockpit takes a camping tent

popular sailing areas, berths for such boats may be scarce or unobtainable.

Motor sailers

Here the rig is less and the engine is more, though easily handled sails and modern high power to weight ratio motors means that many designs can be fully powered under sail *or* motor. There will be a wheel house rather than an open cockpit. Sailing performance will suffer because of such features as the large fixed propeller (causing drag) and high deck structures (causing windage, drag through the air at least when steaming into the wind). Performance under power means carrying a superfluous rig. Unlikely for long range voyages, but a compromise for week-end and coastal work.

Trailer sailers

Because of the shortage of berths afloat, this is a growth area. Quite simply the boat must be capable of going to sea, at least in semi-protected waters, and must be capable of being towed behind a family car or, if big, behind a field car such as a Land Rover. In order to fit the trailer without it being high in the air or impossible to launch in shallow water, it needs a centreboard or retractable keel. Yet it will be possible to live on board for short periods ashore, for instance when on a long tow to a new cruising ground. Yes, it means that there is wide choice of place to sail because of the land mobility, unrestricted by weather at sea. Obviously, the *size* is limited. So it is mobility and freedom from berth problems versus limitation of sea-going capacity (because of smallness, restricted draft and lightness).

Motor sailer type with big wheel house and small sails, the Berger Rogger design

Sheba trailer-sailer is also a midget racing boat of Micro-Tonner class

Sailing boats for fishing and beach

This category is as previously described. The main point is to identify it and not sail such a boat in the belief that it can make extended trips. The result would be unsatisfactory and probably dangerous.

Cruising multihulls

On these boats, there is less angle of heel and more space below, though the advantages are not always conveniently arranged. The reputation for speed does not apply to the cruising versions: this is the prerogative of the

Built in the 1980s, but to appeal to the vintage cruising market, the Cornish Trader is of wood construction

lightweight racing trimarans. The disadvantages are that they take up awkward space in harbour (though in tidal waters they can lie level on the mud) and have an inherent stability defect. At first they heel less in a freshening breeze, which is preferred by many people, especially those who are not dedicated sailors. Beyond a certain angle a multihull (which has no ballast keel) loses all stability and can remain permanently inverted. They are very much in a small minority for cruising and are likely to remain so.

Vintage boats

If you want to go fast from one place to another, you are better off in a jet plane or on the sea at least in a high speed power boat. So, sailing is not for those looking for absolute speed. What is the point in buying a sailing boat with the latest modern design to gain a fraction of a knot more on a basic average of 5·75 knots? Sailing boats are an anachronism, so enjoy the pleasure of a boat that looks like a boat. This is the argument for the vintage yacht. Varnished topsides, gaff rig and topsail, wood and hemp and not a piece of plastic to be seen! There are occasional rallies and races for 'old gaffers' or vintage craft. They can cruise with the best of them.

What kind of selection is available?

There is a huge selection of production boats for the potential buyer. Tom Webb, chief executive of the British Ship and Boat Builders National Federation, has explained why. 'In principle it is fairly easy to set up a plant to build boats; just a mould and some fibre glass and resin are needed. When a buyer is found the builder can add the fit out.' Some are in it

A Baltic Trader type converts for charter and other yacht use

because they like the idea of a life spent building boats. The unromantic result is over-production around the world, but a vast choice for the buyer. The danger to the latter is a steady small stream of boat builders going out of business, sometimes with the loss of deposits or progress payments by customers.

For instance at the beginning of 1980 it was possible to list around 450 different, production sailing cruisers on the market, which were being built in Britain (note, this does not include sailing dinghies and motor cruisers, but does include production ocean racing boats). In Australia these numbered 160 and in New Zealand 40. At the same time the number of sailing cruisers of all types listed by the French magazine *Bateaux* for its readers was 976. This number listed imported boats and so represented the market. It would not be very different for any other European country. In the United States, the magazine *Yachting* tabulated all sailing boats with some form of living accommodation on the American market at the beginning of 1981: the total number was 467. These were graduated in size from something called the Wilderness 21 of 21ft 6in length (6·5m) and displacing 1000lb (454kg) to the standard glass fibre Swan 76 (76ft/23m) with a displacement of almost exactly one hundred times that of the Wilderness.

9

The cruising boat

The Ocean Cruising Club is one of those select societies without a club house to which it is a privilege to belong because of its exclusivity. You are excluded unless you can show that you have cruised under sail at least one thousand sea miles without putting into port. It has an international membership and a secretary in Britain. Some years ago all its members were circulated to ask them what they thought was the ideal cruising yacht. The results of the comprehensive questionnaire were published and it is fair to say that they represented distilled experience. One of the persons replying had sailed over one hundred thousand miles under sail; together the three hundred who answered had sailed just about everywhere and over seven million miles!

It might be thought that they would select a boat fit for deep sea and the worst weather. But many having sailed one or another voyage, subsequently indulge in week-end and holiday cruising on the same scale as the average cruising owner. Having said that, the fact is that when we choose our ideal we think of the riskiest conditions in which we have sailed and ensure that we have features that will bring us through again safely.

The table (p. 90) indicates what preferences were shown by the majority. They chose a boat between 29 and 40ft (9 to 12m). It would have been more revealing if the span of dimensions had been narrowed. Experienced sailors will have a precise idea on length, connected to their previous boats and financial potential. The vast majority chose a single hulled yacht: only five per cent opted for multihulls. For hull material wood came out on top for the ideal with a teak deck—there is no doubt you cannot better it for appearance, insulation and non-slip properties. Ketch was the rig; the cockpit was aft rather than central and it was to be self-draining. Steering was to be by wheel rather than tiller. The main anchor was a CQR type

and it would use all chain rather than warps. Electrics had to be comprehensive with a battery capacity up to 200 ampere hours on a 12-volt circuit. The auxiliary power would be a single diesel engine on the centreline of around 30 hp. Such were the ideals (together with those in the table) of the majority, though there were plenty of opposing views on some topics. To take two details as examples of division and consensus respectively: the preference for canvas or wooden bunk boards was nearly evenly split. But when it came to bilge pumps, the diaphragm type was a firm favourite over piston, semi-rotary, mechanical and electric. (The latter, presumably because of the lack of reliability of electrics in wet conditions, was bottom of the poll.)

Size

Neither aircraft in the air, nor cars and trucks on the land have the variation in sheer size that pertains to waterborne craft. The range from a coracle (as still used by some Celtic fishermen) to the million-ton tanker, encompasses a thousand other scales of ship. Even among modern cruising yachts there is a very great choice. Cost to the individual or syndicate is an obvious limit, not just for initial purchase, but for upkeep and berthing. This applies to buying or chartering.

A man of ample means, however, may not and probably will not want just the biggest boat that he can afford. Yet most of us are not in that position. The chairman of a large publicly quoted company had a series of new ocean racers, and then a hefty cruiser. Then, recently the author met him on the walk way of a yacht harbour. He and his wife were taking delivery of a new Contessa 32. Apparently he had been sailing an older boat of the same class for several years and had decided on a new one. Relaxed, confident in the boat, not wishing to get something different or the latest, he continued to

Three hundred members of the Ocean Cruising Club expressed their preferences on the best type of cruising yacht. Here were the preferences of almost every aspect of the boat, where there is a choice in seaworthy alternatives. It will be seen that only in a single case did the factors apply to a boat under 29ft. The sailors had cruised a total of seven million miles.

Type of hull
Single	95
Catamaran	4
Trimaran	1

Ballast
Iron	11
Lead	80
Other	4
Unballasted	5

LOA
Under 7m (23ft)	0
7m–9m (23–29ft)	1
9m–12m (29–40ft)	58
Above 12m (40ft)	41

Draught
Under 1·5m (5ft)	12
1·5m–2m (5–7ft)	80
Over 2m (7ft)	8

Type of stern
Transom	33
Counter	49
Pointed	18

Overhangs
Long	1
Medium	71
Short	28

Material
Traditional wood	24
Traditional wood/composite	11
Moulded wood	8
GRP	15
GRP/Foam sandwich	13
Welded steel	15
Welded aluminium	10
Ferrocement (concrete)	4

Deck
Mainly flush	34
Short coachroof	28
Longer coachroof	18
Coachroof and house	20

Deck surface material
Teak	65
Plywood	3
GRP	17
Vinyl	0
Paint	3
Sanded	12

Keel
Conventional long fin	81
Short fin with separate rudder	10
Twin bilge	1
Centre-board	6
Other	2

Rig
Sloop	14
Cutter	17
Ketch	47
Yawl	16
Schooner	3
Chinese type	2
Brigantine type	1

Sails
Terylene (Dacron)	98
Cotton	1
Flax	1

Running Sails
Spinnaker	15
Twin Spinnakers	20
Squaresail	4
Boomed-out foresails	61

Mainsail reefing
Roller	66
Points (slab)	30
Special	4

Steering
Tiller	37
Wheel	63

Self-steering control
Sheet load	6
Horizontally pivoted vane	32
Vertically pivoted vane	44
Electric	10
None	8

Self-steering operation
Direct to tiller	32
Servo tab on rudder	24
Separate servo blade	44

Cockpit position
Central	28
Aft	72

Cockpit drain
Self-draining	93
Watertight	7

Cockpit type
Deep	55
Shallow	45

Bilge pumps
Piston	12
Semi-rotary	7
Diaphragm	68
Mechanical	10
Electric	3

Sea anchor
Essential	12
Useful	26
Not wanted	62

Auxiliary engine
None	0
Outboard	0
Single inboard	
(a) centreline	94
(b) offset	1
Twin inboard	5
Inboard/outboard	0

BHP
Under 10	2
10–30	44
30–60	43
Over 60	11

Fuel
Petrol	1
Diesel	96
Paraffin (Kerosene)	3

Range
0–200 miles	16
200–800 miles	70
Over 800 miles	14

Starting
Hand	18
Electric	76
Inertia	4
Air bottle	2

Generator
Off main engine	39
Separate auxiliary	22
Wind driven	1
Solar power cells	0
Combination of methods	38

Generator capacity
0–1 kW	29
1–6 kW	60
Over 6 kW	11

Electrical system DC
6v	2
12v	69
24v	27
32v	2

Electrical system AC
110v	16
240v	18
None	66

Battery capacity DC
0–100 amp hr	6
100–200 amp, hr	45
200–400 amp hr	40
Over 400 amp hr	9

Navigation lights
Electric	87
Paraffin	13

Anchor light
Electric	45
Paraffin	55

Main Anchor
COR	60
Danforth type	27
Fisherman	12
Other	1

Anchoring with
Chain only	66
Warp and short chain	44
Warp only	0

Scope chain
20–40	46
40–50	41
Over 50 fathoms	13

Scope Warp
30–50	23
50–75	56
Over 75 fathoms	21

Tender
Solid	33
Folding	0
Inflatable	67
None	0

Size
Under 2·5m (8ft)	14
2·5m–3·5m (8–12ft)	84
Over 3·5m (12ft)	2

Normal propulsion
Oars	52
Outboard	42
Sail	6

Construction Materials
Wood	16
Metal	2
GRP	34
Other plastics	48

Main compass
Quadrantal	0
Points	6
0–360	94

Bunkboards
Wood	44
Canvas	56

Bedding
Sleeping bags	67
Blankets	27
Other	6

Cabin heater
Solid fuel	8
Paraffin (Kerosene)	14
Gas (Butane)	13
Charcoal	16
Oil (diesel)	38
Electric	2
None	9

Fire extinguishers
CO_2	30
Dry chemical	60
Other	10

Would you have
Refrigerator	52
Ice-box	32
None	16

Cooking fuel
Paraffin (Kerosene)	31
Gas	52
Charcoal	0
Methylated spirit (alcohol)	11
Electric	2
Diesel	4

Would you have
1 companion	20
2–4 crew	75
More than 4	5

Would you expect to take
Liferaft	95
Radar	16
Decca Navigation	4
DF Wireless	91
Loran	5
Omega	6
HF R/T	12
MF R/T	25
VHF R/T	24
UHF R/T	7
2182 kHz R/T	49
Echo sounder	96
Masthead anemometer	51
Masthead apparent wind direction indicator	43
Radar reflector permanently rigged	80
Electronic speedometer/log	61
Trailing spinner log	72
Taped music	49
Pressure water system	26
Hot water system	27
Deep freezer	18
Sliding anchor weight	39
Pets	13

cruise extensively in this standard sloop that he could handle happily without a crew.

Size does though stand for comfort at sea and speed on passage. These are its basic advantages together with space and facilities below decks. By comfort at sea, we are inevitably thinking of bad weather: strong wind, rain, cold. Each of these is improved for the individual on a large boat. The degree of discomfort in force 5 in a boat of 25ft is equal to the force 7 in a boat of 40ft. Less water comes aboard and the laws of naval architecture ensure that there is a scale effect, so that the larger boat is less pressed. Sail does not have to be reduced in the same strength of wind and there is altogether a more solid feeling.

Even rain is easier to deal with as there will be a separate place to peel off oilskins. In the smaller boat facilities are just jammed too close together. To keep warm a solid fuel burning stove can be fitted and places made to hang wet clothing and gear. In hot weather, too, there will be more places to shade from the sun.

Quite simply, a longer boat is faster but few cruisers are sizeable for this reason alone. It would be more perceptive to say that small and especially heavy boats are slow and cannot get through contrary tides or currents quickly; they usually just miss a good breeze taking them

into harbour and generally mean longer at sea in less comfort anyway. Size comes into its own in the passage time stakes when bad weather is prevalent. It is then that the large boat keeps going, when the smaller one is hove-to or barely fighting her way through it.

From these remarks it might be thought that the bigger the better; but one should remember that the majority of Ocean Cruising Club members said that 40ft was an ideal largest length. Our company chairman went for 32ft and no crew—and there is your answer about size. Ease of handling is not really the point. With proper design and ample power, the yacht can be handled, *as long as there are enough competent people to do it.* So size comes back to crew, and who are these crew the owner of the large boat needs? They are friends or friends of friends, or people off club crew lists, or they may be family or a couple of families. Hauling out and work is not a fundamental problem, because the owner of a big boat will go to a harbour or boat yard that can deal with such a size. After all, he can afford it. If he cannot, then money is the problem: so it is cost that is the limiting factor—that is the logic of it. The crew is the *only element that cannot be purchased* (it is assumed that an all professional crew is not contemplated). Thus cost and crew are the reasons for keeping relatively small. In the following pages, unless otherwise mentioned, the author has in mind the OCC popular 29 to 40ft. More exact than that, he is more often visualizing half that range, say, 33 to 38ft. Examples of such cruising boats are the Rival 34, Nicholson 35, Swan 37, Moody 33, Comfort 34, Dufour 35, Oyster 35, Contest 36, Amphora and plenty of others new and old.

Yet the smallest boat to have cruised around the world was the 18ft 4in (5·6m) Caprice class bilge keeler *Super Shrimp* sailed by Shane Acton and one female companion. This was no sudden stunt across one ocean—smaller boats have crossed oceans—but a leisurely genuine *cruise* from port to port. The voyage began and ended in Cambridge, England (19 August 1972–7 August 1980). As for a really handsome sailing cruiser, that exceeds the length of five of *Super Shrimp* placed end to end, how about *Whitehawk?* The largest racing boats under current rules (see part III) are around 75ft (22·8m); these are often considered too big for even a skilled crew to get maximum

Super Shrimp, **smallest yacht to have sailed around the world nears the end of her voyage in 1980**

91

Norena, **a standard Nicholson 30 designed by the builders in 1972, beats to windward**

speed out of. But *Whitehawk* is built to no rule. Her dimensions are LOA 92ft (28m), LWL 78ft 6in (23·9m), beam 20ft 6in (6·2m), displacement 170 000lb and sail area 4484ft² (416·5m²). She has a centreboard and when it is down draws 16ft 10in (5·13m) and only 7ft 3in (2·21m) when it is up. She took three years to build of wood (epoxy saturated system) at Lee's Boat Shop, Rockland, Maine, USA to a design by Bruce King. As this is written she has changed hands

once and has not cruised anything like the distance of *Super Shrimp,* despite talk of various plans. Crews? . . . cost? The comparison may have a lesson.

Speed

Speed when cruising is to some extent a luxury. The author has raced many miles at sea and again inshore when neck and neck with centreboarders and keel boats. What a problem it is to find that extra little fraction of a knot to edge ahead of the others; what a worry offshore to know if the ocean racer is at her maximum. But when there is no competition, and yet the boat is surging forward with the wake hissing astern then you can enjoy what you have and there is no one to tell you that it is still not really fast enough. It is always fast enough if you have cruising speed. This feeling is best appreciated when cruising back to a home port after a race, or on a larger scale when cruising for a week or two after a season's racing.

In other words speed in the cruising yacht is a relaxing commodity, but since it is not compared with other boats, the comparisons are with the owner's previous boats, or the boats the crew have sailed at other times. Apart from feelings and the sensation of a reasonable performance and not being 'glued to the water', what is really wanted in cruiser speed is performance in certain sorts of conditions.

For instance *maximum* speed is usually attained when conditions are far from comfortable, though it is useful to quote that your boat averaged so many knots. For displacement yachts, the maximum sustained speed is between 1·4 and 1·6 times square root of length waterline. The length waterline is in many cases imprecise, but so is the figure (the speed-length ratio). So, it means that a 35ft (10·7m) boat which has an LWL of about 29ft (8·8m) will again have a maximum speed of about 8·0 knots. What use is *maximum* speed? It is a nearly unattainable figure on a passage of any distance, but one may assume the boat will sail at it for an hour or two. It can be used as a point of reference being maximum potential. 'Maximum is eight knots, so we could reasonably expect to average 5½ knots on this trip . . .' What really matters is how soon a given boat reaches the maximum in an increasing breeze. One boat quickly picks up speed and sails very near the theoretical maximum without too much wind: another requires a gale over the quarter to attain it. Maximum speed can also indicate what scale of boat speedometer to install.

Light weather speed is closely related to the point just made about picking up speed at an early stage of a freshening wind. This would seem to be a more important quality. After all the weather we want to go sailing in is settled and sunny, with winds less than about 25 knots. So, an easily driven hull is required that, in 10 to 15 knots of wind, will (in the case of our 29ft LWL example) sail at 6 to 6½ knots, which is over three-quarters of the theoretical maximum. *Light weather* speed is obviously helped by ample sail area, but here we are considering the basic qualities and the object is to get this speed in fair conditions without having to pile on sail like a racing boat.

To keep going in really light air, say, wind less than 6 knots for a considerable period, there is no alternative to big sail area. But a boat of high displacement and large hull area (wetted surface) below the water will need more of this sail area than a light displacement low wetted surface boat; in other words, the easily driven hull, and of this type more in a moment.

The third basic speed quality in a cruiser is *speed to windward*. This is a combination of boat speed through the water and the angle to the wind. What matters is the speed (or distance) made good to windward, usually known as Vmg. This is a prime quality of racing boats compared with cruisers, yet it is the most important quality of all. It is partly a question of safety. The cruising boat must have the ability to beat away from dangers to leeward. It is also a matter of cruising range. It is all very well saying 'We'll sail where the wind takes us', but the time comes when windward work is needed to get home or get round some great headland and into warmer waters or a more suitable cruising ground. Windward ability is only incidentally related to maximum speed. It depends on keel shape, draft, stiffness of hull and the actual design of the sail plan. More than in other points of sailing the setting and shape of the sails are critical. But in terms of the basic quality of the boat, certain ex-racing types are immediately seen to be a better proposition for *windward speed*. The table shows the possible good and bad speed potential of our sample boat. The windward sailing, because it depends on angle as well as actual movement through the water, demonstrates contrasting ability in passage making.

Likely times on passage for a cruising of yacht of between 29 and 35ft overall length. With a waterline of 28ft the theoretical maximum speed is 8 knots; this is from the traditional formula Maximum speed = 1·5 multiplied by square root of waterline length.

Times likely to complete a 100-mile passage

	Light weather		*Sailing to windward*	
	good	bad	good (40°)	bad (50° to the wind)
boat speed knots	6¼	4¾	4¾	4½
time in hours	16	21	28	34

Accommodation

Designing your own accommodation plan is something that can be done without any training or ability in naval architecture or yacht design. But it is only too easy to forget that a hull has the most uncooperative curves when it comes to siting lockers under the berths or compartments in the ends or close to the side. Even bunks cannot be drawn to the edge of the deck plan: most boats are narrower at bunk level than at deck level. The point being made is that accommodation is greatly dependent on the boat's displacement. The two sections show the varying possibilities for boats with the same length and beam but of different volume (displacement).

At once one sees that there is a compromise to be reached between ample accommodation and the easily driven hull needed for trouble free speed mentioned above. Fortunately it is

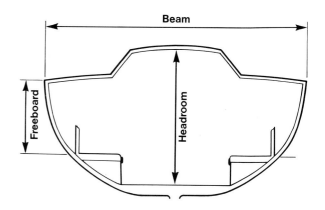

Accommodation depends largely on beam and freeboard. Headroom is achieved in centre of yacht by coachroof or deck design

not sheer volume that provides pleasant cruising accommodation, but the way that it is designed and arranged. Attention to detail is a major factor here.

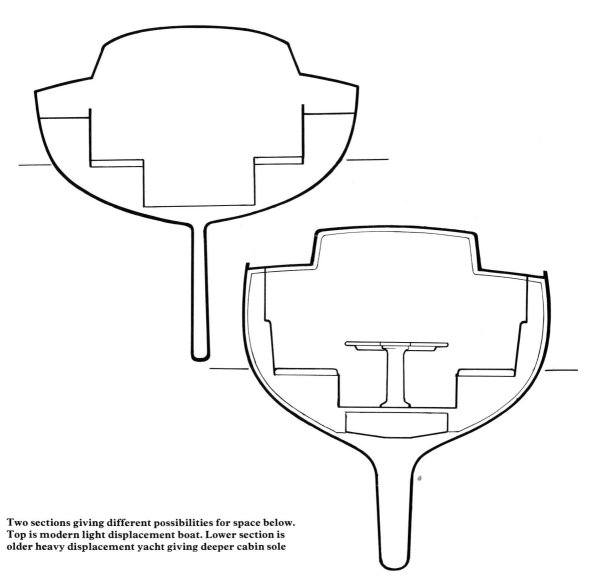

Two sections giving different possibilities for space below. Top is modern light displacement boat. Lower section is older heavy displacement yacht giving deeper cabin sole

Accommodation is a semi-technical term, meaning the design and extent of the part of the boat in which you live and, by usage, below deck generally. (The engine is not thought of as part of the accommodation, but it has to slot into it.) In USA the word is accommodation*s* and means the same: only the spelling differs.

Look over different boats and you will find a marked contrast in 'room'. This is partly due to design, as mentioned, but also caused by the geometric fact that small linear differences (in length, beam and so on) give *cubic* changes in space available. For this reason living in a boat of 25ft (7·6m) is markedly different to being on board a boat of 35ft (10·7m)—and so on with 45, 55ft (16·8m), the latter having a saloon which does not have to double for sleeping quarters with washing and heads facilities at least duplicated. Comparing the 25 and 35ft vessels, it is not just the extra ten feet, but ten times say, eleven (the beam) times six (the height within the middle of the boat). There is plenty of sense in an owner of a 35ft boat thinking in terms of selling her and getting a 38ft one in order to get substantially better accommodation. Besides more living room, the interior volume is also required for *access;* in other words, to be able to move around without squeezing round corners. Then there will be demands for places for the following:

Sitting room (with table for eating etc) for the entire crew.

Enough bunks for the whole crew when in harbour

Enough bunks for all those liable to be off watch when underway (these must be bunks which can be used at sea).

Galley, simple or elaborate, but which is bound to have a cooker, sink and stowage for utensils and ready use stores.

Lockers for food and an ice-box.

Toilet compartment, which must be shut off, even if the rest of the boat below is very open plan. The door needs space to swing. There will be a lavatory and basin and, except in the smaller boats, a shower and lockers.

Stowage which must be ample, convenient and accessible.

An engine compartment which must be accessible for maintenance, sound and vibration proof.

Space for a fuel tank, cooking gas bottles and space taken by the cockpit or other deck areas which scoop out the interior volume.

Space for fresh water tanks and plumbing. Plumbing means piping from the tanks (which may be solid or flexible) to the galley sink and toilet(s) sink(s), drains from basins and pumps on fresh water inlet, perhaps the sink outlet and for bringing in salt water (rather than the inconvenient, wet and sometimes dangerous method of a bucket over the side).

Stowage covers many needs and is the classic omission on a so-called 'boat show' boat. It could be that such a boat, not in commission,

The effective interior of an Impala 28

seems pleasant enough below, but when essential and required gear comes aboard there is nowhere to put it.

The whole question of stowage on board is affected by the fact that heeling, pitching and rolling must not upset the arrangements. Here 'ample' comes in because places suggested by the builder may not cope with movement or may not stay dry. Pots and pans, for instance, on a shallow shelf, may not be secure; on the other hand it does not really matter if they get wet. Water is going to be prevalent in certain parts of the boat anyway whether bilge water slopping up the sides or damp brought down below on oilskins and sails. Personal gear in bags may get wet in some spaces behind the bunks, even though it seems secure there whatever the boat may be doing in a seaway. There have to

be ample places which are both dry and secure. This, in general terms, means high sides stowage away from the side of the vessel.

It may well be drier forward, but not convenient and accessible. Lockers that are so secure that they are difficult to access will be a cause of irritation. It will be found that designers and boat builders have used considerable ingenuity and sometimes shown remarkable stupidity in coping with demands of stowage within the inconvenient shape of a cruising yacht. The main requirements for stowage below will be personal gear of crew, bedding, fresh and tinned food, drink, boat equipment like warps, anchor cable, anchors (if not on deck), fenders, chunky gear such as a bosun's chair and tackles, tools, emergency equipment like life-jackets, first-aid box and flares, personal harnesses, some spares, say sail battens, halyards, shackles, spare line and rope for various purposes.

A simple interior with wallets for stowage and a 'caravan' galley for use in harbour only

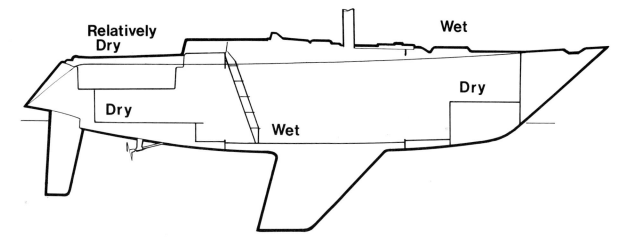

Likely parts of a boat which will remain dry

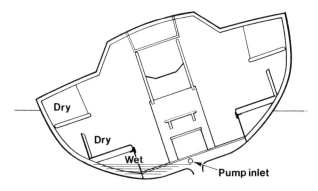

Wet and dry areas when heeled. In modern flat bottomed hulls it is difficult to pump out all water

Some of this equipment might be stowed in the ends, right forward and right aft, which is not being used for living room. Weight in the ends affects performance and this is discussed under the subject of racing boats; but in a cruiser there is no objection to such stowage, provided the basic fore and aft trim of the boat is not so upset that steering becomes unbalanced. Generally, stowage of gear has little effect on stability, though obviously the higher up heavy weights go, the less the stiffness and power to carry sail. But what a pile of stuff one does load on board. Try taking out all the loose gear at the end of the season: even in a 30ft (9m) boat it will be more than several car loads and weigh many pounds. Yet, a 30-footer herself will weigh 10 000lb, so 900lb of gear, say, though quite a load on a dockside, is still relatively minor.

The linear dimensions of freeboard and beam are makers or spoilers of accommodation. Freeboard, of course, is strictly the distance between waterline and deck line; head room below is largely a matter of the distance between the cabin sole and the deck or coachroof, yet freeboard implies the deck has 'room under it'. Freeboard needs to be carried along the length of the boat and a sheer line which reduces the freeboard amidships spoils the space available in the very part of the boat where it is usually needed.

Beam simply gives width in the cabin and avoids that railway carriage effect, found in older boats. Converted ex-metre boats and cruising yachts of pre-1950 vintage are often lacking in beam and the resulting accommodation is long and narrow. There is nothing intrinsically wrong with this; it probably means a couple of saloon berths without wide shelves or pilot berths as well. Yet humans are not used to living in corridors and anything that can even 'width against length' below is more pleasurable.

Deck space

Open deck is less attractive in the sailing cruiser than on racing boats, for the cruising family or crew should have a comfortable cockpit where they can enjoy the sunshine or gain protection when conditions are less pleasant. A cluttered deck is to be avoided. The crew should be able to move fore and aft without stepping up or down on different levels and if there is a coachroof it should leave side decks wide enough to walk along. Some of the available space athwartships will be taken up by toe rails or bulwarks and stanchions for life-lines. These fittings keep you on board, but decrease space for standing, though this is not a factor on larger boats, over 40ft long. Whatever the design of the deck plan, the essentials are that it should be watertight (see below) and non-slip. The latter is often not the case on production GRP boats. Glass fibre is slippery, even if moulded with a pattern. Only some surface with sand or abrasive in it is safe on a wet and heeled deck. A satisfactory arrangement is therefore non-slip paint (which has sand incorporated) over GRP. A smart alternative is bare teak on the GRP structure. The well equipped cruising yacht will have on deck (and by this term is included raised portions such as the coachroof and skylights) hand holds as well as foot holds. On small yachts and on coachroofs they will be the traditional wood or metal rail grip: on larger craft tailored steel bars or banisters near mast and cabin entrance may be found. Fairleads and eyes for handling sails with plenty of back up support will vary from boat to boat, while up forward every cruiser requires a stemhead fitting for leading and then hauling up the anchor. The main cleats or post for the anchor cable or mooring could

be a vital fitting in difficult conditions. The fairleads forward should allow a really heavy warp to be passed through, such as might be passed from a ship giving a tow in emergency. Wooden yachts used to have a 'samson post' which passed through the deck and down to the keel, but metal and GRP boats usually have cleats—a pair of big ones is best—because these latter materials can take the shearing strains imposed along the line of the deck.

Watertight integrity

It is fun on the water . . . as long as water is kept in its place. Beating to windward it will be thrown over you; in rain it will descend on you; when heeled it will run along the deck.

The cluttered deck layout of *Japy-Hermes,* **which raced round the world; ketch rig increases the amount of gear. Note plastic dome for sheltered look out**

Right: Hand holds are a vital aid on deck

Below: Winches and attendant shock cord for stowing the coiled ends of halyards. Simulated teak decking adds secure foot holds

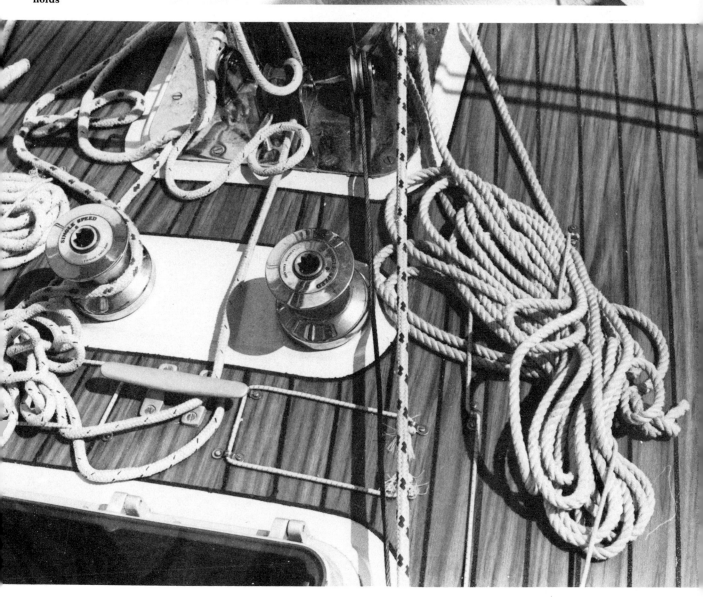

Bulwark rather than toe rail (with drains at deck level) and heavy rigging on *Tzu Hang*, a famous cruising yacht which has been sailed several times around the world. Note solid dinghy on deck

It goes without saying it must be possible to secure the cruising boat completely against ingress of water. The deck, the hull, the mast must shut out water. The mast? Light alloy masts can act as ducts leading rain and spray down the mainsail groove or inside the mast via halyard sheaves and convey it below. The point where the mast passes through the deck also seems difficult to make watertight: neoprene collars on suitable fittings are able to keep things dry.

The hull appears to be easy to keep dry, despite the holes in it! Outlets and inlets can be many in a cruising boat for the toilet (in and out), sinks (out) and engine cooling water (in)

for instance. There will be cockpit drains as well. Each inlet or outlet below the waterline must have a sea-cock. Sea-cocks are among the unseen yet important pieces of equipment on a boat. In the event of fracture of a pipe connected to the sea, they can be turned off to shut the hole, so are an important safety item. Three types of sea-cock are used in yachts: the traditional bronze tapered-plug type, the ball valve which may be synthetic or bronze and the gate valve. Holes above the waterline, which may include the bilge pump outlet and engine cooling water outlet, need not have cocks, though if they are close to the waterline it is a wise precaution. Among the yacht's equipment should be tapered wooden plugs, that can be driven into a cock fitting which has failed. The only other place where water may enter in a sound hull is through the keel bolts. This might happen if they become loose after hitting an object or when the boat is new and they have not been fully tightened down. A common cause if leaks do occur is the joint between the hull and deck. There are a number of ways in joining the two mouldings, ways which are so well developed that this should certainly not be a defect. A system of flanges should be designed so that by bolting and gluing with epoxy resin the two mouldings become as one.

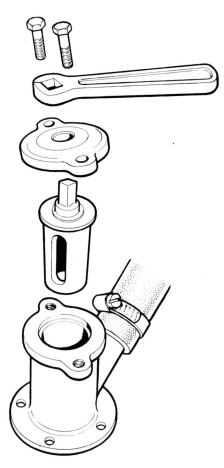

The simple but important tapered bronze sea-cock. It must be precisely made and is an essential safety device for all below waterline connections to the sea

Lastly, there is the deck itself via which water is most likely to find its way below. If you are buying a new boat, close all hatches and test it by using a high pressure hose all over and then inspect for dryness below. Unfortunately, even this is not a complete test as the sea seems more formidable than any representation of it. Likely places for water to enter 'from above' are damaged or ill fitting hatches, edges of windows and bolted-on deck fittings which have not been properly bedded down with soft waterproof compound.

Most of the above remarks apply to glass fibre and metal yachts. Wooden hulls and decks have their own possibilities for leaks in the actual mode of construction.

Cruising boat profile

Below the waterline the profile of modern sailing cruisers has immense variety. The length of keels varies from the full length to bolted-on type fins of minimum chord. Between these two there are compromise lengths favoured by many designers and builders. The narrow fin has been designed for racing: it has been found to give best performance especially to windward for minimum drag (that is minimum friction of water on what is frequently referred to as 'wetted surface'). This not always favoured by the cruising man because (a) it necessitates a flat bottom, so there is nowhere for bilge water to drain; (b) methods of securing such a fin to the hull are less simple than with a keel that moulds easily into hull shape; (c) in some forms it will not permit the boat to dry out alongside a wall as it could on a long, flat keel and (d) it is thought that a narrow fin means the boat is difficult to steer, requiring continual attention, or is difficult to make respond to self steering gear. None of these objections is conclusive and it is the author's opinion that length of keel is not an important factor in design. But it is an immediate visual property of any boat and so many cruising sailors will have instant views on the 'correct' length of keel.

Rudder design depends to a great extent on keel profile. On a long keel which runs with its base right aft, the rudder can only be hung immediately on to this. Where the keel is a compromise and cut away to some extent aft, the rudder will be independent. The curve of the keel can arch round to form a skeg which gives the forward edge of the rudder support for whole or part of its length. Cruising sailors will prefer a skeg, because it takes some of the strain off the rudder stock and protects the rudder in the case of hitting a submerged object. The alternatives with a completely independent fin keel are a spade rudder or one with its own narrow skeg ahead of it. Although the spade rudder appears vulnerable, it is after all protected by the fin keel travelling through the water ahead of it. Yet it depends for its strength on the stock which pivots within the boat and so must be made impeccably and of the right materials (steel, aluminium and plastics all have their part to play).

101

Propulsion under power

The word 'dependable' is the one most frequently used when a cruising person tells of his requirements for a power unit. What matters most is that the machinery carried inert through a salt-laden damp atmosphere, or left steaming in a warm and humid interior of a boat on her mooring, should start and then keep running. For it is when the wind fails or an approach becomes too narrow to negotiate under sail that the motor must spring to life.

Other requirements are secondary but include the ability of a suitable propeller to push the boat at a speed of at least 1·1 times the square root of waterline length or a minimum of 5 knots even in a boat of 20ft (6m) or below. The unit should not intrude on the accommodation and should be low in noise and vibration. The propeller should not be a drag under sail. For this reason a three bladed propeller, which may well be efficient, is ruled out: instead a two bladed propeller which will line up behind the stern post or keel should be installed, or a folding propeller. The blades of the latter lie fore and aft until the rotation of the shaft throws them open by centrifugal force. A feathering propeller by which the angle (pitch) of the blades can be varied for forward, astern, neutral and sailing is sometimes found, but not often as it has several disadvantages.

As for fuel, today diesel wins hands down on every count against petrol (gasoline). It is not combustible like petrol, it is economic on fuel (not only in terms of cost, but for range under power per capacity of fuel tank), it has electrics less sensitive to damp, requiring no ignition system. Petrol engines are lighter and accelerate faster, but the motor is invariably sited low down in the boat where weight is permissible and the second quality is of little interest in an auxiliary engine. An engine will be fitted with an alternator, one designed for marine use; this will charge the batteries which are used for starting the engine and for the yacht's lighting and other electrical needs such as navigation instruments and perhaps a refrigerator and auto-pilot.

To what extent do the owners of sailing cruisers use their motors? Boats with poor performance to windward will tempt their owners to keep the engine ticking over to make a respectable speed. Undercanvassed boats, those with little drive in the sail plan, may be seen with the sails down and motoring direct into the wind. Yet sailing, heeled one way, is more comfortable than the rolling while motoring in a seaway. For instance, some slow motor cruisers have a short mast to carrying a compact rig—known as a 'steadying sail'.

When an owner takes his cruising yacht on an extended voyage, across an ocean or even on a passage of several hundred miles, then he will, because of fuel conservation, have to use sail in both head winds and light weather. The use of power will usually be restricted to periods of flat calm, as well as at the beginning and end of the passage when leaving and entering harbours, estuaries and anchorages.

A sea mark for many extended cruises from Europe—Cape Finisterre, north-west Spain

10

Living on board

The habitable part of a sailing cruiser has several purposes. First, it is to add to the pleasure of cruising. It should be as pleasant to be below as to be enjoying the sunshine on deck, particularly in adverse weather, cool evenings or at night. Then there are more functional roles and on passage the accommodation is for those off watch to partake of shelter, rest and refreshment. Then in harbour or at sea, it is a place for socializing, cooking, eating and sleeping. It also provides a toilet compartment and space for navigating.

Already we have talked of this size of boat as it affects the living room on board and the special problems of stowage and watertight integrity. There must be security against the sea (not just wetness but its violence as well) and against intruders (hatches, doors and windows must be thief resistant).

Every yacht that calls itself a cruiser will have a main saloon—even though it frequently may not carry such a pretentious name. The settees around this may simply be arranged along each side, such an arrangement being usual if the boat is less than 32ft (9·7m). An alternative is a dinette where a table is set between athwartships seats in railway carriage style. Other possibilities are at least one settee being L shaped, or a horseshoe if space allows. The saloon is in the centre of the vessel with just the odd exception where it has been worked in aft (this is where a horseshoe settee might be found), so there is light, air, access and least motion. A cabin table is a centre piece for meals and drinks, or card games and books. All sorts of designs are met and there is no one standard. If the table is to be permanently rigged, then it must be strong enough for use as a support at sea, or having a man flung against it. If it folds away when out of use, this may be done against a bulkhead, or sliding up or down a pillar to lie flush with deckhead or bunk. In the case of the dinette the table comes down flush with the two opposing seats, all three components then becoming, with suitable upholstery, a double bunk.

Some cabin tables of the type that remain rigged have a lift off trap which discloses deep stowage for bottles of spirits. This is a reasonably safe place, though not for long passages where there is the possibility of a knockdown. A well-stocked drink locker is some owners' idea of one of the main pleasures of coastal cruising. In such cases either the table well or a locker in a bulkhead, easily accessible to the saloon, contains these bottles. Joinery is usually made up so that each bottle slips into its own recess: it is easily lifted out, but at sea cannot escape, nor will there be dangerous glass against glass contact.

In some conditions a saloon will become hot and humid. If electricity supplies allow a fan, this will help; but sailing boats are usually short of electrical storage and so a wind dodger, which allows air to be diverted down a hatch

Dinette arrangement on a Southerly 33

and into the accommodation, can be used. This is for harbour only; at sea there must be adequate water proof ventilators to pass air below. Most varieties of vent are still based on the old Dorade principle, so named after the famous Sparkman and Stephens ocean racer on which the design orginated nearly fifty years ago. Both air and water sometimes enter the vent; this only happens in bad conditions of salt spray and/or rain. Liquid drops down and then out via drains: the air on the other hand spreads round baffles and down through a tube into the boat. Vents can be small, large, directional, all-round or powered. It is in bad weather, when hatches are kept closed, that such intake of air is important to alleviate trying conditions. In dry weather air will enter these vents anyway. If solid water comes on board, a Dorade vent can be flooded, water will rise over the baffle and pour through the inlet to the cabin. For this reason even such ventilators must have plugs which can close them completely.

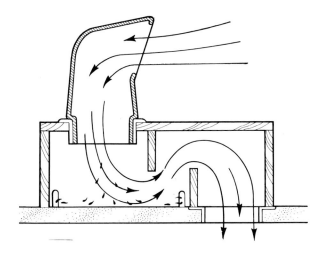

The principle of the Dorade vent: lets in air, filters out water

Modern boats in general do not suffer from lack of natural light below. Older craft with little port holes and dark woodwork tend to suffer from this complaint. Indeed, when off watch by day the usual problem is too much light: trying to sleep in such a glare sometimes means crew have resorted to eye masks (and ear plugs). The coachroof or other deck structure will have

Top left: Dinette in an aft cabin position
Bottom left: Cruiser racer layout shown in this exhibition hull and accommodation without any deck in position
Below: Centre saloon table arrangement

Left: Special boards should be held in reserve to clamp over windows broken in heavy weather or accident

Right: Dorade type vent with low profile in GRP and soft plastic

Far right: Lee cloth on bunk with tightening tackle

windows in armoured glass and it is hardly necessary to say that this must withstand really hard usage by crew and sea (falling on it, kicking it or seas breaking on it). Such windows will be secured on the outer surface of the coachroof moulding and watertight sealed, as already mentioned. Severe forces are not liable to be applied from the inside. If any window is more than 2ft² in area, the yacht should be equipped with emergency boarding that can be used to block the space in the event of breakage. This is simply a pre-cut piece of wood with battens that will clamp it in position. The sea-going pretensions of a boat are sometimes apparent at first glance by the amount and area of glass windows. For serious offshore passages it must be right to keep such an area reasonably small.

Artificial light will invariably be electricity. Years ago, when alternators for charging and storage batteries were less efficient, paraffin (kerosene) lamps were to be found below, burning away in glass cones and neatly gimballed in brass. As they had to be hung low enough not to burn the deckhead and from a vertical surface such as a bulkhead, they projected and were liable to be bumped with one's head or shoulder. At sea it was advisable to stow the glass cone away; yet at a recent boat show there was a boat equipped with oil lamps in this way, billed as a traditional attraction! The tip with electric lighting (and there is an excellent choice of differently designed fittings) is to have plenty of lights to illuminate the many awkward corners in a boat; but only use those which are needed at any time to conserve battery capacity. Yachts will normally have a 12-volt or sometimes a 24-volt circuit. Light fittings of 20 watts are ample and use 1·6 amperes.

Seamanship below decks

No cabin furniture or fittings should ever have sharp corners that can injure, though one still sees such dangerous building at times in production boats. It must be possible to move around effectively below when the boat is heeled, rolling or pitching. Therefore, a system of handholds everywhere is essential. There must be no question of leaping from one safe position to the next which is just out of reach.

Entrances to the accommodation need handholds on deck, in order to give one a firm hold when going below. Then the cabin entrance should have grips either side for lowering or clambering up: these are normally found. Once below, the best handhold is one on either side along the underside of the coachroof (the deckhead). The great attraction of this is that when the boat is heeled, you can work along on the windward side, suspended as it were. Upright pillars growing from half bulkheads or from the cabin table are excellent. Easy to grab at any height, they can be held with an arm even, leaving hands free and cannot injure. In more awkward corners, simple grips of wood or alloy fittings can be bolted (never screwed) on where they could add security. Apart from the positive advantage of adequate handholds below deck, provision of them is also preventive. Their presence means that people will not grab at something quite unsuitable such as a curtain or door handle.

Down below, and especially in the main saloon. tidiness must be the rule. It really consists of putting things back in their correct stowage after use. Again, one's own personal gear should not be left lying around. It is amazing how pleasant a saloon can remain at harbour, or at sea, if this routine is observed. However, talking to experienced owners, it always seems to be the owner or skipper that ultimately ensures all remains in order below! On some boats, stowage positions on a list up on the bulkhead are to be found. Probably this list consists of vital and emergency equipment and is certainly advisable. It may be remembered that a

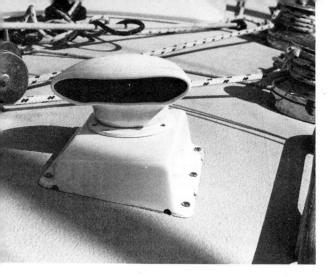

contributory factor to the loss of *Morning Cloud III* off the Sussex coast, in September 1974, was that the storm jib could not be located on board by the delivery crew. Even with a regular crew, such items should be listed somewhere conspicuous: the skipper may forget, the crew may not know where to replace gear, or the skipper or owner may be out of action.

So, even the main saloon, a place of enjoyment, needs planning and organization. When these are taken care of it certainly can be a place to enjoy on any cruising boat.

Sleeping arrangements

Cruising yachts of more than 50ft (15·2m) can be equipped with separate cabins containing a bunk with at least space to stand beside it and perhaps a built-in dresser and lockers. In any sailing yacht the bunk must lie fore and aft, or else when the vessel heels the sleeper will be tipped head over heels. One form of double cabin may have a second bunk above. Every bunk must have adequate boarding or fabric to prevent the sleeper falling out; is is assumed one side of the bunk is against a bulkhead, the side of the ship or structure which holds the contents, including the person in it. This idea is simple and essential, yet many production boats are not adequately equipped in this way. In smaller boats, when bunks have to double up as settees by day, lee cloths must still be fitted and they can be folded out of sight when not in use. When a lee cloth is fitted, it must be strong, otherwise there is the danger of a sleeping man being flung out of his bunk with serious results. Even in a permanent berth where there is a deep board, a lee cloth should be fitted in addition, so that it is not possible to be toppled over the board in severe conditions.

To avoid accidents the following points should be adhered to in fitting a lee cloth.

Where it is attached to bunk level, it should be doubled and a batten run through: two thicknesses of cloth round a batten are thus secured to the bunk. The shape of the cloth should taper towards the centre at its top edge. This will give a fair pull to the securing lines. If it is simply cut at right angles, as is sometimes seen, then the cloth will not pull taut. The securing lines should be set through stainless steel rings sewn into the corners and edge, not through pressed-in brass eyelets which will pull out under strain resulting in torn fabric. Finally, the securing points must be beyond suspicion. They should be treated the same as other important fittings above and below deck: in other words, they should be bolted through or be structural members.

The best conditions for sleeping at sea are when the boat is slightly heeled in a moderate breeze. Then one is chocked along one side of the bunk. Bad conditions for sleep are violent motion, obviously, especially rolling and also in a calm, even when the swell is slight. On land most people sleep on their sides. This is often not easy on yacht bunks because firstly the motion rolls one off one's side, the body being balanced on an edge; secondly, many yacht bunks made of foam on boards do not have the absorption of bed springs, so the hip and side become sore against the hardness of the underlying board. The author has trained himself to sleep on his back with head turned to one side to avoid snoring and discomfort: it seems a sound method of getting sleep in conditions at sea. Sleeping bags are the rule except on the largest boats with separate cabins. They can have an inner sheet on long passages, which can then be washed during the voyage. In tropical or hot weather, the sheet can be used on its own. A pillow helps, but it is bulky: try stowing even six pillows on a 40ft (12·2m) yacht! One idea is to cut foam pillows in half and make pillow cases for them.

107

Nothing can be done to prevent noise in heavy weather; but when rolling in light airs or calm, it is infuriating, when trying to sleep, if some item is rattling or going 'clunk' every forty seconds. It is usually in the galley and such culprits should be dealt with immediately. In harbour it is tapping halyards that keep people awake. At night on an anchorage or whenever the boat is left all halyards should be taken away from the mast. They can be led well clear to points on the pulpit and life-lines. This includes a thin masthead burgee halyard, whose tap-tap is the worst of all!

It is traditional to recommend a narrow bunk and settee for best comfort; however, if using the sleeping method mentioned above the width of the bunk is not relevant at sea. In harbour extra width is helpful. The standard design is around 1ft 10in (550mm) and this may be needed because of the restriction of limited beam of the boat. Apart from bunks in cabins already mentioned there are seven types of berth in sailing yachts. Most yachts will have two or more of these designs.

A *saloon* or *settee berth* converts from sitting accommodation. For comfort it needs to be 6ft 2in (1·87m) and this length measurement applies to all berths. A *quarter berth* usually tapers from ample width at the head to narrowness at the feet, because of the berth's position tucked under the cockpit in the ship's quarter. Such berths are in a position with minimum motion at sea and the occupants are not disturbed by crew moving about in the saloon. A *pilot berth* is another type where the sleeper is undisturbed. The name comes from berths rather like deep shelves let into the cabins of sailing pilot cutters used during the turn of the century. The pilots could rest in these until required for duty. In a modern yacht the pilot berth is more open, but the user is still snugly stacked away. As it is right outboard and raised up it can be difficult to get in and out of at sea. Some people do not like sleeping when the pilot berth is to leeward when heavily heeled and it is certainly more pleasant up to windward and gives the boat better performance. A *pipe cot* is bunk shaped piping with Terylene laced inside it to take a mattress. The advantage is that the cot can be folded against the side when not in use. If properly designed it can be very comfortable, with more give than a settee berth. Invariably, a pipe cot is in the fo'c's'le, so it is not used at sea and does not need lee cloths. A *root berth* is not so commonly seen today. It consists of a Terylene stretcher with a pipe

along the outer edge anchored in a chock each end: adjustable chocks can permit change in camber (for instance deep for sea, flat for harbour or an inboard chock to stow it away). *Fo'c's'le berths* are constructed like settee berths except that they taper towards the bow and the feet probably meet well forward. This is a harbour only arrangement: the motion is unsuitable for sleeping at sea except in very light weather. A *double berth* can be worked into various ingenious places in quite small yachts. In larger vessels it does not present a design problem. In a boat under 40ft (12·2m) there can be a double in a small after cabin under or to one side of the cockpit. Additionally, the fo'c's'le berths can become a double if a filling piece is put between them. A dinette also becomes a double berth. Depending on the location within the yacht of the double berth, it can be made usable at sea, if the berth mattress is split down the middle from which a lee cloth emerges. Without this rather anti-social fitting, a lone occupant will cover rather a lot of distance when the boat tacks.

The galley

In French it is still called *cuisine*, but the cooking area in a boat is certainly no kitchen. The cook who likes to spread the work out will not be able to and therefore preparing a meal on a cruising boat is not easy. But design and some planning by the cook can alleviate potential difficulties. Years ago, when yachts had paid hands, the galley was forward; cooked meals mysteriously appeared for the owner and his guests already seated in the saloon. Today it is all much more visible. Galleys are usually a little aft of the centre of the boat. Far from being mysterious they owe something to open plan living at home where one might eat in an attractive kitchen, or perhaps utility has given them a functional attraction.

Common layouts for the galley area are on one side of the accommodation, and so very roughly rectangular or L-shaped when at the aft end of a main saloon and adjoining the companion way. On very small cruisers the galley may be spread across under the entrance to the cabin. Obviously, there are variations on these.

The galley area will usually need to provide space for the following: stove, sink, ice-box, working tops and storage (or stowage). Nearby there should be a bin for gash or trash—depending on which side of the Atlantic you sail. The

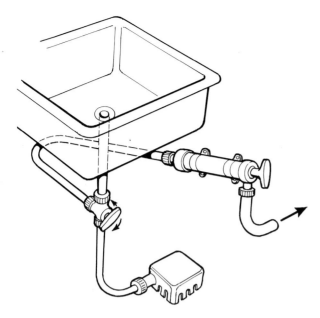

Yachts are not caravans and a good sink will pump, not drain, out. Two way cock enables same pump to be used to extract bilge water

sink is invariably stainless and there may be twin sinks in larger boats. The only differences in sinks on boats and those on shore are the water arrangements. Both a fresh and salt water pump are useful and the outlet should also pump rather than just drain. This prevents back pressure releasing the plug when the sink is being used and obviates flooding when the boat is heeled towards the sink drain. One or more pumps can well be operated by foot rather than hand; this allows the user to hold on in bad weather or use his hands to grasp other galley equipment. An *ice-box* is now customary on all yachts, though older British yachts were not so equipped. It is invariably a deep bin made of glass fibre, with insulation around. As it is usually flush with the working top and indeed part of it, there should be provision to prevent liquids seeping down into it. A gutter and small drain round the edge are advisable.

The *working top* itself is the visible galley area and is usually covered with melamine or other hard washable plastic. Around its edge

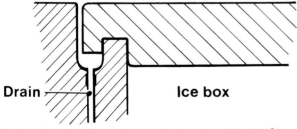

Ice box top should even have a drain to stop ingress of liquid from working top

and across it fore and aft there should be effective fiddles. Fiddles are essential to prevent utensils, plates, mugs and cutlery sliding off the working top. They are of course used elsewhere besides the galley and sometimes seen on main saloon tables; the latter seems pointless as the table should not be used at sea except in flat calm conditions. Fiddles should be vertical on both sides, but if one side has to slope because of the method of fitment then it should not be the side which supports the objects. The vertical height should be about $1\frac{1}{4}$in (32mm), certainly not less. There should not be gaps in the corners which allow knives and forks to slide out like missiles. Such gaps are sometimes left for cleaning purposes, but are incorrect. No apology is made for somewhat labouring the construction of fiddles: they are frequently seen wrongly designed and are then a continuous cause of annoyance at sea.

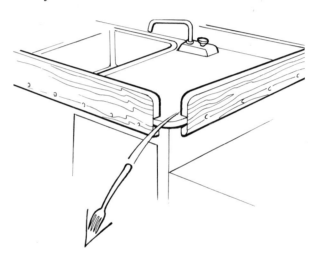

Fiddles are essential, but should not have gaps for 'cleaning', which allow items to fall out

The stove on boats over 28ft (8·5m) will consist of an oven with a grill and two or more burners on the top for saucepans. On smaller boats there will be smaller equipment with burners and grill, or burners only. The whole stove must swing freely in a fore and aft line and well beyond the expected angle of heel. The pivots must be secure so that the stove cannot jump off them in any circumstances. Cooking gas (propane, butane) is the most common fuel in Europe, but not so in America where there are more stringent regulations. In any case the gas bottle should be in a separate locker in the cockpit, where any leaks drain into the open air. There will be cocks on the gas bottle and where the pipe enters the galley. In some small stoves the gas bottle is integral, screwing up under it

Lockers with sliding doors are best, but should reveal deep fiddles inside

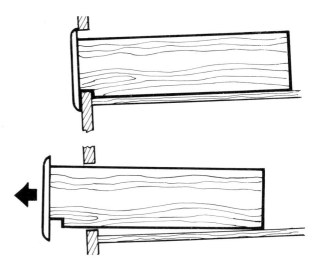

Standard yacht drawer, which cannot slide out, unless required

and swinging with the stove: this obviates the need for any piping. However, in some countries this may not be allowed. In the USA alcohol (methylated spirit) stoves are widely used. It is necessary to prime them by allowing the burner to be heated by the spirit itself in a tray below the burner. The main supply under pressure is then switched on and the burner uses vaporized spirit. The same principle is used in paraffin stoves—the famous Primus. Both types of stove can flare up if raw liquid fuel is allowed to burn before vaporizing, but in the case of alcohol, water will rather easily extinguish this.

In front of the stove where the cook is working there should be a crash bar. This prevents the cook or anyone else sliding on to the stove. When the stove is to windward the cook can have a strap to support him, leaving both hands free. Some skippers do not like a cook's strap because of the danger of being unable to get out of the way quickly if hot liquids are spilt.

Storage in the galley area will take up the volume below the sink and under the working top. Items such as tea, coffee, sugar and bread should be easily accessible from where the cook is standing. Open shelving with extra deep fiddles, or small bins are best. Plates of different sizes and mugs will invariably be fitted into holders of exact size. A T-shaped recess is a favourite for plates as they cannot be dislodged whatever the motion and cannot rattle. Mugs should be behind tight fitting deep fiddles. Sometimes there are recesses for the handles, but never on hooks. If you see a galley with mugs on hooks, then you can take it that the

boat does not sail very much. Lockers with sliding doors are preferable for food, because they save space and ensure better security when they are slowly opened. However, stores should not fall out because even these lockers should have fiddles in them. Cutlery can well be in a drawer. Whether the drawer is fore and aft or amidships, it must be notched. That is to say, it is necessary to lift it about a quarter of an inch to open it because a small cross brace stops it from pulling straight out. Any drawer on board should be fitted in this way.

Lavatory and shower

Even in completely open plan interiors, the toilet compartment or head is shut off. With boats 40ft (12·2m) one lavatory is usual; over this length two are preferable and in larger yachts further plumbing will be installed depending on the cabin arrangements. Some double cabins may have their own shower and lavatory. As to the type of plumbing installed, the builder or owner is largely in the hands of the manufacturers and one selects the lavatory of one's choice. For sea-going use it will have some system to pump salt water in and then pump both waste matter and this water out. For extra flushing merely pump more sea water in and then out. Marine lavatories seem to have more than their fair share of difficulties. Whatever the pump system, there is a potential for waste matter to block it and such a blockage is fairly unpleasant to clear. To avoid this make sure it is only used for disposing of waste for which it is intended. A further difficulty occurs

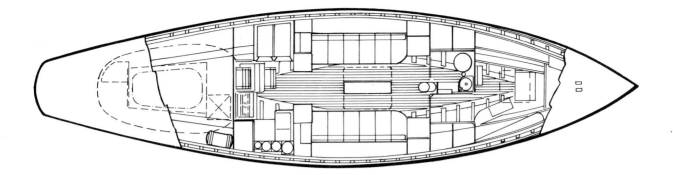

at sea if the system is on one side or the other. Centre line installation is preferable, otherwise on one tack the inlet and outlet are out of the water, while on the other the pan will flood unless sea-cocks are shut off smartly. Offset positions are used because of the inconvenience of the centre position when planning a boat's interior layout. Other forms of marine lavatory include simple chemical closets, as used in camping, and holding tanks. The advantage of both these is that no plumbing and holes in the hull are required; the disadvantage is the unpleasant notion of having to carry the waste matter around as you sail, and having to allow for special disposal at some point in harbour or at sea over the side.

Most toilet compartments will have a hand basin with a fresh water pump or pressurized pump and possibly a hot water system. A shower is advisable in other than cool climates and the water can drain through a grating into a sump for pumping out. The rest of the toilet compartment will consist of lockers, of which a set of lockers for the washing gear of each member of the crew is a useful touch. Separate

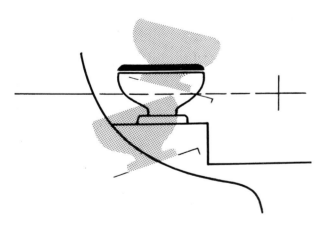

Side installation of the lavatory means that on one tack flushing water cannot be pumped and on the other that it floods when sea-cocks are opened. Centre line siting is best

How did they manage? This is the 40ft (12·2m) cutter Binker built in 1932. The beam of 10ft would be 2ft more today, but the lack in today's terms is of any chart table (there are 'dressers': for what?). Amazingly there are only three berths in this yacht. A 1980s 40 footer would have eight or nine

ventilation is advisable for the toilet compartment. A more convenient name for the toilet compartment (cabin is seldom appropriate) is the *heads*, but in the USA it is known as the *head*.

Navigation area

Somewhere for the navigator to sit and work on his charts with his instruments is now considered essential in a sea-going sailing boat. It was not always so and cruising yachts which made impressive passages half a century ago appear on their plans to have no provision for a chart table. They seemed to have strange pieces of joinery called dressers or sideboards, for what purpose (except to provide extra horizontal space in harbour) it is difficult to imagine. Presumably navigation was plotted on the cabin table, or a makeshift board rigged over a bunk.

A detailed discussion about the chart area will be found in the ocean racing section, because it is in ocean racers that navigation has been developed. In terms of the general layout of a cruising yacht a sizeable chart table is no disadvantage, for in harbour it provides another table, while at sea it can make a difference between an accurately navigated passage—and therefore a safe one—and a trip with developing anxiety over the yacht's position and her future course. On a long cruise space will have to be found for numerous charts and pilot books. With so many cruising yachts on long voyages across various routes in the world, some voyagers have found that they can swap charts with sailors in harbours where routes meet. One crew will have finished with the charts along a voyage where a second yacht is about to traverse in the opposite direction.

II

Pull, haul, slide and press

The deck and working equipment on a sailing vessel somehow epitomize the sporting aspect of being aboard. Do we not find riding lights hanging in the porch or pictures of hauling on ropes to typify sailing people in advertisements? The act of varnishing an oar in the spring sunshine, turning it to gleaming gold, yet making it proof against sun and salt water, is to anticipate the whole season. Sailing gear is not only essential to working the ship, but has a fascination of its own. It can also be the cause of expenditure on its own account and used to renew the ability of an existing hull. In times of recession, when the sale of boats is lagging, there is often a brisk sale in equipment which is then applied to existing craft.

Design detail

Every piece of equipment needs close attention to design. 'Sod's law' is well known on boats, which means that if something is going to go wrong it will; often this takes the form of something fouling or jamming if it has the chance. Drag a loop of rope along the deck and it seems destined to catch some fitting or other, yet try and capture a cleat or other object with the same loop as a necessity and it will obstinately fail to engage. Careful design will obviate most of the causes of 'sod's law' and give continuing pleasure. Take, for instance, the stem head fitting, an item which varies considerably between different boats. On boats above about 45ft (13·7m) the fitting is usually serviceable; it has to be, or handling large anchors is impossible. On smaller boats there is more option, but how many have desirable design features? These include: a roller which runs smoothly when warp or chain pass over it, whatever the effects of dried salt; side checks so that the anchor cable does not jump off the sheave; a drop nose pin to lock it; a lead from the roller to a winch, cleat or hauling position clear of other gear especially

the forestay; and not least a pleasant appearance, perhaps with chromed stainless steel. Allied with the fitting will be the need to allow for very secure anchor stowage, either at the stem head or in a self draining anchor box in the foredeck. It is no more costly to fit a well designed stem head fitting to a deck structure and in the long run, it is, of course, less costly.

It is detail that matters with deck gear in its design, specification and fitting. The smallest snag can lead to a chain of events which are irritating or even dangerous. It is the old story of the nail in the shoe of the horse. A key type ring secures a clevis pin, a clevis pin is the link in a rigging screw fork, the rigging screw tightens the stay and the stay is an essential component in securing the mast. If the mast goes, it could be at the best very expensive and at the worst the cause of injury or shipwreck. The answer to this little sequence of events is never to use key rings on cruising boats: they are a dinghy fitting. A split pin (cotter pin in US) must be inserted and preferably opened out about 30 degrees so that it can be easily removed when required. This also does not damage it. If this will snag lines or clothing then both ends have to be bent right back and it should not be used again: plenty of split pins to fit all clevis pins should be carried as spares—and as substitute for those fittings which are supplied by manufacturers with key rings!

Because of the great variety of production boats and the relatively small numbers (compared with the car industry) in which they are built, there are invariably points of poor design and fitting which need to be corrected by the owner. There is no great expenditure on research and development in the sailing world. It is left for the user to discover flaws and the builder or supplier can then correct these in future boats. In fairness to the industry, it must be said that the use of boats, even of the same type, varies immensely. One owner may be fully

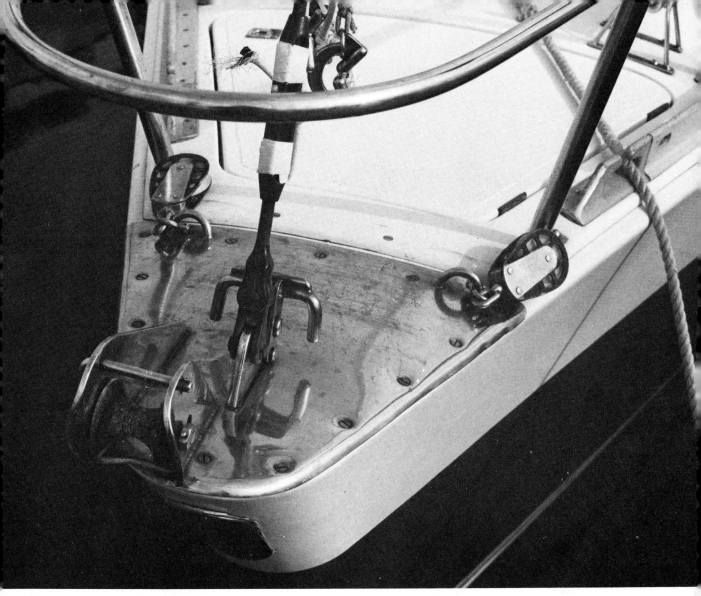

A good stemhead fitting with roller fairlead and pin to stop cable jumping, hooks for headsail tack and integral eyes for spinnaker fore guy blocks

satisfied, because he only sails his boat on Sunday afternoons. Another, who has made a three thousand-mile cruise in a long summer vacation, finds some things are not so good when caught out in heavy weather or when trying to take the ground alongside a wall in some foreign port. The latter probably puts them right himself and says nothing, while the first owner meets the builder one day and says that everything works fine. When a third party complains, he is genuinely told 'So far we have had nothing but praise for the way she is equipped'.

Even if boat builders had the resources to pre-test boats extensively, they might spend a long time until they met the weather conditions which tested a particular item. In some cases prototypes are raced or cruised extensively and then a production boat is based on such experience. But even this is not a complete answer, and there are several reasons. One is that a knowledgeable crew just does not allow some of the snags to occur, or crew members put something right without fuss and hardly noting. Then commonly, when the boat goes into production, small changes are made for manufacturing and costing reasons and quite by chance poor design aspects may creep in. There is also the matter of time. Some defect may not come to light until wear or corrosion have developed over a period of a year or two. So, every owner must expect to have to improve or alter a number of pieces of gear on deck or in the rig.

Hull materials

Yacht hulls are made in four principal materials: glass reinforced plastics, wood, metal or ferro-cement. Straight away it can be said that the most popular and practical of these materials for modern cruising boats is *GRP*. This name is an accurate description because the concept is simple. It is resin (polyester carefully formulated and steadily developed by manufacturers, of course) reinforced by strands of glass, properly and specifically cured to give a material homogeneous for large structures and highly resistant to impact. It is often called 'glass fibre', but this is only one of the components, or in the US 'fiberglass'. (In Britain 'fibreglass' is a trade mark). GRP has many uses in industry, but boat construction is one of the largest uses. One reason is that it is not a cheap material, while skilled labour is required to mould it *correctly*. Thus, boat hulls and GRP go together (but not masts or spars despite some attempts over the years). Some boats have GRP hulls, but wooden deck structures. This has no special advantages and the advantages of a GRP hull can equally well be applied to a moulded GRP deck structure. If a wooden deck is desirable for non-slip and aesthetic reasons, strips of teak are glued over the moulding. A purely wooden teak deck is sometimes difficult to keep leak proof.

The advantages of GRP include:
(a) For the builder, a production line technique from one or more female moulds. The costs of the mould are recovered over a building programme. (The mould will have been made by making a male plug, the shape of the boat, very accurately in wood covered by resin, and then shaping the female mould of GRP on it. The plug is kept as the 'master' so more moulds can be set up, if required.)
(b) For the owner and builder, saving of cost and pricing because of production line methods (not possible with other boat materials).
(c) Little maintenance: annual cleaning and waxing of topsides. GRP is impervious to organic decay. The homogeneous structure is waterproof (subject to good engineering of joints and sound lay-up of the laminates of which a GRP hull consists).
(d) Strength against impact.
(e) Smooth and smart appearance, with coloured 'gel coat' permanently incorporated.
(f) Basically simple repair by filling or patching with epoxy resin and more glass fibre which give as much strength as ever when cured.
(g) Long life: the first GRP boats were built in the late 1940s and writing in the eighties, these earliest craft are still usable. Therefore, the life span is not yet known.

Wood. Before 1945, 95 per cent of yachts were built of wood; today it is in the region of two per cent (world wide). The main reason for this is that wood has been driven out by GRP, on almost every ground except aesthetic, for cruising boats, and lightness (when certain methods are used) for racing boats. With the decrease in the number of wooden yachts, craftsmen are scarce and costs rise. The wooden boat is invariably a 'one-off'. The hardwoods (teak, mahogany, oak) used in boat building are not easily obtainable and are expensive. The traditional method of construction with timbers (like ribs) and planking (piece by piece) has been the same for hundreds of years. Thus the wooden boat in the last thirty years has become rare, traditional, deliberately beautiful and select. Sadly it is more logical to list the disadvantages of traditional planked yachts:
(a) High cost of materials and labour.
(b) Annual painting and varnishing, and weathering of exposed surfaces.
(c) Numerous joints and edges, difficult to waterproof.
(d) Potential movement between members causing leaks.
(e) Difficult to fashion into complex shapes.
(f) Repairs require skilled carpentry.
(g) Absorbs moisture, which increases weight.
(h) Is attacked by various forms of rot in marine environment.

All wooden boats are not of traditional construction and there are more modern methods of using wood. *Marine plywood* (that is ply laminated with waterproof resins) had a vogue, especially for 'do-it-yourself' sailors. A few cruising hulls of hard chine shape (with 'corners') were built and many more dinghies. GRP has ousted this method as well; it was always a compromise on shape to allow for the panels of ply. It was, and is, very suitable for decks. It remains extensively used for the *interior* of cruising yachts, for bulkheads, locker fronts and other furniture, where a flat, evenly stressed panel can be used.

Moulded plywood is used by several specialized builders. Laminates of veneers are built up on a mould using marine adhesives (resins) resulting in a strong, light and attractive hull. This obviates disadvantages (c), (d) and (e) above, but not the other problems listed. Moulded plywood craft have been built since the early fifties when marine adhesives (particularly resorcinol) have been generally available.

A refinement is the WEST system of wood building, invented in the mid-seventies. This stands for wood epoxy saturation technique and is patented by a company in Michigan, though the system can be used by any boatbuilder. The principle is that very dry wood is saturated with certain synthetic resins, which drive out humidity for ever. It is humidity in wood that is responsible for many faults in boatbuilding. Similar resins in the WEST system can be used for gluing and filling, yet the actual method of putting the boat together is optional. Obviously, moulding veneers is one way, but it can be traditional (planked) or hard chine. Some layers of GRP can be used as well, perhaps in parts of the structure where there is chafe or wear. WEST saturation increases the naturally poor compression strength of wood, without lowering the tensile strength ability. What WEST have in effect done, is to invent special sorts of epoxy resin for the particular conditions of boatbuilding and subsequent use in the stringencies of a marine environment. Why use wood at all in view of its inherent disadvantages? The people who build using WEST and have spent so much effort in producing the resins to transform wood would say, rightly, that wood compared with GRP has greater rigidity and lightness for given structural strength and is more suited for 'one-off' building, where elaborate moulds are therefore not required. These properties are naturally of less interest to the cruising sailor and boats built by WEST are usually racers, either offshore or dinghies. But this shows that wood is not obsolete and in conjunction with modern chemicals will continue to be seen in boats of the future.

Wood combined with GRP is found in several building systems. A GRP outer and inner skin with balsa wood blocks between give a light rigid structure, but poor impact resistance and complications if water gets between the skins. Cellular foam is used in the same way as the balsa but has the same disadvantages and rather less stiffness. In both cases, it is hard work to get a good outside finish as the outer skin is applied last on a male mould and takes much smoothing down (in contrast to the shiny hull out of a female production mould).

Metal hulls mean in effect either steel or aluminium. Bernard Moitessier sailed one and a half times round the world in 34ft 6in yacht (10·5m) (*Joshua*) built of 5mm *steel*. Yet the material is not widely used. The main objections are weight and corrosion. Moitessier says corrosion and electrolysis are no problem, if proper precautions are taken. When the hull is bare, sand-blasted and shiny in the building shed, a coat of special zinc silicate paint is applied everywhere and on every steel piece, it is then overcoated with zinc chromate. These have the same effect as galvanizing and further paints are over coated. With such treatment and welded (not bolted) anodes on the hull below the waterline, a steel hull can last ten years and longer. If it is scratched or worse, it must be treated before rust can cause any damage.

In other words maintenance must never be neglected and great care must be taken with any metal fastenings to avoid electrolysis. (A contrast to the inert GRP, but wood can suffer electrolysis between two fastenings of contrasting electrical properties.) The appeal of steel? Its immense strength when a boat is welded like a metal box. It can withstand seas bursting over it, or bumping against some inhospitable quayside. For instance, the chain plates, so vital for the support of the mast, are sold with the boat in contrast to the ways which have to be found to fit them to GRP and wood. Steel resists impact well, being dented but not broken and this can be rectified with a rubber mallet. More serious damage needs professional help in the form of cutting and welding equipment.

Aluminium has many of the above characteristics of steel. It is, of course, much lighter. It can be applied to smaller boats than steel, where the thickness of plating makes boats below 30ft (9·1m). Marine grade light alloys will corrode only slowly, but require treatment at fastenings and special protection from electrolysis. The same strictures as to steel apply to the maintenance of this hull material. Aluminium deteriorates (pitting and decay) rather than rusts, and scratches are not of immediate consequence. Like steel, aluminium can dent, but it is stronger and more rigid for its weight than any other boatbuilding material. A limited number of yacht building yards can undertake construction of boats in this metal: it is expensive to cut, fit, weld, shape and finish. Again major repair needs a specially equipped boatyard. The properties of aluminium (by which, it is emphasized, is meant marine grade light alloy) are of appeal to racing boats (lightness for strength and rigidity) and it is of less appeal to the cruising owner. Boats commonly made of light alloy are light runabouts (kept ashore, which minimizes deterioration), ocean racing yachts over 40ft (12·2m) and, since 1974, all 12-metre class yachts (see Chapter 7), which were formerly always built in wood.

Ferro-cement construction at steel framing stage

Ferro-cement boats are built in a few yards, but the material is primarily of interest to the amateur who wants to construct his own hull. The component materials are the cheapest of all the building methods reviewed here, but the hull takes a long time. The latter may not cause an amateur any problem. The hull is made by first constructing steel pipe (½in diameter—12mm) as frames. On these are stretched ¼in steel rods longitudinally and vertically and some eight layers of steel mesh, such as chicken wire. The effect is of a complete hull built of wire. The ferro-cement is introduced into this mesh until it is thoroughly impregnated and finished smoothly with further layers. The curing process is allowed to take up to four weeks; then the hull is turned over and the bare hull finished like boats of other materials. Probably a wooden deck is fitted. Later advantages are easy repair, with a bucket of cement. There is good resistance to impact damage. Disadvantages are the considerable weight (twice as heavy as wood), potential rusting of the metal skeleton (if

finishes do not protect the hull at all times) and the initial difficulty of getting a smooth, even surface.

Material for fittings

How the varnish makers must have lost business! Time was—before, say, 1960—when every season there were fittings to be varnished. As well as the coachroof (cabin trunk—US) and covering board (the outer plank on deck), there were the cockpit sides and cabin bulkhead. There was the mast and the boom and the spinnaker pole, and all sorts of small fittings. Even blocks were often still of wood, cleats, the samson post by which the boat could anchor or be towed, the hatches with all their elaborate watertrap joinery, the hand rails, the cockpit coamings, the toe rail, the boat hook and all the bits and pieces of the yacht's dinghy and the dinghy herself. The latter might be painted, but that would not be too good form. Indeed in some parts of the world, especially where the sun is hot, a light coloured paint used to take the place of marine varnish, but it still had to be applied every season. As for rope, it was either 'best yacht' hemp or manilla, natural fibres grown and twisted into lines as it had been for hundreds of years. After a season's hard use it rotted away. It was brown or off white. Some rope and twine was tarred; it was dark in colour and smelt of seamanship!

Now deck equipment is made of synthetic materials: stainless steel (shackles, tracks, fastenings stanchions, pulpits); aluminium alloy, often nylon coated (cleats, toe rail, forehatch, tracks, blocks and their sheaves, spars); laminated plastic (some blocks, handholds); neoprene (mast collar); nylon (hinges, stops, pads of various sorts); thermo-plastics (ventilator cowls, winch holders, various covers). Rope is invariably synthetic and what an improvement in strength, durability, resistance to chafe, easy running and appearance with the added facility of colour coding bought off the shelf with types and colours ready for selection at the chandler!

Such modern materials need very little maintenance—no varnish, no paint—just sometimes a drop of oil on a track or moving part. If the design is a sound one, it will go on for years. Because they are strong, it is fastenings which require attention. An old wooden cleat might have split in a way that is impossible for an alloy one, but the latter could pull poor fastenings. Under a GRP deck there must be doubling and bolts with nuts resting on big diameter ('penny') washers. Although boats vary greatly in design, and there is a wide range of fittings available from equipment manufacturers, this range turns up time and again on cruising yachts. The rules for selection and fitting change little between boats. If a wrong way is chosen, it will not be for the first time and the 'dos' and 'don'ts' mentioned here apply again and again.

Modern above deck fittings and their use and misuse

Once *cleats* were just two horned pegs, but jammers of several kinds have grown from light use on sailing dinghies to heavier duty on cruising yachts. The common cleat is for mooring and small cruisers will have two forward and two aft for mooring and towing. Larger yachts start to sprout them along the deck for mooring, towing, securing smaller craft at anchorage, or deck gear. A wide base for the fastenings and soft edges and corners for the lines or warps are the basic need. Cleats with less massive bases can be used for halyards or other lines coming off winches, because there is no direct load and the friction of the line on the drum of the winch takes the strain. (Winches are needed on cruisers, but have been grouped together in part III, as their development is for racing.) For sheet winches, horned cleats with non-symmetrical sides are useful: the line jams under one horn and is then wrapped straight round and not in a figure of eight like a traditional cleat.

In the past there have been a number of devices to jam ropes, which can then be quickly released. Quaint systems may be found on old boats, but basically, there are three modern types. The *cam jammer* merely has cams with teeth: the harder the pull, the more they conspire to prevent it moving. It is released by pulling up, the cams shut below the rope and away it goes without further obstruction. It is very suitable for use with blocks and common on mainsheets and mainsheet travellers. The patented *clam cleat* is very clever. It has the advantage of no moving parts. The stronger the pull, the more the line is pulled down into the 'V' of the cleat by the slanted grooves. Both these types can be damaged by overloading. If a line pulls through under excess load, the teeth will be damaged (ie blunted) and then become less effective. Both have the disadvantage that under heavy loading it may be impossible to remove the line by hand. Then it must be winched out, or extra man power applied—keep the hands well away from the cleat when heaving! Nor can the lines be surged, a useful technique on an ordinary horned cleat. An additional problem with a clam cleat is that the line can fall back into it and jam, or any line can fall into it and jam: this does not happen with closed cam jammers.

The third modern type is the *single cam with lever*. The rope can run through it at all times except when the user closes it by means of the lever. It can bear a heavy load and is released by throwing the lever. When shut it is the strongest system and best for permanent requirements such as holding halyards. It may also be impossible to open by hand under heavy load. In that case hit the lever with, for instance, a winch handle; or winch the line out until the lever comes free.

Blocks should be mentioned briefly, if only for their relative absence on modern yachts, yet where there is rope there will be blocks of one

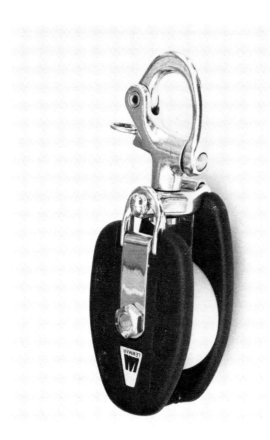

Left: A snap shackle swivel snatch block; a delightful name for a useful standard piece of sailing gear

Above: Sparcraft spinnaker sheet snap shackle. Unlike side action model, this one cannot open accidentally

Below: A trysail and storm jib in use by a yacht in a gale. Note mainsail stowed on its boom on deck

sort or another. Today ropes tend to run over sheaves in specialist fittings (for instance there will be a hinged sheave at the base of the mast under which a halyard runs from above and then is directed towards a winch on deck) and turning blocks fastened to the deck for headsail sheets. The old wooden ash carving with its galvanized steel sheave is only used to make a desk lamp and the modern block is of stainless steel and light weight compressed synthetics. There is a great variety—single, double, treble, beckets and links of all types. Indeed, it appears that chandlers have great difficulty in stocking the exact one you need: they always seem to have every other kind. One important point is not to use a block with swivel fastening, unless strictly necessary. Such swivels are a point of weakness, and a secondary objection is that the lines through it may tend to twist it, so that it does not run smoothly. A non-swivelling link will hold it in alignment. The most common uses for blocks on a modern yacht are in the mainsheet and the kicking strap. The latter runs from a point along the boom to the base of the mast on deck and prevents the main boom from rising (the mainsheet cannot perform this function once the sheet is eased for reaching or running). In the US the term 'vang' is used instead of 'kicking strap'. Every boat should carry at least one 'handy billy'. This is a tackle made up with a couple of double blocks to apply force anywhere. It is frequently used as a vang (both British and US usage) to hold the main boom forward when running in a seaway.

Shackles are another basically ancient fitting, which are seen in greater numbers on old cruisers. Present day rigs and deck gear have specialist linkages instead. An old boat may well have a shackle to link the shroud to the mast tang aloft: modern masts have a swaged 'T' fitting, which is inserted into a slot and turned through a right angle—less wind resistance, simpler, less vulnerable components. Forms of snap shackles have been around for a long time. Side hinged versions are invariably used for headsail halyards, spinnaker gear and anywhere else that frequent connecting and disconnecting is required. They are not suitable for the head of the mainsail, where a D-shackle is used and should *never be used* to make fast a genoa or jib sheet to the clew of the headsail. A snap shackle in such a link will invariably open when the sail shakes.

Snap shackles with a top opening hinge have been developed from racing boats, so that they will release under heavy load. They are not intended for halyards, though often fitted. Their primary use is for spinnaker sheets. Even there they can open if the sail shakes violently. Sometimes they open at the wrong moment because the release line is snagged and pulled by some other fitting. A type invented by Sparcraft always remains secure.

Tracks and *chain plates* are two permanent fittings to be found on the decks of most yachts. The tracks port and starboard are for the sliders or cars carrying the headsail sheet fairleads. Gone are the fixed eyes of something called *lignum vitae* (a very hard wood) which were sited with some difficulty. Tracks enable the sliders to be positioned correctly for different headsails and are fortuitously a method of spreading the load which is considerable. One check that should be made is that the storm jib, whose lead will be well forward, will set with the car on the track. There is a tendency to forget to test this sail until it is needed in a gale (the last circumstance to be 'trying something out'). If it does not lead to a position on the track either make special provision on deck with a special eye bolt and block each side; or change the cut or height of hoist of the storm jib. Tracks, like other deck fittings, have to be bolted through with well fitting pads under the deck to spread the upward pull. Any number of sliders or cars can be used on a track: for changing headsails, for spares, for making something fast, perhaps a main boom vang.

There have to be chain plates. This seventeenth-century term is still used for the tie bars which secure the shrouds to the boat. In old ships and yachts, they were bolted externally to the topsides (using chain bolts, now an extinct term), but racing practice has now seen them moving inboard so that they sprout from the deck. This system goes with shorter spreaders which enable the headsails to be sheeted (closer in) more efficiently. Having chain plates through the deck in this way poses a problem of waterproofing, which is not difficult to solve and another of siting the steel tie bars in the cabin: they are liable to descend through bunks or lockers. The designer has to ensure that they coincide with some member like a bunk edge or locker side. They can then pass down to the inside of the hull where they are very strongly and structurally tied.

Stanchions, life lines and *pulpits* are a tremendous safety aid to prevent crew falling overboard. Their current design is almost entirely borrowed from racing practice and they are discussed in part III. Personal harness lines

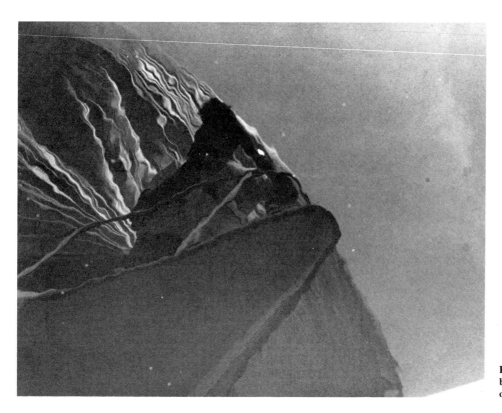

Force 0. Nothing to do,
but look at the reflection
of limp sails

should never be clipped to such life lines, though clipping through a loop in the stanchion base is safe enough. For harness lines, a special wire jackstay close to the deck should be fitted each side.

Hatches have been mentioned as an important aspect when making the yacht structurally sound and watertight. As well as being totally watertight when fully shut, a hatch must be strong because, in a sense, part of the deck has had to be removed to insert it. *Sliding* hatches are the most usual for access to the saloon (the main hatch) and are sometimes also seen forward. To waterproof such a hatch, a box recess for it to slide into is a favourite system; otherwise when it is shut it is difficult to find a way of closing the front slit where the hatch meets the frame on which it slides. Along the side baffles will prevent water entering there. An important little item is a live gum rubber hatch stop at each corner. A smoothly shutting hatch acts like a hammer and well fastening resilient stops are an essential detail. (The author was in a boat in the 1979 Fastnet race, which was improperly equipped in this way and the inadequately fastened stops sheered off. He had to secure temporary ones (screw heads) in the storm conditions otherwise the hatch might have been pulled clean off.) *Hinged* hatches, usually on the foredeck and in larger yachts around the deck, are also for access, though

small ones may be fitted for ventilation. Hinged hatches may also be used for deck or cockpit lockers. The desirable properties of any hinged hatch are as follows:

(*a*) a system to raise the hatch partly, so that it cannot close by accident on someone's head or fingers;

(*b*) hinges facing forward, then a heavy sea cannot force open a hatch which has inadvertently been left not fully closed;

(*c*) opening from both inside and out, except when locked for security (it must never be locked when persons are on board as it is a means of escape—indeed a boat without any forehatch is unsafe for this reason);

(*d*) inside opening ability also applies to large locker hatches where a man may get inside to sort out gear. There is a danger of being locked in and it may be desirable to shut it down in rain or at sea in bad conditions;

(*e*) some (small) ventilation hatches and others have double hinges, so that the hatch can be hinged up either way. In this case, there should only be one set of pins, so that, for safety reasons, both sets of hinges cannot be shut simultaneously;

(*f*) a hood over hatches in the after part of the boat enables the hatch to be left open in rain and when going to windward: hatches forward may have flush storm

Twin sliding forehatches on an aluminium boat with welded boxes for watertight integrity and heavy plastic storm covers

covers of Terylene which help withstand intense spray and moving water on deck;

(g) avoid flush designs which level neatly with the deck, as they are difficult to keep watertight.

Rope is a word not heard afloat. 'Strings', when used, is actually a joke-word. *Cordage* is called by its name of sheet, halyard, warp, spring, guy, up-haul and many other appropriate terms. Three types of basic plastics in effect cover the materials used on yachts cordage. Polyamide is in cordage as nylon; polyester filament is sold as Terylene, Dacron or other proprietary word, depending on country of origin; polyolefins include polypropylene, the 'hard' rope, which is cheaper, floats for certain applications, but is less hard wearing than the other two kinds. With excellent modern finishes, it is sometimes difficult to distinguish between the types. Nylon is used where some elasticity is required and is invariably suggested for anchor warps, but the author is not convinced of its superiority as the 'springiness' makes it difficult to haul in; also, Nylon is more prone to chafe—at the fairlead or below water on a rock—than Terylene (Dacron). Three strand Terylene has immense strength, great resistance to chafe and remarkable longevity: it is a good investment for the week-end sailor or long voyager. It can stand many years of hard use. For halyards, sheets and all running lines on the boat braided polyester is usual. Where necessary it can be spliced to wire to give a Terylene tail to a wire halyard. It winches smoothly and is best for handling and coiling. Manufacturers bring out various braids (eight plait, sixteen plait and so on) and recommend specific uses. Pre-stretched halyard is available, but wire is preferred and pre-stretched line tends to kink. Polypropylene was widely advertised when it first came out; but it remains inconvenient because of the way it kinks and will not 'relax' when coiled and stowed. It is best left for those applications where a floating line is essential, as on the hook up for a mooring buoy, for certain uses in safety equipment and for floating a line down to another boat when some operation demands it. In its softer forms, it can resemble Terylene, but has nothing like the strength life. Colour codes are now the rule. There is a mass of different colourings, solid and flecked, in all sizes. As a result, a mass of line on deck, or in the cockpit, no longer requires the services of a snake charmer! One's hand goes instantly to the control line that needs attention. How did we ever manage with those yards of natural light brown hemp, indistinguishable and wasting towards the end of its life with every application of salt water and sunny weather? Why, you could not even use a hot iron or a lit match to seal its end.

12

The competent crew

'Wake up. It's time for your watch.' 'All right. All right. I'll be with you in a moment.' Is this really fun? Is this the enjoyment I came for? What the hell am I doing out here at 0300, the water rushing past the hull a few inches from my ear.

Such are the feelings sooner or later, when on passage. Whether they will be amplified or modified, depends on the scene that greets me—having struggled, sitting at a fair angle of heel which tries to press me against the back rest of the bunk, into my weather proof clothing and safety harness. It may be a moonlit night with smooth water and the log reeling off the miles—or it may be a punch into the blackness to windward, rain tipping down from time to time and the ETA undetermined. Usually it is some situation (always different, that is one intriguing aspect) between these two. Anyway, daylight in a few hours may show us a sun of a special clear sort that is found at sea. Later will come completion of a passage with all the satisfaction that it brings.

The fact is that physically unpleasant conditions at sea do nothing to deter. Every long distance voyager and those who sail less far, says to himself or herself at some stage the well known phrase in yachting 'Never again!'; but not long ashore, or sooner with a change in the weather, it is the next trip or voyage that is being planned. Mundane physical descriptions are only the surface of the feelings of magnetism, which sailing the sea promotes. They are the equivalent to a description of cricket as throwing a piece of leather at three pieces of wood. These latter objects are but the vehicles for a sport that provides opportunity for skill and invention, companionship in pleasure and adversity, and for some a way of life. So a competent crew is a visible reminder of the deep satisfaction of the cruising game.

Acclimatization

Coming straight from an office job, or even a land based manual one, to a boat and then putting out to sea, is bound to be hard in anything but the finest weather. Many a cruise has met failure for this reason. If a two week holiday cruise is contemplated, the crew naturally wants to make use of every hour, but the fact is that life at sea takes some getting used to. A reasonably fit person will soon be in the rhythm and accustomed to the motion and effect on bare hands and different muscles—about forty-eight hours is all it takes. The answer to this is obviously for some members of the crew to be hardened already; sailing at week-ends and then returning to the office still builds up 'sea legs'. For others, remember that the first two days may be hard, but after that everything on board will get easier. Alternatively, be on guard at this early stage and take it easy. The unhappy possibility here is that too long will be spent waiting for the weather and you will not get anywhere. By the way, the wind whistling through masts in an anchorage or yacht harbour can give a worse impression than it should. It is frequently worth going outside and setting off, even if it means putting back: frequently it will be less bad than expected and you will be glad you went.

Crew's own gear

Foul weather clothing, still known in England as 'oilskins' after the pre-PVC treated fabric, has yet to be perfected. New models continue to come on the market and it is necessary to ask around and observe how the other man's gear stands up to use. Ruggedness varies roughly with price and the cruising man should not buy light weight oilskins, which are ideal for dinghy sailing, but unsuitable offshore. (Nor should the dinghy sailor, who might well find a one piece suit useful, go for the heavier cruising gear with separate jacket.) The material is not usually a problem; there are many excellent synthetic fabrics with good flexibility which are coated with waterproof PVC. The plastic coating must cover the seams. Hold a seam up to the light and stretch it sideways: if you see pin holes for the thread, reject the garment. It will let water in.

A conundrum not yet solved, despite some manufacturers' claims, is that what keeps rain and salt water out, also keeps perspiration in. In dry weather when oilskins are worn to keep the wind out, they will often be found to be quite wet inside when taken off because of perspiration, which is unpleasant. But when the spray is flying this is still an advantage, since water will force its way in through the smallest ventilation hole. In a cruising boat a jacket where the front can open rather than a smock is preferred, as it is easier to take on and off in cramped conditions below in bad weather. A hood is almost a necessity, certainly a great comfort. Pockets are useful: they may fill with water, but they are somewhere to put a knife or small tools and bits of line when working on deck. But not steel objects which may be magnetic and have an effect on the steering compass! Inner cuffs will keep inside garments from getting unduly wet; the neck arrangement should be supplemented with strips of towelling kept for the purpose.

Trousers need reinforcement in the seat and knees. This is where PVC inside is preferable, for when it is coated on the outside of the garment, it can be chafed and rapidly lose watertightness. Trousers must come chest high and be supported by braces, otherwise the suit will certainly have a disastrous gap. No pockets are needed as they cannot be reached when the jacket is on. A draw string keeps them snug. The legs must be wide enough to pass *outside* seaboots which come just below the knee. Even then it is quite possible to get a frequent boot full on the foredeck. As for sailing boots themselves, they should be light in weight and initially loose so that thick seaboot stockings can comfortably be worn inside. It is the soles which are most important. These must be truly non-slip; a fine zig-zag pattern is one of the best. All the boots seen with varied patterns on the sole are, unfortunately, by no means non-slip. Ankle or half calf length is insufficient for cruising and below the knee is the required type. However smart or efficient the seaboot, it is always a pleasure to cast them off as the weather

improves and put non-slip sailing shoes on instead. The other side of the coin is to get those boots on early, as soon as the spray shows any sign of flying, if wet socks and feet are to be avoided.

Although safety harnesses are worn individually, it is the duty of the owner to provide these for the entire crew and they are not a cheap piece of equipment. There has been a lot of discussion in recent years, following fatalities where harnesses have been in use. Undoubtedly, these accidents have led to improved design. In Britain there is a standard BS4224, and it is best to get these. There are few makes to this standard and others are not necessarily dangerous, nor, of course, are harnesses in other countries which have no official approval. Points to look for include the line for the harness which should be at least $\frac{1}{2}$in (12mm) diameter three strand Terylene/Dacron and on its end should be a heavy carbine hook or special harness hook. The webbing should be lock stitched and braces should have a minimum width of $\frac{3}{4}$in. An important aspect is to have adequate hook-on places around the deck. Wire jackstays are often used, running close to the deck from somewhere near the cockpit to within 5ft (1·5m) of the stemhead. Carbine hooks on harnesses should never be clipped to 'U' or 'D' bolts, as these can lever them open: this cannot happen on a jackstay, so a short jackstay can well be incorporated in the cockpit for the helmsman. This can be used to hook on *before* emerging from the main hatch. The yacht's life lines must not

Deck fittings. Note jackstays of plastic covered wire harnesses running from top to bottom. Also large Dorade vent and prism for light below

A combined safety harness and life-jacket. Such combinations are available from only a few manufacturers. This is the Crewsaver Survivor

be used to hook on, as a man's weight is too risky in terms of leverage when applied at a single point above the stanchion. There is also a risk of two or more members of the crew slipping on to the same life line.

There are harnesses inside oilskin jackets, which have the great advantage of being already on as the weather deteriorates and avoiding what is always a slight struggle to don an ordinary harness. But with this pattern, it may be found to be a belt in the lining with the whole jacket acting as harness. Then it is essential to check there is a strong crotch strap so in the event of going overboard, the whole jacket is not wrenched off. The author has found most jackets require modification in this respect, pathetic little buttons sometimes being supplied. Harnesses will not be worn at all times at sea, but the cruising skipper must make it plain when they are *de rigueur* on deck. Experienced cruising men have their own views on yacht safety harnesses. Frank Mulville, who has crossed the Atlantic five times single handed, says that all harnesses need modifying in some way or other. Eric Hiscock's latest advice was that they were probably not necessary for yachts, like his, which has life lines 30in (760mm) above the deck. Most yachts have 24in

height. He insists on any crew using a harness, but prefers not to have on one *himself* as it hinders his work on deck.

Like harnesses, life jackets are ship's equipment. In Britain those carried on a well found cruising boat will be invariably to British Standard 3595. Such jackets are usually inflatable, have 35lb minimum buoyancy (for children 20lb), float the wearer with his head clear of the water after self righting, if necessary, are rot proof, fuel oil proof, resist extreme temperatures and are of 'low flammability.' Other countries have their own standards and systems: in the USA, the Coast Guard have varying grades of PFDs (personal flotation devices) for different recommended use and legally enforced. Life jackets are a controversial subject, but the author believes that they should be kept dry and ready for use and not worn except in dire emergency. One reason is that they do not combine well with harnesses. At the time of writing combined harness and jacket systems are coming on the market in several parts of the world; these may in due course find general favour.

Saving crew power

In giving directions for hoisting a spinnaker, the nineteenth-century yachting writer and designer, Dixon Kemp, at several points in the sequence directs 'Clap all hands on the foreguy'. With modern winches 'all hands' are no longer necessary and an aspect of cruising has progressed in recent years, where less and less crew are needed. The early reasons for this were that paid hands at extremely low wages became scarce and are now very rare or employed on a different basis (eg college men before taking a regular job), latterly short handed techniques enable a couple of people to sail a boat with guests who may be novices. Then there is actual single-handed cruising, mostly unsung (though single-handed racing enjoys all the publicity); statistics are impossible, but one sees these single-handers sooner or later in all waters. Aids to saving crew power include vane self steering, an auto-pilot, a dead reckoning indicator and roller furling sails.

Wind vane steering is simple in concept. For a given course of the yacht, the vane is set into the wind: when the course diverges from that chosen, the vane swivels in relation to the boat. This rotation is used to activate at once a rudder, which corrects the course. To get this working really well in all conditions at sea, a surprising amount of development work proved

A pendulum type self-steering gear in action

necessary and there have been many different
designs since about 1955 when the gears began
to make their appearance in any quantity.
Before that they were used on model yachts and
by individual experimenters. There are now a
number of reliable proprietary makes. Incidentally vane steering is banned in fully crewed
ocean racing. The four types of vane are (a)
those which act directly on the rudder; (b) those
which actuate a small auxiliary rudder; (c) those
connected to a trim tab on the main rudder and
(d) pendulum wind vane gears. Type (a) is seldom seen as it requires a big vane to turn the
rudder. One of these was used by Sir Francis

Chichester on his first transatlantic voyage and
it even had reefing facilities! Type (b) has not
much power, but the main rudder can aid by
being lashed so the boat nearly sails herself
already. Type (c) is a servo blade, so when it
turns one way the main rudder turns the other
and it is best for a stern hung accessible rudder.
The pendulum type (d) was the invention of
Colonel 'Blondie' Hasler. The Hasler-Gibb gear
has been continuously improved for nearly a
quarter of a century. The vane turns an independent blade hanging over the stern; when the
blade turns it is forced by the water to swing
sideways on a fore and aft axis—hence the 'pendulum'. This swinging action is strong and

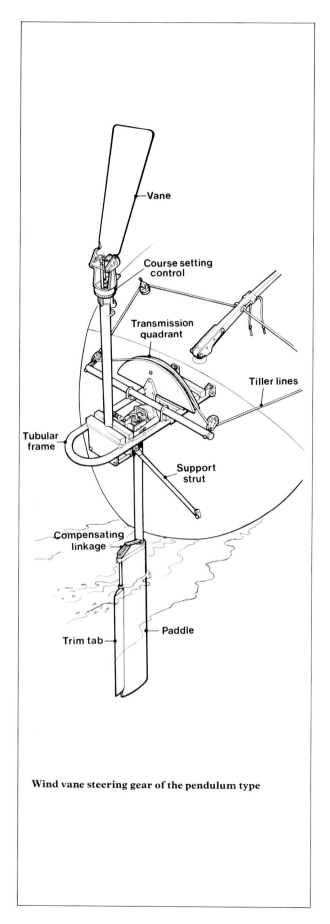

Wind vane steering gear of the pendulum type

actuates the main rudder to restore the desired course. It now seems the most popular type and the British Aries is a particularly rugged version. The French Navik is a pendulum gear, again widely used, as it has proved to be reliable and is easy to fit to existing yachts.

A major asset of the wind vane steering is that it uses up no power, but an *auto-pilot* requires electric current. On the other hand it can be set instantly under power or sail and does not require any above deck structure. A compass course can be used, so once sails are trimmed, the auto-pilot literally puts its arm on the tiller (or its connection to the wheel) and steers the set course. A miniature wind vane is incorporated in some models: it merely senses wind direction and transmits course changes, which are actuated by electrical power. Large yachts, and of course ships, have had auto-pilot for many years, but it is the self fitting weather proof device such as the Autohelm, which has made auto steering widespread on tiller equipped yachts. Extra controls may be incorporated such as varying the sensitivity to allow more course alteration in rough going without instant correction. Drain on the batteries must be allowed for and obviously more charging by running the engine is needed, as with every extra electric device on a sailing yacht. With any self-steering device, it will be appreciated that any change in direction or strength of wind means adjustment of the steering gear and/or the sails, but the crew are relieved for a period from the tyranny of the tiller.

A *dead reckoning indicator* is invariably part of an electronic system of showing speed, wind direction and other displays referred to in part III. However, dead reckoning calculation electronically is often banned under racing rules. So it is of primary interest to the cruising navigator and also demonstrates a significant aspect of navigation. When using auto-pilot or vane steering, there is no helmsman to report the mean course steered (essential information for plotting the dead reckoning); the same applies with inexperienced helmsmen, or a weak crew where the course made good is not properly recorded. The electronic device records the actual course of the ship's head (not that merely attempted) in relation to distance run. At any moment the navigator can read off the distance of the preferred course and plot it on the chart. The significant point is that this eliminates one of the major uncertainties (one of human error) in navigation of yachts. Of course, this only detects the path through the water and any

Left: Auto-helm control for the wheel on the trimaran
Moxie
Below: Medium weight headsail furler

allowance for current or tidal stream and actual sideways drift (leeway) must be an additional calculation.

Headsail *roller furling* sounds so ideal that one might wonder why it is not very widespread. As the wind increases, instead of going forward to a wet foredeck, one merely pulls on a line, thus rolling up and reducing the jib in area. Instead of lowering it when entering harbour, it rolls completely round the stay and virtually disappears. There can be snags to this. As wind increases one needs a flatter sail, yet the roller sail will tend, if it changes shape, to go baggy. Then the weight of cloth cannot be right for both light and heavy airs. Either it will pull out of shape in strong winds when it is partly rolled, if of light cloth; or, if made heavy, it will look heavy and miserable in the pleasant light weather when most sailing is done. Then there is always the possibility of mechanical failure especially at the head roller mechanism where it is difficult to deal with. Then the sail may be neither in nor out. Weathering is another potential weakness, for the rolled sail is exposed along one resultant strip at all times. A second sail must still be carried, in case of serious damage which can happen to any sail. All these objections have been known for years. As a result modern headsail furling gears have been developed which overcome, to a greater or lesser extent, all these difficulties. Grooved headstays invented for racing have helped in this as it has been possible to hoist and lower the roller sail into its own groove. Few cruising people will have the roller jib as the only headsail. A two-headsail rig is preferable, one stay of which is a roller furler and the other a conventional stay with a selection of jibs on ordinary piston hanks. Which is the outer sail and which the inner is a matter of choice and subsequent design.

Roller furler mainsails are something sharply improved in recent years, when special alloy spars have been made into which the sail can be rolled. Instead of lowering or reefing on the boom, the mainsail is gradually rolled into the mast where it is safely out of the way. The great advantage of conventional reefing methods is saving of crew power: no more scrambling over the coachroof and threading reef points to clear up yards of Terylene obscuring the helmsman's view. Unlike a roller jib, this sort of mainsail cannot be fitted to an existing rig. A completely new mast is required: it will therefore take time before such models as the Hood Stoway are widely seen. *Moxie*, winning yacht of the 1980 single-handed transatlantic race, used a furling mainsail as well as a furling headsail and her owner Phil Weld said 'Mainsails such as these will revolutionize short handed sailing. Gone is the terror from 45 knots of wind. Soon the joy came home to me of never hesitating to shake out a reef when the wind dropped for fear of having to waste all the energy that had gone into reefing.' He mentions the slight disadvantage of a cupped leech, because sail battens cannot be used, but any lack of speed is more than made up by the time saved by rapid adjustment to optimum sail area.

Wind and visibility

When the seaman talks of weather, he may sometimes think of rain and sun. At sea in a cruising yacht, the features that matter are first wind and a close second, visibility. All the weather phenomena that matter fit under these two headings. Waterspouts and prolonged calm obviously come under the wind heading. Mirages and convection fog classify as visibility.

Heavy rain may well also affect visibility. The fact that it runs down your oilskin collar is incidental.

Wind directly affects the rig and sail plan rather than the hull. Spars and sails are more fully dealt with under racing because most, though not all, spar and sail development was started in racing boats for the ultimate benefit of cruisers. In relating cruising yacht spars to the racing requirements there are some differences. Margins can be greater: the next size up can be used if there is any doubt, though excessively heavy spars make the boat tender (heels more easily and demands early reefing), which is not only uncomfortable but means power to carry sail is lacking, which may be a vital need when beating away from a lee shore. Some halyards can be outside rather than internal for easy replacement: components like spreaders and the gooseneck may be heftier, but the principles of masting are the same as for an ocean racer.

Again, sails for windward work are little different from a racing boat in their needs. Both cruiser and racer need to sail to make the best possible speed to windward (Vmg). Slab or jiffy reefing has all the advantages over boom roller reefing today. But off the wind the cruiser has rather different needs. The fact is (despite amazing feats by single-handed racers) the conventional spinnaker is a handful, needs constant attention and nine or more control lines (two sheets, two guys, foreguy, topping lift, inner end up-downhaul, release line and halyard). Twin triangular sails, each of easily handled size, are more pleasant to use in a cruising boat.

For long passages, an old favourite is the twin staysail system. One specially designed jib is boomed out each side: the two sails equal the ordinary mainsail and jib in area, but when these twin staysails are in use the mainsail is lowered altogether. Before the days of wind vane steering, the sheets were connected aft to the tiller and as the course varied the one sail or the other pulled the tiller in the desired direction. The big advantage was that it was impossible to gybe under this rig, but it really only works when the wind is well aft and not round on the quarter by more than 20°. Disadvantages include the tendency to roll heavily as there is no fore and aft sail to steady the vessel and quick alteration of course, for instance to avoid a ship, is not easy. Methods of rapid lowering, taking in and so on vary and can be devised. Such sail area is bound to be on the small side in light weather, but then the conventional rig with a large headsail and steered by a wind vane is best. It is an advantage to 'tack down wind' in light weather when the required course is dead to leeward.

In the late seventies a new down wind sail for cruising boats made an appearance—the cruising spinnaker. It is also known by a number of trade names, such as 'cruising chute', 'easy rider' or 'MPS' (multipurpose sail). It is made of the same sort of cloth (nylon) as racing spinnakers and the cut is based on the experience of sailmakers in designing light running sails. Cruising yachts will not carry these sails in any weight of wind, but they do keep the boat going when she would otherwise be hardly moving with her normal heavy working sails, or would have the engine on. Remember, too, that the wind always appears lightest from astern and this is when more area is needed. Surely, fine light weather is just when you want to be enjoying the sailing and not be turning on the noisy motor. For the cruising chute there is no spinnaker boom, so a number of controls can be dispensed with, the area is less than a racing spinnaker but considerably larger than a genoa. It is cut full like a spinnaker, but is not symmetrical. The tack is on a pendant and the sail is allowed to 'fly' well out from the boat, the sheet is taken right aft and off you go. As the wind comes further aft the cruising chute can be 'goosewinged' so that it is on the opposite side to the mainsail. A perfectly cut sail will stand well and even further out than a conventional spinnaker on a boom. It can be gybed without lowering.

With roller sails in the fore and aft rig and some form of cruising spinnaker to increase area off the wind, the modern cruising boat can keep up good speed and sail steadily and is more conveniently equipped than her racing counterpart. There are rigs, outside racing rules, which are seen on cruising boats and these include the junk rig and the cat ketch. They have their adherents, but have not gained wide popularity. The junk rig, developed by Colonel Blondie Hasler, has been in use in some boats for over twenty years and has been used to cross oceans. Like the cat ketch, its area is not easily increased off the wind and so it lacks area to keep going at an acceptable average speed.

Whatever the system, the necessity to be able to vary the sail area is what the cruising sailor needs. A modern yacht will keep going to windward even when the wind is up to 45 knots across the deck. It will be very unpleasant and sail will be reduced to a minimum. Once the wind becomes even higher, it will be better to heave-to under storm canvas (storm jib and trysail or heavily reefed mainsail). The next stage (55 knots?) may be to get all sail off and lie a-hull. This tactic allows the boat to drift with the gale, but the danger is that the crew have no immediate control. Then, if seas become particularly steep, the yacht may be knocked down. The results of this can be damage, dismasting, flooding or crew injury. If the seas are bad or the wind is greater than 60 knots, the better practice is to run before the storm under bare pole with a helmsman steering to avoid the worst of the breaking seas. Because in these conditions the yacht will run very fast, even with no sail hoisted, it may be advisable to tow long warps in a bight to reduce speed and thus keep more control.

Visibility

Some would say that fog is worse than a gale, because at least you know where you are in the latter. Actually, you may not because a bad gale is accompanied by lack of visibility due to rain and spray. Fog, in light weather at least, means there is no discomfort from cold and motion, but it is potentially dangerous because circumstances may be beyond the control of the crew. In other words the boat may be run down by a ship or run into danger (rocks or shore) because the position is not known. Fog occurs by no means always in light weather, although that is one type of bad visibility. It is quite normal to be sailing in moderate or fresh winds without being able to see more than a couple of boats' lengths. On land any wind means that any fog is 'blown away', but at sea there is so much moisture available that it can move about in great banks. Ahead of a frontal system there is often fog and indeed wherever warm moisture-laden air crosses cold sea. This is known as advection fog and is almost permanent over the Newfoundland Banks where warm air from the Gulf Stream meets the cold Labrador current. It can occur where there are turbulent currents resulting in cold water being brought to the surface from lower depths of the sea. Thus it adds a second peril to an already tricky area.

The kind of fog met in fine (anticyclonic) weather can be radiation fog. This is near land or in estuaries and is the result of the land cooling at night and the water vapour in the air just above the land condensing. It is particularly dense near dawn; this makes arriving or leaving harbour near impossible and obscures a landfall

129

which is sought and coastal lights and other navigational marks.

The arrival of fog is a test of the yachtsman as a seaman in a way that perhaps strong winds do not make so apparent. For in a breeze one must just cope with the weather as it comes, but in fog courses of action must be chosen. Does one go on? Turn back? Reduce speed? There are a number of things to be done when visibility closes in. If in a shipping lane, on the high seas or in the approach to a port, one must sail out of it as soon as possible. The preference here is to make for shallower water, where larger vessels will not operate. In order to make for shallow water, it is necessary to know one's position in the first place! This is not as obvious

as it sounds, because it takes an experienced skipper to spot the onset of fog. A fix by visual means before visibility clamps down is worth a lot. Navigational instruments which do not require visual range are those which the navigator will turn to. Radar is invaluable, so is any position-finding electronic device such as Loran-C, Decca or satellite navigation system. Small yachts without these devices will have to be navigated by depth sounder and radio direction finding, if suitable beacons are available. In deep water, the yacht will have to rely on dead reckoning navigation and the crew must keep an ear open for ships. Ships unfortunately do not take heed of collision regulations in these days of radar and may not be sounding their fog horns as they should. A power-driven vessel is required to give one prolonged blast at intervals of not more than two minutes.

Strictly, the yacht should sound her own fog signal—under sail this is one long and two short at intervals of not more than two minutes—but most yacht devices carry very little distance. They are of some value in restricted waters and close to other small craft. Precautions that can be taken on board, however, are hoisting a radar reflector, having extra hands on deck (to keep an all-round look-out and prevent anyone being trapped below in the event of collision and starting the engine so that if a ship suddenly appears close the yacht can be steered clear regardless of the wind). The cruising yacht can either run the engine, have it turning over in neutral or at least have it checked for starting and ready to go instantly. The latter is often preferable because then the crew can listen for ships' engines in the fog.

When listening for fog signals, whether from ships or navigational marks, it must be remembered that such signals are not reliable. They may be deceptive in the direction from which they appear to come, or they may not be heard at all even when close. Reasons for this are that the variable density of fog can cause inaudible areas; fog may not be present at the light ship or mark, but may, a few miles off, be surrounding the yacht; some fog signals may be slow to start up for technical reasons, and there are other causes such as a signal with a combination high and low note or bell that may be only partly audible. Such knowledge as this shows that even a common phenomenon gives scope at sea for mistakes; or, preferably, a demonstration of several facets of seamanship in a cruising yacht.

Summary of action on board a yacht in fog

Fog creeps up unexpectedly and quite suddenly the watch on deck can be aware of lack of visibility. Then alert skipper and navigator.

● Hoist radar reflector.

● Have fog signal to hand. Under sail sound one long and two short blasts at intervals of not more than two minutes.

● Check engine can start immediately. Run in neutral if necessary, but then switch off to listen for ships and fog signals.

● Make for shallower water if possible (where big ships cannot possibly run a yacht down). At least get away from shipping lanes and routes.

● Life-jackets to be available and worn if there is a serious risk of collision.

● Hands on deck as required to keep an all round look out and so as not to be trapped below in the event of collision.

● The crew should be instructed to report all relevant sounds, engines, fog signals, bells on buoys and anchored ships, sounds of the land, but sound is deceptive in fog as explained in the adjoining text.

Fog can be forecast by observing both air and sea surface temperature together at regular intervals together with the humidity of the air (by wet and dry bulb thermometer). If the sea surface temperature converges with the dew point fog will probably form.

13

Charter anywhere

Even those who could afford to own a boat may choose to hire one (or rather charter) for reasons not hard to find. Capital is not tied up and there is an immediate choice of cruising ground, not restricted to a limited range of the home port of an owned boat. Then there is all the enjoyment of a holiday cruise without the cares of maintenance, security and the difficulty of finding a berth or mooring (in most popular yachting areas of the world) and its rising cost when acquired. Chartering is obviously not so suitable if the users want the boat every week-end or are planning an extended cruise of more than, say, three to four weeks. For many owners working on and planning for the boat is a part of the hobby. Charter boats are mainly thought of as sailing cruisers, but there is boat charter where cruising is not the purpose: it may instead be under water exploration, motor cruising, business conferences (where the vessel is unlikely to move far). There is increasing charter for racing yachts, but because of their specialist nature and the risk of damage at close quarters, this is bound to remain a very small sector of the charter business.

For the potential charterer of a sailing cruiser, three types of charter business will be met. These are, as already mentioned briefly, crewed boats, 'bareboat' and private craft. *Crewed boats* are for those with little experience or who want a leisurely holiday afloat. There may be a skipper and hand, or a married couple. Larger boats may have a bigger crew. Such a boat will be from one of the larger firms. They pay the crew and know that the boat is continuously maintained and is likely to be returned to base on time, ready to go out on the next charter. *Bareboat* is a term simply meaning that the charter party take the boat themselves without any crew supplied by the charter firm. It is the most common kind of charter and means that charterers must have some ability. The agreed readiness of the yacht varies. It may be

necessary for the charterer to get his own stores and prepare the boat in various ways. In other cases there may be an inclusive fee for air tickets and other transport to the charter station, to find the boat fully provisioned and ready to sail. Most bareboats will be between these two extremes, with the charter firm assisting the users in various ways up to the time of departure on the cruise. *Private craft* are chartered by their owners to help defray the cost of running the boat which is primarily for their own use. Rather than leave the boat lying on her mooring when the owner is away at work, it is chartered. This can be satisfactory, especially if chartered to recommended clients, who are sure about the boat which they are using. But obviously this amateur approach could often be unsatisfactory and such chartering is selective. Sometimes such private chartering has led to the owner ending up making a business of it. In other cases, where the owner hoped to get some tax relief on his boat, it has proved more costly than ever because hired boats invariably suffer damage and excessive wear and tear that does not appear to occur when the owner is on board. To charter the boat with owner on board rather defeats the purpose of letting it out when he cannot use it, making money elsewhere. There are private yachts, especially larger ones, which are chartered through brokers or charter firms and this is more satisfactory.

Chartering by the day is a feature in tourist areas. It has the advantage that more persons can be taken, and cooking and overnight accommodation are avoided. In a suitable area the boat can make a minicruise to some pleasant anchorage or stretch of coast. It is a useful system for the owner of a private boat as it may be linked with a big hotel, which handles the promotion and bookings.

Increasingly found in the bareboat charter world is cruising in company, known by such names as 'sail together cruising', 'flotilla cruising'. It has many advantages as each party is independent, but a pilot boat with experienced people from the charter firm is never far away. It means that small sailing cruisers can be used which gives flexibility to the charter bookings. This seems particularly prevalent in the Greek islands, where the charterers are mainly European and therefore used to smaller boats; and geography also lends itself to this kind of activity.

Charter areas

Wherever there are yachts there is charter activity, but it is more common in certain places. Perhaps the charter capital is the Caribbean with its tropical climate, steady winds and almost perfect sailing waters. It is in reach of the huge potential market of the United States, though the Americans are no longer the only charterers, as was once the case. Second on the list would come the equivalent playground for Europeans, the Mediterranean. Here the big charter areas are the south of France, Adriatic and Greek Islands. Elsewhere, the north east coast of Australia is becoming an established charter area and in the Pacific the Fiji Islands, and Hawaii.

Less exotic, but meeting a strong home demand, are charter firms in the customary yachting centres in the United States and Britain. In *Britain* around half the charter firms for sailing yachts are based in the west of Scotland. Despite the uncertain Atlantic weather this area is extremely beautiful and has numerous cruising anchorages and protected stretches of water.

In Britain a body called the Yacht Charter Association has been formed by 31 (at the time of writing) firms to ensure minimum standards of service and equipment. These firms are also concerned with finding a scale of charges to avoid the cut price scales, which very small firms, hard to distinguish from private owners, were able to advertise. Apart from these YCA firms there are hundreds of private owners and small firms, which are bound to vary in dependability. A number of firms, established for many years, are not members of the YCA. Charter firms spring up and disappear with some rapidity. A major problem is investing in the right sort of boat; if a boat is chosen which does not generally appeal to customers, the firm or individual has no alternative but to sell it, and this may be a slow process while revenue is lost and capital tied up. Many charter firms in

Britain do not last very long. A bad summer can have a serious effect, a factor which does not arise in the warmer climates mentioned above. In Britain only two charter companies have survived since 1964, four since 1967, five since 1972 and 15 from 1975 to 1980. In the last 15 years 56 out of 94 companies have gone out of business.

Charter business in the *Caribbean* was a sizeable business long before it emerged in strength elsewhere. Many were the ocean voyagers who expected to make a living on their arrival at the other side by chartering, though today efficient and established companies have most of the market. The climate allows boats to stay in commission all the year round, though the main season is December to March and hurricanes are possible from July to September. The charter bases run the extent of the West Indies from the Bahamas in the north, through the Virgin Islands (American and British), down to the Windward and Leeward Islands off the coast of South America. If there is a centre to all this it might be said to be at English Harbour, Antigua. The much publicized Antigua Sailing Week attracts some of the world's finest racing yachts and numerous cruisers. The guaranteed fine weather and the scantily clothed female crews are particularly of appeal to photographers. Antigua is well served to Europe and the US by its Coolidge airport.

Much of the bareboat business is to be found in the Virgin Islands. There are sheltered anchorages and no island is out of sight of another in the sparkling visibility. An active firm in the American Virgins is Caribbean Yacht Charters Inc, whose boats are based in the east end of the island of St Thomas, though the head office, which obtains the customers in the USA, is at Marblehead, Massachusetts, far away in the north east US, but in an important yachting harbour. For a bareboat 50ft (15·2m) ketch the weekly charter fee in 1980 for six persons was £2000 ($4700 at that time) per week, or in more permanent form, one per cent of the price of the vessel. This firm has about 110 yachts, some of which are crewed. Some of the boats are well-known racers or cruisers, left by the owners to be chartered for one or more seasons.

The Moorings Ltd is in the British Virgins at Tortola. It is really a yachting complex with hotel, restaurant, swimming and beach clubs and 67 yachts on the books. The latter are supported by a boat yard and sail repair loft. They say that some 7000 persons enjoy holidays with them every year. Like most charter firms the rates vary with the time of year and the hurricane season has a typical special offer with payment for one week and up to 14 additional days free. However, the Virgin Islands have not been damaged by a hurricane since 1926, though the risk (albeit with ample warning these days) is always there. In fact the main threat is the warning, which keeps the boat in harbour, even if the hurricane does not come anywhere near.

South and a bit east of the Virgins are the Windward and Leeward Islands. These include Guadeloupe, Dominica, St Lucia and the French yachting centre at Fort de France at Martinique. At the southern end is the island of Grenada. The Windward and Leewards are less developed than some other parts of the Caribbean. One major charter firm, Stevens Yachts with its headquarters back in the United States, has boats, mostly between 43 and 65ft (13m to 20m) based at Admiralty Bay in Bequia. Flotillas of about six of these boats are common, while Caribbean Cruising Ltd, with slightly smaller sailing cruisers, is based at St Lucia. Because of the different nationalities of the islands in the chain, whether independent or colonial, there is rather a lot of customs checking and clearing; this applies especially in the Grenadines which stretch immediately north of Grenada. The other problems in this part of the Caribbean are insects, for which repellent and screening in hatches is essential, and the deep water anchorages. All these things are eased by flotilla sailing, the guide skippers knowing which tree to make fast to in an anchorage!

In the *Greek Islands* the boats are smaller, reflecting the usage of European sailors and the smaller distances on a sea rather than an ocean. To the east of mainland Greece is the Aegean with its myriad islands; and to the west the Ionian Sea with the islands closer to the coast and the big resort of Corfu to the north. The headquarters of several of the fleets, when not in Athens, are in England. British companies operate there with standard boats such as Westerlys, Sadlers and Moodys. A common size ranges between 25 and 40ft (7·6m and 12·2m) and flotilla sailing is the most likely system. There are negligible tides in this, as in all parts of the Mediterranean. Summer is reliable for sunshine, though winds can blow hard if a Meltemi begins, a wind that may be over 50 knots and blow for several days. Many of the islands are isolated and without the noise and mechanization of other sailing areas in Europe, but in

moderate weather anchorages are numerous. One company which has been in the Aegean since 1970 is the Yacht Cruising Association Ltd. With a fleet of nine to 12 boats, the flotilla might spend some four or five hours sailing in a day during the April to October season. The warm nights in the anchorages encourage beach barbecues, or depending on the surroundings visits to tavernas. Outside these there might be found a spit, roasting a sheep or pig, which can be washed down by local wine. In settled weather there will be only the sound of crickets and an occasional sheep bell to disturb the warm night air.

One of the most unusual chartering areas in the world is the *Galapagos Islands*—there are 134 of them and 26 reefs. They are completely unspoilt. Because of their isolation, 600 miles off the coast of the mother country Ecuador, the sailing is in 49ft (15m) schooners which are based at Academy Bay. The price for this sort of chartering per head, including a flight from Europe, a week in Ecuador and a total of 18 days' sailing was £1250 in 1980.

By contrast *Australia* has its own market of potential charterers in the big cities of the south. Headquarters, for instance, of Whitsunday Yachting World Pty Ltd is in Sydney, but the boats are based at Shute Harbour. This is on the mainland opposite the Whitsunday group of islands, on the Great Barrier Reef, which is inside the tropics at 20 degrees south. The Barrier Reef is a thousand miles of coral reef lagoons, the water is clear and most spots are safe for swimming and diving. The south east trade wind keeps temperatures comfortable. To reach the yacht base a small aircraft is taken from Sydney to Airlie Beach. The Whitsunday Islands are maintained as a national park and largely uninhabited. Being in the tropics, sailing is possible all the year round, though like the Caribbean, winter is the most popular time. The middle of the summer, January and February, can bring tropical revolving storms. The boats used by Whitsunday are Mottle 33s which sleep six with an after cabin. By 1980 there were ten of these boats and three 40ft sloops.

The charter yachts only sail by day, because of the lack of lit channels in the abundance of coral reefs. It seems there is a pattern in chartering world-wide consisting of short day trips and warm evenings in pleasant spots. After all, the charterer is usually new to all the harbours he visits, in contrast to the cruising owner who makes an extended passage to reach a new cruising ground each season in the same part of the world.

A new dimension

Cheap air flights, easily maintained GRP boats and more people able to afford a fortnight in the sun mean that chartering is established as a regular feature of the world sailing scene. The sailor can come to it in two ways. One is as the charterer, saving money by not owning a boat, but taking several weeks a year in widely varying parts of the world. On a more modest scale, he and his family or friends may charter nearer home, so his boat is indistinguishable from the mass of owned sailing cruisers.

The other way he or she can come to chartering is by making it a way of life. Buying a boat and living afloat by chartering the boat out has its attractions, though the snags have already been hinted at. Chartering part time in order to use the vessel at other times in the season also has its pitfalls. Though some individuals, provided they are not looking for large profits, will continue to charter quietly as a way of life, it is efficient, relatively large charter firms that will look after most of the demand.

Comparative novices will be able to take a package sailing holiday, supervision being handled by crews or flotilla sailing. The location will be in a warm and sunny climate and the choice of boat and shore organization will ensure that most of the ruggedness, thought to be associated with cruising under sail, is eliminated.

Most yachting magazines will carry several pages of advertisements of charter firms, while there are often special numbers or special publications which list the charter holidays available all over the world. Back in the creeks of Essex, Mike Peyton, sailor and artist who charters out several cruising yachts every summer, says of his charter work 'I won't deny there have been a few Friday nights when I have regretted having to cast off, but never once have I regretted going by the end of the charter'. If this is how the harassed owner feels in the inclement climate of the North Sea, then how much more is the appeal for the charterers themselves in the crystal clear waters and holiday atmosphere of the Mediterranean, Caribbean or chosen part of the Pacific Ocean.

Part Three

Offshore racing

'Sailing vessel design has remained a "mystery and an art",
as it was described in the old apprentice-shipwrights'
indentures, and this has made it so fascinating a profession
throughout the ages . . . . Attempts to apply mathematical
methods to such complex problems as sail carrying power,
dynamic stability, total resistance and even seaworthiness,
continue, even though it is admitted that such calculations
are very inadequate and even unreliable.'

Howard I. Chapelle (late senior Historian,
Museum of History and Technology, Smithsonian Institutions)

14

What shapes the ocean racer

While the cruising sailor chooses his voyage and perhaps subsequently varies the route, the offshore racing man must select one and then another of the world's ocean racing courses. These courses have each a character, yet there is a repetition about the sea and its behaviour which makes a good boat as suitable for sailing over one course as another. Some of the courses and series (listed in Chapter 17) have a definitely expected weather pattern, and for such it might be thought that a special sort of boat would develop. Even where it does (such as in the trans-Pacific race), by no means all the boats entered are of one type, any good ocean racing yacht still being eligible. So, the design, construction and sailing of ocean racing boats produces a unique seagoing sailing machine of the late twentieth century. The reasons for current design will include tradition, the effect of rating rules, the improvement of materials and their limitations, personal prestige and a number of other factors. For this boat is a pleasure boat—though sailing men would wince at the term—a toy for a rather serious game. The most famous courses have a disproportionate effect on the development of design and sailing techniques for this reason; the type of boat which wins or reported incidents on the course come to be taken as guides and turning points. The boat which wins the SORC (Southern Ocean Racing Conference) or the One Ton Cup will have direct descendants the following season. This is true even if the design of the boat were not the main factor in the success.

The purpose of the ocean racing boat is to beat her competitors. Yet she is more than that. If she is a one-off, she is an extension of her owner's personality in terms of concept and details even if he thinks she is purely functional. If she is a production yacht, even then she represents what each owner or customer thinks a yacht should be, for unlike cars the numbers are never so large that the owners do not have

a 'collective personality'. A production yacht will also be to some degree suitable for cruising in terms of handling, deck layout and accommodation. Some yachts will represent the status, or financial attainment of their owners, though in sailing this is more subtle than in, say, a large motor yacht moored in a Mediterranean harbour. Even in the biggest ocean racers, there is an element of discomfort and risk and rich men seldom buy such a boat merely for status. The satisfaction of what money brings is more likely created by being first home on a long course (the biggest, fastest boat is needed!)—or first home for tea on a short one. Perhaps the patronage and attention of the latest fashionable designer is a spur. Some inexperienced, wealthy sailors who have bought the finest sailing yacht have been rapidly disappointed and have sold her quickly. In other words, whatever the personal resources of the owners in the ocean racing scene today, if their boats are large, fast and expensive, it is a safe bet that they have started with something more ordinary and worked their way in terms of sailing ability to the 'yacht of the moment'.

There are a proportion of modern, well designed boats which are not expected to win races. The owners would deny this but the urge to beat the rest of the fleet is not there. They enjoy their sailing and sail hard, but evidently not hard enough. Their presence swells the racing numbers and they will find good competition against each other. However, to some extent this type of relaxed owner has been driven out of the sport in recent years. The intensity of competition has meant that the 'out-to-win' owners fill a greater proportion of the places and the easy-going owner gets pushed to near the bottom of the results list.

This talk is of owners but for every owner there are on average about seven or eight crew. They sail first for sheer enthusiasm, though naturally once each man becomes experienced

The terms used in the broad description of ocean racing yachts are not clear in the English language. The kind of vessel could be accurately described as an *ocean racing yacht* or *ocean racing boat*, but this is long-winded. Ocean racer is an abbreviation, but *ocean racer* can also mean a person engaging in the sport. The latter is more common in the US than in Europe. *Offshore racer, offshore yacht, offshore boat* all mean the same thing with a feeling that the boat does not actually race across oceans, so it is frequently more accurate. Offshore racer will be used often in these pages—it is a species of boat (as opposed to an inshore racer or dinghy, cruising boat or motor boat). This description is demonstrated by the entry of a short handed race (like the two-man round Britain), where an entry (though it is an *offshore race*) might be 'a cruising boat', 'a catamaran', or again 'an offshore racer'. We know what is meant by the last term and can vizualise it. Tall rig, smart winches, fairly modern . . . *Cruiser-racer* is a rather unsatisfactory term, for a yacht which has racing pretensions but is comfortably fitted out below. *Fast cruiser* is much the same. The terms are not rigid though and some use them to describe any habitable racing boat.

As for the races themselves, the term *ocean race* is a race across open water out of the immediate control of the race committee. It certainly does not have to be across an ocean. However conscious of the pretensions of the term, many refer to *offshore races*, for shorter events, say across a stretch of water of sixty or one hundred miles. Racing round marks (regatta or inshore racing), even if it involves offshore racers is not offshore rac*ing*. It may well be part of an inshore/offshore series.

there is a tendency to go for the sort of boat which is exciting and likely to be successful. But not always, for many prefer to sail with friends and with a happy crowd and do not merely want to have experts and brawn suppliers as companions. Fortunately, in sailing there is a sizeable band of men and women, who fit between the legendary foredeck gorilla and the clueless cousin; competent friends, who soon form a team on a boat, such teams, as in any other sport, having various grades of ability.

Much is heard about a minority of people who are sailing and racing for the purpose of promoting a particular make of boat, mast or sail. Sometimes such crews have more resources than the private owner in the comparable size of boat. Often they are more expert because they spend more time (sometimes all their time) sailing and racing. This is a difficulty which the sport has not yet resolved. However, these people have invariably taken up sailing as a full time occupation because they were, in their early days, so enthusiastic that they wanted to make a career of sailing. Since there is no professional in the way that there is in football, they are obliged to do this via a sailing product manufacturer.

Such committed people only go to demonstrate how offshore racing can grip the enthusiasm, taking up as much time and effort as one may wish to give it. In a kind of way, it explains the rest of the owners and crews. The sea really is a magnet for those who are drawn to it and this is remarkable because many would subscribe to the saying that 'those who would go to sea for pleasure, woud go to hell for pastime'.

Despite the emphasis in the pages which follow on the description of the yacht herself and her technology, the human element remains all important; otherwise why apply science and development to this game on the water? Why sail around the world just to win a trophy? Why start a race in a gale? Why drift for many hours in blistering heat and calm with an unused engine and a tankful of diesel below, trying to coax another quarter knot? This is the nature of sailing—and ocean racing in particular. This is shown by the ingenuity and industry which, in comparatively few years—starting in about 1925—has shaped the ocean racing boat.

Why the shape it is?

So the purpose of the design of the ocean racing boat, whatever the motives of those who manage her, is to beat her competitors. She has just got to be faster, but 'faster' in any sailing boat is a word that grossly oversimplifies what the designer is seeking. Here is a list of the fundamental qualities required in an ocean racer. The winning yacht of any race of standing has to be to a very high standard in all of them.

The hull and keel must be fast through the water in the conditions of the race or in all-round conditions.

The sail area in its magnitude and design must provide the maximum power for the strength of wind.

It must be possible to handle the rig for optimum performance. It must be changed as necessary, so all gear in the rig and on deck works without any snags.

The interior (and deck design) must accommodate the crew so its members give of their best (eg there must be adequate cooking, sleeping and resting arrangements).

It must be possible to navigate the yacht to cover minimum necessary distance at best speed over a set course.

The yacht must be able to withstand heavy weather and other hazards of the sea. The design must conform to the requirements of the safety and emergency rules of ocean racing authorities, international, national and club. The yacht must carry a rating or handicap, whatever the system may be.

Some boats give of their best in certain conditions, say a particular wind speed and direction (eg close hauled in a 14 knot breeze), either because they have been designed for this, in expectation of certain courses, or because they are just found to perform like that after some experience in varying conditions. The science of yacht design being what it is, the latter is quite common. The right design for specific conditions is a challenge to designers. An offshore racer might be specifically designed or more likely special emphasis given for such conditions as:

Inshore events, which implies Olympic type course layouts, of which much is beating in smooth water.

Very long events, where the longevity of gear is more important than its initial performance or light weight.

A high proportion of down wind sailing—sailing free and not closehauled.

A high proportion of stormy weather.

A high proportion of use in light wind areas of coast and sea.

Despite such contradictory requirements not only is the all-round (at least intended as such) boat more common, but it exemplifies those contradictions which are at the root of the designing of racing yachts.

Other vehicles are designed to operate at a best speed. An airliner climbs to a specified height and accelerates to a designed economic speed. Even a racing car on the flat just goes at its maximum potential; among ships a freighter steams at her designed cruising speed. Yet a sailing yacht is denied this commonplace demonstration. This is because the amount of her power source is unpredictable and variable in its effect. The wind may provide any potential speed and it follows that 'fast' becomes a word without much meaning. One boat may be at her best when the wind is light (say, 5 knots); another will take the lead when the wind gauge records 20 knots. Apart from the strength there

are the varying qualities of boats in different wind directions—directions to the boat, that is. Though there are an infinite number of directions over an angle of about 270° we can for practical purposes divide the performance into three circumstances—beating, reaching, running.

An interesting demonstration of the necessity for the all-round yacht, at least to a high degree, was the experiments conducted by several designers in 1975–76 with bulbous bows. These excrescences are used on oil tankers and other large ships—a conspicuous ram bulb on the stem just below the waterline. This was tried in Denmark and Australia on a cruising yacht and inshore racing yacht respectively. As with the oil tanker, it gave an increased performance, but only at a single narrow speed range. On other speeds, it actually spoiled speed. For similar reasons, radical experiments with sailing yachts seldom succeed, especially in the necessary constriction of measurement, rating and other rules for racing boats.

What the yacht needs when beating

The contradictory qualities for each point of sailing (beating, reaching, running) will now become apparent. The basic requirement for beating to windward is *speed made good to windward*: this is usually shown as Vmg. It can be seen that this is a vector quantity and a combination of boat speed and close-windedness. Sailing close to the wind, but at a comparatively low speed, may well be equivalent in its effect to sailing fast through the water, but at an undesirably large angle to the wind. For a particular boat and set of wind and wave, there is an optimum Vmg resulting from an ideal angle to the wind and ideal boat speed (meaning actual speed through the water of the hull). Traditionally, this is the classic test of the performance of a yacht (roughly speaking anything, an orange box on the surface, will blow down wind), so yacht racing courses should, and usually do, contain a substantial proportion of beating. Where for instance the wind changes to give reaching and running throughout, this is not considered to make for a fair race. The design qualities in a boat to give the best Vmg include the following:

Power to carry sail

In a conventional ocean racer (that is not a multihull or unballasted centreboarder), the pressure of the wind on the sails when she is beating

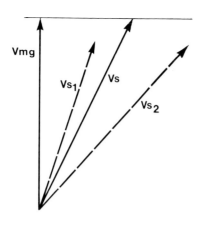

Vs is the course that gives best speed made good direct to windward, Vmg. Vs1 is closer to the wind, but slower. Vs2 is faster, but makes less ground to windward

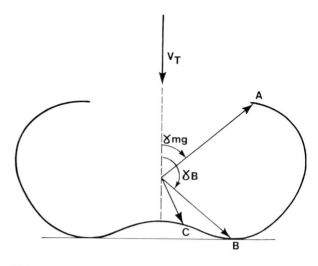

This is the polar diagram of a sailing yacht. A is the best course to windward: it is at an angle of Xmg to the wind. B is best course down wind. C is slower, because yacht is running away from the wind. XB is best down wind angle. (VT is true wind direction. The boundary line is the performance on every point of sailing)

causes heeling, which is resisted by the form of the hull and the distribution of weight within the hull. The heavier the lead ballast keel the more upright she will sail: saving of weight on deck and in the rig has a similar effect. The crew sitting to windward helps, but in larger boats the weight of a man becomes of less importance in relation to the yacht as a whole. The more upright the boat the faster she sails; this is partly because the less heeled posture will give better steering and less hull resistance, and partly because a greater area of sail is projected to the wind to supply forward driving force. If the boat easily heels, sail must be reduced and power is lost. A stiff boat is said to have power to carry sail.

Low windage

With the wind blowing at 30° from the bow, speed is directly affected by every part of the yacht and her rig which offers wind resistance. Of course, water resistance is there as well, but it is present at all times, whereas wind resistance does not matter except when the wind is forward of the beam and specially when beating. This is why there is every motive to make deck houses streamlined, freeboards moderate, masts, spreaders and standing rigging thin.

Crew weight and placement

This is mainly of importance in small ocean racers, under say about 32ft (9·7m). In principle

it applies in all boats, especially as bigger boats obviously carry more crew.

Helmsmanship

The yacht must be steered skilfully on all points, but on the wind, it seems easier for the boat to slip out of the groove. It is an exaggeration to say that sailing to windward is what helmsmanship is all about, but if one thinks back to one's days as a beginner helmsman, it was keeping the boat going to windward which was at first a major puzzle. On a more advanced level, a crack helmsman, however well the yacht is equipped with instruments, keeps her going by steering skill, especially when the run of the sea is difficult. This may well not apply on, for instance, a reach along a given compass course in fair weather.

Tacking ability

If a boat is slow when actually in the process of tacking, then she is going to lose time on a beat to windward, in which there are presumably a number of tacks to be made. In practice, modern ocean racers spin about easily and if there is delay it is more likely to be in faulty crewing, especially in winching in the genoa. However, crew variables are not being considered here.

Qualities when reaching

Sailors know the feeling of how the boat 'jumps upright', when the sheets are checked (eased

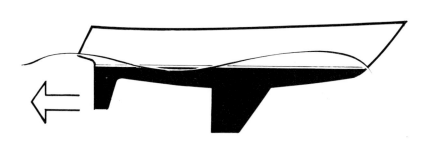

Keel weight. Athwartships it gives stability. Running with the wind, it is weight (displacement) to be dragged through the water

off), even by a small amount from close hauled to a close reach. It demonstrates that ballast ratio, and thus keel weight, are of less importance when reaching. Some power to carry sail is of use, but nothing like that needed when strapped down and going to windward.

Length to displacement

Reaching occurs when best speeds are obtained in moderate conditions (world speed sailing records are always attempted on a reach). Length of a given weight is needed to develop this speed. In other words, for a given length less displacement is wanted—and therefore, amongst other things, less ballast weight on the keel. However, as some power is necessary, excess weight is best removed from higher up in the boat on the rig or deck works.

Tracking ability

Unlike beating, reaching is quickest along a straight line. Some boats are difficult to steer, but the less wandering, the better. Shape of hull and size and position of rudder will help in tracking. Excess heeling adversely affects steering, so power and crew weight help again here.

Qualities when running

Running and reaching merge, when the wind is on the quarter, but the term is used here for when the wind is well aft. When reaching, the apparent wind draws ahead as it increases but when running, it is assumed the yacht is steered off so that the apparent wind remains 50 degrees or less from dead aft.

Length

This is a factor of which the importance increases as the wind gets stronger. The hull wants to surf and plane and it is only displacement which is limiting it in strong winds. The boat is comparatively upright, the keel is doing nothing but cause drag, so the less weight and ballast the better. Nor does the hull shape need stiffness, only lack of resistance to forward motion. For races where running is paramount, boats are designed long, slim and very light. Windage is no disadvantage when running, on the contrary it helps.

Tracking

As the spinnaker will be up with many extra forces on the yacht's rig, tracking is vital. Of course, the best tracking yacht can only cope with so much wind speed before sail is reduced. When racing, the amount of sail carried will sooner or later result in broaching, but the frequency is reduced by a hull with tracking qualities. Rudder failures are most often experienced when running under spinnaker.

So, the basic design qualities in a sailing yacht are contradictory in terms both of the three basic points of sailing (wind direction relative to the boat) as well as in terms of wind strength. In cruisers the hull and gear design can be made suitable for strong winds; for after all, in light conditions the best can be made of the boat as she is and there are no special problems. Possibly the motor is in use anyway. But this will not do for the racer, she must sail faster than the next boat in 5 knots of wind. Will the design aspects, which achieve this, be a source of disadvantage, or even danger, in heavy conditions?

How different emphasis is on the various qualities when beating, reaching and running in five different wind strengths

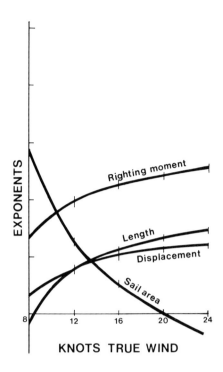

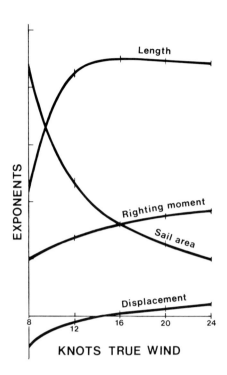

Beat: righting ability predominant, sail becomes excessive in stronger winds

Reach: length is significant, then levels off

On the short racing course

The visually conspicuous features on an ocean racing boat are conditioned by the needs for sailing exposed at sea, and so they contrast with the look of an inshore racer such as an Etchells or Star boat. But these apparent differences today are lessening for various reasons. One of these reasons is the increasing popularity of sailing over day racing courses. It is useful to see to what extent short course racing shapes the modern ocean racer. 'Short' course lasts something between four and ten hours, so it cannot go very far out to sea, though the sea may be severe for all that. It will not involve night sailing or cooking (perhaps just a 'brew up') and navigation will consist of finding the next mark and choosing the correct racing tactics.

The deck area is a platform on which the crew exercises its skills. More and more decks are flush and kept clear for the essentials of 'go-fast' gear. Halyards and sheets do not really like going round corners, each turning block means more friction, slower operating and the chance of a snag when running through. Straight line ropes mean space but in the interests of speed it is allotted to the purpose. Not much moves on the hull except the rudder (unless a

centreboard is fitted), so the gear on deck is all concerned with using the rig. Therefore the fittings consist of winches, stoppers, leads and their attendant track and cleats. There are also anchorage points, perhaps disguised as part of a stanchion or bow fitting. Except on larger yachts, the anchor windlass of the cruising man is absent, while mooring cleats probably double as working gear for some device or other.

Lines do not pass through the deck because watertight integrity must be assured—anyway the rules forbid it. Three deck features are universal: the cockpit, the main hatch (with companionway) and the forehatch. Some very small yachts are without a forehatch, but this is unsafe in case of fire or flooding aft. These areas, including lockers in the cockpit, must all seal absolutely watertight. Once the crew is on deck, it should be possible to operate the boat fully with those accesses to below battened down.

The cockpit will vary from a small well for the helmsman's feet only, to a large affair which can take several of the crew in comfort. It should be separated from the entrance to the cabin by at least a partition, though more likely a bridge deck; then if the cockpit is flooded, water does not enter the cabin. Whatever the

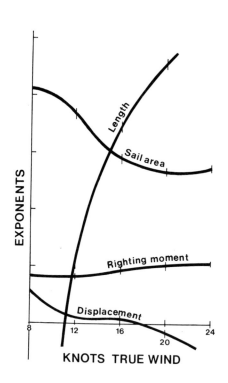

Run: length and sail area both important, but displacement is not wanted

spinnaker and mainsail, sheets of the genoa, spinnaker (2), mainsail reefing pennants. On larger boats this list will be increased. Requiring jammers or cleats (again a basic list) will be main topping lift, mainsheet traveller, all the lines on the winches just mentioned, spinnaker topping lift(s), foreguy(s) and sheets for extra sails (eg spinnaker staysail).

Not only do these essentials fashion the deck design, but also other gear which does nothing for speed but is there for ergonomics and safety and is often to comply with safety rules. Life-lines, toe rails, life-ring and life-raft stowage come into this category. There must of necessity be space for the crew, the size of which is sometimes laid down by rules, but more often determined by the optimum for racing. Plenty of hands during a difficult manoeuvre more than make up for the crew's weight. On a typical 40ft (12·2m) yacht the crew of eight comprises about eight per cent of weight.

On the long course

And so to the more characteristic features needed on a sailing yacht for any course extending overnight to even more days and nights at sea.

When a course extends overnight or longer, certain features require more emphasis. Dryness is needed below, not only for the integrity of the hull, but the comfort of the crew. A man cannot sail the boat for twenty-four hours, so there must be sleeping accommodation for at least half the number of the crew, which is suitable for use at sea. This will consist of bunks that keep one in when the yacht heels steeply and which are positioned where motion is less than violent. Therefore bunks forward of the mast cannot be used when racing—they are for harbour use only.

These bunks, 6ft 3in (1·9m) long each, once again show the purpose of the yacht as contrasted with other types. They may or may not be seats in the day time. Many small cruising yachts have bunks quite unsuitable for use at sea, but some very small offshore racers can have excellent arrangements.

Other features which have become part of the ocean racer because of the long course are:

Navigational facilities

A sizeable chart table is considered essential for the accurate navigation needed to win races.

design of the cockpit, it must enable the man on tiller, or wheel, to steer in comfort for long periods, despite the angle of heel and motion. He must also have a view of the sails, particularly the luff of the genoa when on the wind, a view forward and sight of the compass (for wind shifts in inshore racing) and instruments (speed, wind direction etc). A view forward is not always possible with current sail plans: the low cut genoa and other headsails obscure the view. A lookout may have to be posted forward sometimes.

The most commonly used feature on deck, by the crew, are the main genoa sheet winches. They are the biggest and get used every time the boat tacks and are used continuously to trim, especially when reaching under a headsail. They must be powerful, easy to wind and cleat and possible to throw off without jamming the sheet. Yet another conspicuous feature is the mainsheet track with its traveller or car. Somewhere it must cross the cockpit or the deck. Its siting is a major shape maker and there must be adequate structure to support it, as there must be for the genoa sheet tracks.

On a basic sloop, places must be found for winches in use for the halyards of the genoa(s),

With it will be chart stowage and instrumentation, where the navigator can conveniently have the benefit of such modern aids. There will be seating when working at the chart table and some form of strap to keep the navigator in place. The instruments mean elaborate wiring through the boat from power supplies and to repeaters and mast head.

Cooking

After a day or so, proper meals are necessary for enjoyment and health. Some crews may exist for a week or more on hard tack, but it usually adversely affects morale. Fuel has to be stored for the cooker and a safe compartment must be constructed and designed for it—propane gas explosion is a hazard of small vessels. Stowage for food and an ice box go with this and washing up facilities, which in turn means plumbing for outlets and water tanks with pumps. While considering plumbing, a separate hand basin is desirable and another plumbing need is a sea flushing or chemical toilet.

Stowage

Planned space has to be found for the variety of loose equipment carried below. This includes the crew's effects such as spare clothing, bedding and personal gear. There are spares for the rig, plumbing and engine. Racing boats will try and cut this to the minimum, but the longer the race, the more prudent it is to take at least materials to effect repair and tools to work with on boat and engine. Deep lockers with everything packed in are not adequate. Each item or type of equipment ought to have its place, dry or wet. Among the gear might be distress flares, life-jackets, first aid, sail repair stuff, electronic spares and a heavy rigging cutting tool.

Engine

This is not strictly essential for racing, but very very few ocean racers are not equipped with one. A yacht under 28ft might have an outboard motor. In any case, current rating rules give an allowance for engine and propeller, with more given for heavier engine and propeller with apparently greater sailing drag. It is a safety aid in case of loss of mast or other rig disablement; it enables the yacht to reach the starting line on time; it performs the more normal cruising duty of getting home if the wind drops; it charges the batteries (with shaft disconnected when racing) for lights and instruments. A propeller and shaft on the boat is a major characteristic shared with cruisers, but differentiating

from the pure racer. Twelve-metre boats and Dragons would never have motors.

At first it all sounds elaborate, which it is in comparison with a simple open day sailing boat. Yet each item is essential for living at sea and racing the boat. It reflects a sometimes hard but simple life, which is one of the appealing aspects of offshore racing. So the way of life, be it for just a few days, shapes the ocean racing boat that can be seen sailing today.

Conditions at sea

On the whole it is conditions at sea that shape the ocean racer. Rating rules as interpreted by designers limit and frame the shape to an extent that will be discussed later; but the yacht is a sea vehicle to convey a small number of persons under sail and this simple premise remains the primary design influence. The sailing yacht, and particularly the fast offshore one, is the inheritor of the techniques and way of life of the commercial sailing ship—and the fast pilot cutter and naval sailing frigate. At one time all seaborne traffic, except when rowed, waited upon wind and tide as does the ocean racer today. However, the cruising yacht may start her motor in adverse conditions. Of course, the comparison is limited, mainly because the yacht has no pay load as a commercial vessel had. The weight can therefore be put into the ballast keel to assist performance and the displacement kept low to increase speed for the given sail area. Widespread development of the commercial sailing ship stopped before the synthetic materials and other modern substances appeared. So, in viewing today's reinforced plastics or marine aluminium hull with its light alloy spars, polyester sails and fittings of different plastics and stainless alloys, one can speculate on the look of a fleet of sailing ships as they could have been towards the end of the twentieth century.

Ocean racing is essentially seasonal. Races are not arranged in winter time or in hurricane seasons. It is not that boats could not be made to withstand such conditions, but that it would be a pointless exercise for what is intended to be an enjoyable sport. Conventional ocean racers are sailed from open cockpits and decks on the assumption that temperatures are not unreasonable. It can be cold enough on summer nights in so-called temperate climates, or heavy weather or winds from an arctic quarter, but foul weather clothing as made for sailing should be sufficient to get by in such weather. Inside steering positions are seen on some long distance racers, very often in the form of a dome over a hatch position through which the helmsman looks. Cruisers have dodgers and wind breaks and centre cockpit steering, all of which give protection, but these are not a characteristic of ocean racers.

Therefore there is hardship enough on a small vessel with little protection on deck to make even summer sailing testing. The extra hours of daylight in summer seasons are welcome and advisable. Summer in many climates can bring a wide variety of conditions and it is these which play such a part in shaping the modern ocean racer. In the transatlantic or round-the-world races, it is summer but a yacht may sail close past an iceberg, the crew swathed in thick clothing.

Few parts of the world have the predictable weather that the travel agents would have us believe. Even if weather seems seasonal on land, in a small boat at sea one is much closer to the elements and more sensitive to them. For instance when the sun beats down on the hinterland of, say, La Rochelle on the Atlantic coast of France at 46 degrees north latitude, the wind offshore may be giving a hard beat or a light run, all within a 50 mile radius and depending on the course of the yacht. In light conditions the rig must be able to spread ample sail area or else she will appear 'glued to the water'. Incidentally, it is cruising boats that can rig the most sail, for it is in fine (light) weather after all, that cruising is most pleasant and they can then take best advantage of light winds. Besides, they do not have the constriction of a racing boat, which must pay in rating for larger sail area. Big rigs mean tall masts, which are just what are not needed when the wind begins to blow hard.

Since in boats up to 50ft (15·2m) LOA, the single mast of the sloop rig can be managed without special difficulty, it is on this spar that the optimum sail area for light winds (0–12 knots) must be spread. In the apparently simple foretriangle can be hoisted a selection of light weather sails from gossamer ghosters to full size working genoas, as well as various reaching and running sails. There being only one mainsail, however (the rules insist on this), it must be good for all weather. In light weather it will appear full and loosened off, its maximum area available. Modern ocean racers need remarkably little movement of air to get them sailing. See the light sails perhaps falling in from time to time, while with barely a ripple round the bow the yacht slides forward. Maybe she is heading

to a patch of sea where wind of greater strength will help her on her way. (This is another marked contrast to old sailing ships, whose sail wardrobe did not include sails able to stand in such light air.)

True wind speeds from 10 to 22 knots could be described as moderate. Full sail is then seen—perhaps many boats are designed for just these average conditions. Now the full mainsail is in action but flattened and tightened. The genoa fills the foretriangle, but it will be of a heavier cloth able to take the considerable loads at the speed at which the boat is likely to be travelling at her maximum on each respective point of sailing. Features designed for such conditions include the sheeting arrangements on deck, ways of controlling and bending the rig, the secure stowage arrangements and ergonomics of crew work on a moving deck and in a seaway.

One of the strange aspects of design and construction of ocean racers and other sea-going sailing yachts is the provision of conditions and strains that might be put on the vessel. The building has to allow for circumstances that it is hoped will not occur. One effect is that the cost of an ocean racer is high compared to a small family cruiser of the same size which is not intended to be hard driven in strong winds or ever to be out at sea when extreme conditions of weather arise. Other effects on design are more concerned with equipment or the method of fitting out, such as effective bilge pumps, quality sea-cocks, sound hatches in the event of seas breaking over them, fool proof reefing arrangements and storm sails that can be hoisted when conditions on deck are impossible.

Apart from gales and storms, the other most likely extreme condition is bad visibility, deteriorating to thick fog. This is possibly the most dangerous situation, because a yacht can be run down by a ship and sink quickly without the ship ever knowing about it. However, apart from having the facility to hoist a radar reflector, this is a department which is not catered for in ocean racers. Because of the weight and windage aloft and the power needed, they seldom carry radar. Even reflectors are not kept permanently hoisted as in some cruisers. Engines are not, of course, turned on for quick collision avoidance in calm or light air (although they should be ready for instant use in these conditions). It may be in the future that compact electronic devices will be invented that will improve the present unpleasant circumstances which exist in fog.

2

CHARTER (See Chapter 13)

1: Red Sea charter. A Swedish built Maxi 84

2: Antigua Week, 1981, where charterers seek blue skies and sun

3: Flotilla charter boats in Greece in a typical small harbour

4: Greek islands charter is mostly warm sun and light winds. A charter boat leaves Sivota

5: A chartered cruiser in the British Virgin Islands

6: Red Sea flotilla in a sheltered bay. Typical of modern charter

7: Charter fleet moored at Bonifaccio, Corsica

4

1
3

5

7

15

Designs for ocean racing

The yacht designer

Few drivers of cars could name the designer of their vehicle, while only the owners of a minority of houses would be able to mention the architect. Many houses and cars are more likely to be designed by a team working under the name of a company of architects or the design department of a huge automobile corporation. Yachts and especially racing yachts are quite different in this respect. Not only would the owner know his designer, in many cases personally, but other competitors would as well. If they did not, one of the first questions which they would ask would be 'Who is she designed by?' In some race reports the name of the designer has even been given and the owner omitted!

The important role of the designer springs from the days when every racing yacht was individually designed and built. The builder started every boat on bare shed floor and it was the designer's brain child that he constructed. This 'one-off' tradition still holds good in many cases today, especially among the top ocean racing boats. But even series built boats carry the stamp of their designer. A highly thought of designer is a positive sales asset to the marketing of production boats.

Outstanding among this new breed is New Zealander Ron Holland, who won the Quarter Ton Cup in 1973 in his own boat *Eyethegne*. This caught the eye of an Irish entry for the One Ton Cup in the following year; this proved successful and then came Admiral's Cup owners. By the late seventies, he was inundated

Douglas Peterson, Californian designer of ocean racing yachts built in many countries

German Frers, Argentinian racing yacht designer

with design business—exclusively for ocean racers to the IOR and from his offices (a converted pig farm) in southern Ireland, he catered for leading ocean racing men world wide. His contemporary Doug Peterson, who has always lived and worked in California made his mark in the 1973 One Ton Cup with *Ganbare*. The following year a development named *Gumboots* was built by owner/builder Jeremy Rogers, which won the Cup for Britain. A string of Peterson successes followed as leading owners in America and Europe built to his designs. His Californian base enabled him to create large yachts and include some fast cruisers as well as IOR boats. A leading British designer is Ed Dubois, who in the 1981 Admiral's Cup was responsible for two of the winning three boat British team and seven yachts of other nations competing. In the previous decade Dick Carter set up as a designer in Boston after winning the Fastnet twice, first in *Rabbit* and then in *Red Rooster*. German Frers, after leaving the design office of Sparkman and Stephens, carried forward from his Buenos Aires office the name of his father German Frers Sr; designing large boats like *Scaramouche* for American owners brought him success. Like the others he was active in sailing on board his own creations in important races. This last point is highly significant, for racing yacht design is built on sailing experience and cannot be maintained merely by

working on the drawing board or even in the test tank. By contrast Camper and Nicholsons, the very old established British yacht builder, who have designed as well as built many ocean racers in the past, ceased designing racing boats in 1975 turning to Ron Holland for their series racers.

Such specialization seems here to stay, for not only do people like those mentioned above live on their racing yacht reputations, but more all-round firms of designers would not be into racing enough to cope with such designs and would be unlikely to find the service required profitable. New faces can come forward quickly in the world of ocean racing design, so the faces seen here could well have equally valid additions at any time.

Yacht design on paper

The most secretive aspect of design concerns the *lines plan*. In the opinion of the author it is not the most important factor in speed potential, but it is in a way the designer's 'signature'; lines plans are not published in the way they once were. On the other hand, if a designer provides nothing else he must draw the lines—the shape of the hull. Of course, his drawings usually consist of many sheets and include the following, as well as the lines:

Ron Holland, New Zealand racing yacht designer, (resident in Europe)

Ed Dubois, British designer of succesful ocean racers

149

OFFSHORE RACING

150

6

1: *Panda* designed by Ed Dubois typifies modern ocean racing shape: clean deck, big sail area, weight saving stern. She has raced in England, the Mediterranean, Florida and sailed the Atlantic

2: Offshore racers beat in a fresh breeze. The mainsail, centre, is well reefed. This typifies the pressure under which they are invariably sailed

3: *Revolootion*, designed by Groupe Finot, four times in the French Admirals's Cup team between 1973 and 1979. Sailed all weather and across oceans, consistently beating more modern boats. Owned since launch by Jean-Louis Fabry

4: *Acadia*, built 1981 to the latest ideas by New Orleans Marine to a design by Argentinian German Frers

5: *Robin*, owned by Ted Hood seen here in 1979 was already five years old, but remained a top performer. Note the smooth perfection of her sails made by Hood Sailmakers

6: *Disque d'Or* (**Switzerland**), at the big end of the ocean racing scale

4

5

The sail plan of a fractional rig Three Quarter Tonner
(rating 24·5ft). Three backstays support mast; largest
genoa is limited by rule. Several sails are shown inside
this. Dotted lines on mainsail indicate reefs for successive
reduction of sail
(LOA 33ft 2in, 10·1m. Displacement 7260lb, 3300kg.
Mainsail 350ft² 32·4m². No. 1 genoa 330ft² 30·6m²)

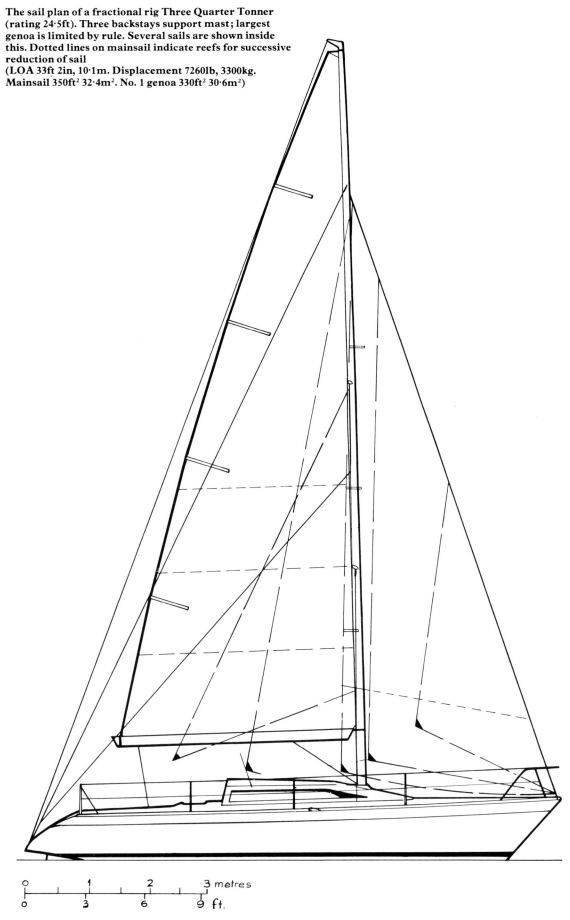

0   1   2   3 metres
0   3   6   9 ft.

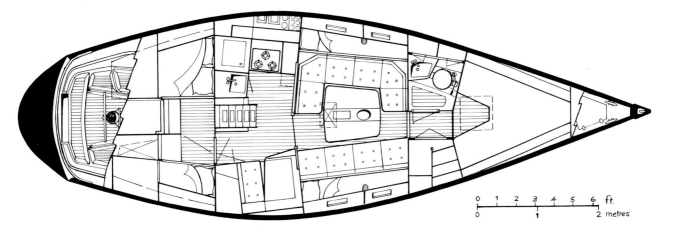

'General arrangement' on a 39ft sloop. There are bunks for eight or nine, large L-shaped galley to port and chart table to starboard. Many designs have very similar layouts to this one (which is a Finnish built Baltic 39)

sail plan

general arrangement (the main accommodation below)

deck plan

construction plan

sections through accommodation

then on a more subsidiary level:

plumbing and piping

electric fittings and electronics with wiring

keel sections and detail

detail such as special fittings, methods of fastening, hull to deck joint, mast step, stem head fitting and so on.

Some of the later drawings are usually made after construction has started and the designer knows that major changes are not then liable to occur. Though there are some drawings of detailed fittings, these are never to the extent found in an aircraft or car design office. The basic reason is financial: there is just not the return on a yacht design. Series designs collect a royalty and a one-off design for a 35ft (10·7m) yacht might have a fee of $5000 (1982). In any case many standard fittings will be used and these are drawn in from traces supplied by the manufacturers of engines or winches, for instance. A designer's fee usually includes two or three visits to the yard, though because of the international manner of design, this may be the subject of a separate agreement. On the other hand an American designer can take into one visit to Europe a number of boats which are being built. It is best if the designer sees the lines 'lofted'; then the deck and accommodation nearly completed and finally has a trial sail. Certain modifications are possible at each of these stages. A designer living close to the builder,

might well look in far more often, while if an owner is arranging building under his own responsibility, then it may be agreed that he gets on with it and can make reasonable modifications of his own.

Yacht drawings have a peculiar fascination and to some extent are a sales aid. A designer might submit preliminary drawings to an individual or a yard, which excite enough interest, resulting in an order for a design. When examining the plans mentioned above a few points are worth remembering.

Lines plan

Lines are essentially slices seen from the side, from above and from ahead and astern. Formerly, great play was made in ensuring that these lines were fair, but modern theories of the effect of rating rules may mean that the designer has decided on certain shapes, hollows and straights. These lines are his great endeavour to push a certain weight and length through the water with least resistance, whether upright or at an angle of heel. Other main considerations of this shape are resistance to heel (stiffness) and sufficient volume to allow for the desired accommodation. The keel and rudder probably begin life on the lines plan, but with modern configurations, they can be redesigned without affecting the hull shape. What is 'fast' in hull shape? When we are talking in terms of ocean racing yacht design, the differences are in the realms of designers' latest theories and opinions—all are fast. Only the heavy displacement cruiser, which is not in this field, is slow. Crewing, weight distribution, surface smoothness below the waterline and a number of aspects of the rig are all (in the opinion of the writer) more important than the minutiae of hull shape. This statement pre-supposes a competent hull shape by any experienced racing yacht designer.

1

2

3

4

5

6

1: *Kriter Lady II*, **a Freedom 70 with wrap round mainsails and no jibs was sailed by John Oakeley and Laurel Holland in the two-handed transatlantic race**

2: *Moxie*, **sailed by Phil Weld at the start of the single-handed transatlantic race (Plymouth-Newport), which she won in 1980**

3: **A Japanese owned Two Tonner to the International Offshore Rule**

4: **An Australian Two Tonner,** *Impetuous*

5: **Maxi-rater:** *Condor* **in a gale**

6: *Sunshine Boys*, **Mini Ton rating IOR**

Sail plan

At its most basic, this shows the size of the mainsail and largest headsail. Therefore, it also gives the key factor of the position of the mast in the boat and its height. Details of the mainsail (eg placement of reefs) may be shown by the designer, though they are more likely to be filled in by the sailmaker. The smaller headsails and sail inventory may be given by the designer, or the owner and sailmaker may work this out. Spinnakers are determined under rating rules and depend on the mast height and distance from mast to intersection of forestay and deck, so when the designer shows these latter features he is, amongst many other things, determining the basic spinnaker shape.

Mast standing rigging will be shown on or adjoining the sail plan. But from these a detailed construction plan of the mast will be prepared by the mast manufacturer for approval. If the rig is other than single masted, the sail plan becomes more elaborate, to include the position of the mizzen and its rigging and its relationship to the main mast. A useful sail plan will show the hull and its structures accurately in profile, so it also gives a view of the boat as she will look on the water. However, even sails are not ultimately two dimensional: for instance headsails take up a curve so that the clew position will be forward of the point as shown on the sail plan once the boat is sailing. Is there any special formula as to where to put the sail plan in relation to the hull shape, keel and rudder? Not really; the designer builds on experience moving the mast a little from one design to another, or raising the mast or shortening it. The sail plan indicates the actual (and rated) sail area. This will increase with the designed displacement for any given length of boat.

General arrangement, the 'GA'

Here are the intentions of the designer for the positions of bunks, galley, chart table, motor and bulkheads. Even for racing there are numerous combinations. This is the drawing most likely to suffer from modification as the yacht is built. When owner and designer are able to climb on board the finished hull and see exactly where various items are placed, they may take off an inch here and put one on there. When looking at GAs, it should be remembered that the plan view shows the bounding hull at about deck level, whereas all the time the volume is decreasing. For instance, stowage space under bunks will be far less than it

appears. Sections through the accommodation are useful for checking this aspect and for relating fittings from the deck (eg the tie-bars from the chain plates must come past bunks and lockers, without, if possible, interfering with their use). Later the use of the accommodation by a racing crew is discussed and it is practical experience in this that will determine the designer's proposal for the GA. Owners frequently have strong views about the arrangements below, when they would not dream of expressing opinions about the hull lines or the keel shape. In standard boats this greatly affects the market. The builder will be looking for an attractive layout which is wider than the out-and-out racer.

If the design is a one-off for ocean racing, or if the accommodation is for ocean racing only within a standard hull (other versions might be fitted out for the wider market), then weight can be saved by fitting only those facilities that are needed for racing. This saved weight can go into the ballast keel, or into the hull for strength, or subtracted to keep the yacht trimmed to her designed flotation. The GA will in such a case show bulkheads and other structural members insofar as they affect space,

bunks, enough to sleep the off-watch crew, possibly all to windward—so there must be enough along one side,

galley, equipped for using at sea, including swinging stove, fresh water access ability and all-weather stowages,

chart table, so that the navigator can operate for maximum accuracy and best decision,

motor position,

sail stowage, the ocean racer carrying a large number which must be accessible and not be detrimental to performance because of the position of such weight,

other stowage space.

The resulting combination of these features will show in the GA to any potential owner the practicability of the design for his own needs.

Deck plan

This basically two-dimensional plan shows the cockpit, coachroof, hatches and every deck fitting. Placement obviously has to correspond with the GA.

Construction plan

In the days of planked wooden boats this used to show every timber and structural member. Since there were many minor variations in the way wooden boats were put together, the builder would cut out the various members (all of different woods in accordance with the specification) and fit them together in accordance with the designer's latest ideas for strength, rigidity and lightness. These principles still apply for modern building systems, but aluminium or glass fibre are homogeneous materials. The plan still needs to show points of reinforcement, where the material is thicker or doubled up and in the case of aluminium the frames and members. For glass fibre there are still strengthening members with wooden or rigid foam cores and these are indicated on the plan. Critical points of construction will include keel attachment, rudder construction and system, mast arrangement and the way in which its thrusting load is taken and deck to hull joint, which, if not perfectly made, will result in leaks that can seldom be cured.

Decisions about the construction methods on a glass fibre hull usually lie somewhere between a complete specification from the designer, which the builder then rigidly adheres to, leaving it to the builder to work according to his usual practice. A one-off boat consultation will continue at various stages, while for a production line decisions can be made during and after completion of the first boat or prototype. A construction plan in such circumstances could then well be the result of building a certain design and the key for subsequent boats.

The yacht builder

Even mass producers will never approach the automobile industry in the way they are run—there just will never be the volume. One basic difference—scale apart—is that engines come from motor manufacturers, often subsidiaries of car and lorry engines. Of course no boatbuilder would ever contemplate making engines: these arrive in their marine versions from Ford, Volvo, Renault. . . . In boating terms big quantities are mainly in outboard runabouts, small motor cruisers and standard sailing cruisers—not ocean racers. Builders of such boats may run a line of ocean racers, but because of design changes year by year, the line will be limited in its run—not much more than two years, perhaps and then a new model must be offered.

These short production runs of racing boats are more likely to come from a medium size builder. He may be independent or the subsidiary of a larger group. Typical is Southern Ocean Shipyard, Poole, England. Its workforce is geared to making glass fibre hulls and finishing them all in the yard. However, many hulls come from specialist moulders and are only finished in the yard; they may even be marketed by a third party. Over the years the first of each range has been campaigned by the builders or experienced yachting friends. One of the world's earlier production glass fibre boats, the Pioneer, was started in this way nearly thirty years ago. She was designed by Ricus van de Stadt, a Dutch designer at top international level, who has now retired, though the design firm of his name continues. Southern Ocean Shipyard followed this boat with a series of design runs including the larger Excalibur, which scored many ocean racing successes. In the early seventies came the Pioneer X, a quite new Van de Stadt design to the old name which won her class in the RORC championship. Meanwhile the yard also went in for a somewhat different market by building (from the board of the same designer) the Ocean 53, then the Ocean 71 and even bigger, the Ocean 75. These could be offshore raced and they were, but it is fair to say that such large yachts were more in demand for long distance cruising and charter work. In 1975, Douglas Peterson was engaged to design a 33ft standard IOR boat, the Contention 33. The first one was successfully campaigned in the closing months of that year and then others were ordered, for the boat rated at the Three Quarter Ton level and the championship for that class was to be held in England in 1976. During the 1976 season the Contention was raced by a number of good helmsmen and a French owned boat *Bilou Belle* won the RORC championship, while others had success in a variety of races. In the Three Quarter Ton Cup itself *Bilou Belle* won the production boat prize and in one of the offshore races there were three Contentions in the first six boats home. These included *Contention*, with different ballast to the standard boats and *Incontention*, purchased by an American team for the series and fitted with a special rig, which failed to stand up.

The history of Contention production is a classic pattern of a standard boat. In the year after top helmsmen had sailed the boat in the Three Quarter Ton Championship, sales continued, but a year after that the yacht was no longer considered a winner. That is not to say that the design was not competitive in the right hands: it is just that the keener sailors will always tend to move, sometimes quickly sometimes slowly, to another sort of design, After successful world wide sales, demand in 1978 was

down to a trickle. It had had a good three-year run, leaving many owners of a fine boat with racing potential and cruising ability.

The smaller sister of this design was the Doug Peterson Contention 30. The yard went into production of this in 1977. Thus it wisely rotated its racing designs, but kept eyes on a wider market with the production in 1978 of a standard 60ft schooner, the Ocean 60. Though the prototype was raced it was designed for charter work. This large cruiser-racer kept the yard busy in the severe boat building recession between 1979 and 1981, a slump in orders which particularly hit standard offshore racers between 20 and 40ft. The Ocean 60 had an international market (and of this it only needed a limited number of rich men or companies with funds) of a more long-term nature. No doubt the pattern will continue to ensure success in this yard and those others who are in the business of building production yachts.

Types of offshore racer

Ocean racers and offshore racing boats follow several streams of evolution. The widest influence is that of the International Offshore Rule of rating. Most of the major events around

Above: An Ocean 60 (pale blue) built by Southern Ocean Shipyard sails against a Freedom catamaran rigged design

Top right: Maxi-rater: *Mistress Quickly*

Bottom right: *Three Legs of Man :* **a trimaran for short handed ocean races**

the world demand yachts rated to it and have done since 1970; its effect is to be seen on most ocean racers and on cruising yachts as well. Racing under other rules or club handicap systems can also be found all over the world, but will be at local, regional or perhaps national level (of a second line nature). Such rules are all different, so they have no influence at all—with isolated exceptions—on designers and builders who therefore have no market.

Strong influence on design and construction does, however, come from short handed transocean races. After flirting with home-made handicap systems these have now become non-handicap, with the first boat home the winner. The winner must therefore come from among the largest yachts, but many of all sizes compete for the achievement. To encourage this further the organizers wisely divide the fleet up into groups of sizes and each crew can aim to be the first home for its class prize.

Multihulls have a very important part to play in these events. Despite attempts from several quarters to create a rating rule for multi-hulls, no such rule has found favour and there is no *regular* racing for catamarans and trimarans of ocean racing type. They are therefore aimed at the long distance, short handed racing and cruising. Additional reasons for this are the problem of accommodating them in more than a few harbours and their unsuitability for numerous crew, because weight is highly detrimental to their performance and stability requirements. Since the main argument for multihulls is absolute speed through the water (as opposed to speed relative to rating or class rules), there has been increasing success for them in 'first home takes all' events. Many of these craft are sponsored by commercial concerns and manned by persons who have become known as professionals of the ocean circuit. Since there is no professional yacht racing as such (although in 1980 there were proposals for spectator yacht racing in California, which at the time of writing has yet to prove viable), trade names or associations on boats, which will be in the lead (symbolic) and make news (good public relations), are the next best thing. Short handed, long distance events have less tradition but more publicity than most other ocean racing and so have become the vehicle for this. An additional reason is that the French sailors have done particularly well in these events and as France is the birthplace of this type of commercial sailing, so it has spread to other leading sailing countries, especially Italy and New Zealand. In Britain, 'names' sooner or later can find sponsorship, a typical example being a trimaran called *Brittany Ferries*. Built for Chay Blyth it won the *Observer*/Europe 1 two-handed transatlantic race of 1981. This boat with exotic materials in the hull like Kevlar, unidirectional glass airex foam, carbon fibre and light alloy was 65ft 7in (20m) length overall, displaced 14 000lb (6350kg) and carried 2300ft² of sail on a single mast. Although one of the largest boats in the race, it was not the biggest and there were six others with an LOA within 3ft of it.

The winner of the 1980 OSTAR (see Chapter 17) was the trimaran *Moxie,* sailed by a very experienced American to finish in the record time (for the event) of 17 days 23 hours 12 minutes. The boat was 56ft (17m), a length limit for the race after giant entries (particularly the 236ft four-masted schooner *Club Mediterranée* had been entered and sailed in 1976—she did not win) had been banned as a danger to other shipping and competitors when sailed by one man. *Moxie* is particularly mentioned as typifying the racing ability of short handed boats; for instance, all her winches were self-tailing and her headsails and mainsail could furl vertically, and indeed were furled and unfurled all the way across the Atlantic by her 63-year-old owner. The contrast to the IOR class yacht with her big and usually young crew described below is immense. His best daily run was 265 miles (426km) which means 11 knots.

Further down the scale are every shape and size of boat with skippers of different motives, some carrying a sponsor's name as an adventure with little chance of winning, some to prove seaworthiness and confidence sailed by designer or builder who hopes his class will be promoted; some, like Richard Konkolski, the sole representative of his country, Czechoslovakia, and a number just there to make that crossing alone but glad of the companionship and organization at start and finish.

International Offshore Rule class

Around ten thousand yachts in the world carry ratings, having each been measured to the International Offshore Rule. The main reason that the rule is so widespread is because of its evolutionary nature. This was not some class officially declared and then looking for recruits. It was instead a combination of the world's two most widely used ocean racing rating rules, those of the Cruising Club of America and the Royal Ocean Racing Club. Both had started as simple rules to handicap yachts between the wars, though the RORC rule was based on even earlier methods of rating. European yachtsmen with international racing at heart saw no reason why quite different designs had to be built for races depending on which side of the Atlantic they sailed, and at a meeting in Bremen in 1967 they urged the two sides to get together. After several years of meetings under the chairmanship of one of the world's greatest yacht designers, Olin J. Stephens Jr of New York, the International Offshore Rule (IOR) became effective on 1 January 1971 with an international body, the Offshore Rating Council (later the Offshore *Racing* Council) as the authority for it. It was to be independent of the International Yacht Racing Union, since offshore men had little regard at the time for the handling of yachting problems by the IYRU. However, relations were always friendly and there were two IYRU delegates on the ORC.

Club Mediterranée, **largest yacht ever to sail in the single-handed transatlantic race**

Between 1971 and 1981 the IOR has changed considerably. In the early days boats designed to the old rules were measured to it in the expectation of fair racing, but immediately the most competitive owners all over the world were commissioning yacht designers to devise boats that took maximum advantage of the rule formula. In the very early days demands were heard, particularly from the United States, for rule revisions to ensure fairness to existing yachts. Revisions followed with major changes in 1972, when IOR Mark II (Mark I had been a draft that was never raced to) became IOR Mark III, and again in 1975 when IOR Mark IIIA was introduced. The latter was for boats already in existence and has given them advantageous ratings. There were further big changes which altered rating figures across the board in 1979. Every year there are some alterations to plug anomalies or try and increase fairness to certain features on boats. The problem is that one man's rating advantage is another's loss and there is always some section of the fleet—new boats, old boats, light boats, boats with more than average sail area, whose owners feel hard done by.

Total numbers of boats rated to the rule have varied, but not violently, world-wide. In 1972, the first year in which European countries were racing to IOR Mark II, the world total was 6924 (as at 1 September); by 1973 it was 9364. Then it settled between 10 000 and 10 500 until 1979 when it dipped to around 9500. Individual countries have shown somewhat different stories (see graphs p162). The USA fleet has dropped in numbers in the face of other regional rules, while some European countries have made up for this.

From the above it will be appreciated that an owner's rating figure for his yacht is something to be treasured and fought over. There is an understandable reason for this, as the rating determines his result at the end of every race. A reminder of how this works would be useful. The rating certificate shows figures in *feet* (even the French and Italian rating authorities prefer to use feet, which is a sailing term and not just an imperial measure; it makes a distinction between rating and boat length for which they use metres). This was once meant

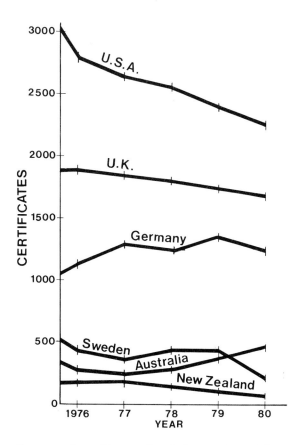

Some numbers of boats using the International Offshore Rule in certain countries. USA has most, but numbers decline. Germany generally grew until 1980. UK has second largest numbers. USA and UK IOR boats have always exceeded all other countries added together

to approximate to the boat's waterline length which in turn has a basic relationship to speed. But that is now forgotten and the figure is a key to potential speed derived from the complex formula—all 64 pages A4-size of it—which is the IOR today. Most dimensions on the yacht are fed into the computer. With a rating figure of, say, 27·0ft rating, the yacht is given a time allowance. In north west Europe and Australia there is a time multiplication factor (TMF) derived from this, the RORC TMF for 27ft being ·9729. At the end of the race, the time round the course, the elapsed time, is multiplied by this to give the corrected time. Another boat with a lower rating finishing close after this first one would have her elapsed time multiplied by a smaller figure so reducing the corrected time. It might be that this time was less than that of the first boat and so the second boat would have better corrected time and beat the first one. The boat in the race with the least corrected time is the winner. Thus owners are keen to have as low a rating as possible: for racing success, personal pride, crew enjoyment and second hand value.

In the United States and the Mediterranean, tables are used to find a time allowance per mile for each rating against a scratch boat, so for a course of a certain length there is a fixed number of hours (if any), minutes and seconds for boat A to beat B (which is smaller than boat A) if she is to save her time. This system is called 'time-on-distance' as it is fixed for the course. The RORC method is called 'time-on-time' as it depends on the time taken, which will vary for the course depending on wind strength and if there is much windward sailing which, because of tacking, increases actual time taken. Each system has its advantages and drawbacks, time-on-time appearing to be favoured for tidal waters where distance as such means less; but in truth it would appear that tradition has a say. The ORC for several years in the seventies tried to combine the systems, as the rules had been combined. They did devise an experimental combination, but it had no appeal and was dropped, partly because of its complexity. The RORC formula for devising TMF from rating is

$$TMF = \frac{a + \sqrt{R}}{1 + b\sqrt{R}}$$

where R is rating in feet, and a and b are figures depending on the rating. 23ft and above, $a = 0.2424$, $b = 0.0567$; 22·9ft and below $a = 0.4039$, $b = 0.2337$. A four-figure decimal is used for the TMF. Ratings are taken to the nearest 0·1 of a foot. Ratings can be in metres and this is used in Scandinavia.

Whatever the time allowance used, there is frequently a less than satisfactory feeling at the end of a race even if the ratings and time allowances allotted are fair. A large yacht and a small yacht on the same race, both being sailed to the same high standard, will gradually separate in distance. Therefore they cannot experience the same weather and tidal conditions and regardless of any allowances, one or the other will obtain a natural advantage. Secondly their very separation means that there is a lack of direct competitiveness between boat and boat, crew and crew: instead each boat is sailing against the clock. To be fair on time allowances, these negatives may not apply where the ratings are close, the boats in sight of each other and the adjustments at the end small, for instance a few minutes after several days of racing.

Evolution of rating rules leading to the IOR can be found in *The Guinness Book of Yachting Facts and Feats*.

But there are many who prefer not to race under time allowances. Then an IOR rating can be used without it and this is called *level rating*.

Level rating

It was a simple idea, much simpler than all the trappings of time allowances. First boat home the winner! The control would be by maximum

Right: Measuring beam under the IOR
Below: Adding IOR 'bumps' to the hull to increase measured dimensions

rating. Jean Peytal of the Cercle de la Voile de Paris took the old One Ton Cup, a beautiful piece of silver from 1898, dusted it down and presented it in 1965 for ocean racers in a combined inshore-offshore series for RORC rated yachts not exceeding 22ft rating. (The boats were about 36ft LOA.) From 1902 to 1962 the cup had been used for the international 6-metre class which had become obsolescent. The first race in the English Channel, and based at Le Havre, was in existing boats near the rating, but the idea excited top owners and designers and they were building One Tonners to the RORC rule. With the introduction of the IOR in 1971, competition heightened, because here was an international class of boat for boat racing and intense effort was put in. Each nation could enter up to three boats, although the winner was an individual yacht. Designers made and lost their reputations in the One Ton Cup. From 1965 to 1973 only boats designed by Sparkman and Stephens of New York and Dick Carter of Boston ever won the series, but in 1974 the British owned *Gumboots* won at Torquay, designed by Douglas Peterson. Subsequent design success in the One Ton has been more evenly spread between America, Europe and New Zealand.

The One Ton Cup is now under the auspices of the Offshore Racing Council as are the other level rating classes which have derived from it. There are rules for the conduct of the races which consist of a long offshore race (to last about 54 hours, the length in miles depending on the class) and a short (27 hours). There are three inshore Olympic shape courses, again varying in length per class. There are brief accommodation and equipment rules. These include minimum headroom above a certain surface area. Other IOR boats have no such accommodation rules. There are also rules on equipment and prohibitions of certain advanced electronic devices to facilitate navigation.

These are the level rating, or 'Ton Cup', classes by rating with an indication of the likely overall length. The latter may vary considerably, depending on how the designer chooses the factors in the rating formula. The boats under all ratings tend to get slightly larger year by year, as designers learn to extract advantage from the measurement and rating.

The Mini Ton, established only in 1978, has slightly different rules and does not have offshore races out of sight of land or out of immediate control of the race committee. The longest race is planned to last only 15 hours.

One Mini Ton rule is a maximum beam of 8ft 2in (2·5m) to enable it to comply with road trailing regulations: this shows the sort of activity envisaged for the smallest offshore racing class. The minimum rating for any IOR boat is 16ft.

Trophy	Rating IOR in feet	Number of crew allowed	Approximate LOA in feet	(m)
Two Ton	32	8	42	13
One Ton	27·5	7	38	11·5
Three-quarter Ton	24·5	6	33	10
Half Ton	22·0	5	30	9
Quarter Ton	18·5	4	27	8
Mini Ton	16·5	3	23	7

Maxi raters

At the very top of the IOR scale are boats owned by very rich men, who want to be first home in any fleet. They delight in really big sailing machines with crews of 25 and a length of perhaps 80ft. The maximum rating under the IOR is 70ft, so if the computer finds a higher figure for the rating, it is not valid. There is no official maxi rating class, but the few boats with ratings at or close to the maximum will tend to race each other to be first home even if there is a small time allowance adjustment. In 1981, a specific series was held for them on the south coast of England, on a level rating basis. In theory the advantage lies with the boat which is right up on the maximum rating. Sail area and some other features can be adjusted to get up to this figure.

Such boats really come into their own in the longer races, where their size can cut days off the time such as the Fastnet race, Bermuda race or even the Round the World race, where, with a trained crew, size means security and speed. Such boats do not usually have limited seasons as do most yachts: they roam the world from one major fixture to another. Part of the crew may be permanent, paid men; others amateurs who have joined for a long or short period. The owner flies out to join the boat, as and when he wishes, probably for all or some of the races.

Top right: *Waverider* **(New Zealand) winner of the Half Ton Cup in 1978 and 1979**

Bottom right: The British yacht *Solent Saracen* **(J. S. McCarthy) which won the Three Quarter Ton Cup in Norwegian waters in 1975**

Top: Half-Tonners in action. The boats are about 29ft – 31ft (8·8m – 9·5m) (compare size of crew with yacht)

Bottom: *Oesophage Boogie,* **a successful Three Quarter Tonner of 1977. Note IOR stern development with big sloping transom**

Admiral's Cup limits

Several series are run for boats on time allowances, but they keep the size of yacht within a narrow rating band for fair sailing, and to maintain the character of the event. Longest established (since 1957) is the Admiral's Cup, but others along the same lines are the Sardinia Cup, based at Porto Cervo, the Onion Patch which is a series within the Newport-Bermuda race, the Rio circuit in South America and the Southern Cross Cup which is held every other year within the Sydney to Hobart race. The rating restriction for the Admiral's Cup is from 30·0 to 40·0ft, which means boats of between about 39 and 52ft LOA (12m to 16m). Time allowances are applied, but not Mark IIIA formula or age allowances for date of building. There is a simple accommodation rule for the series.

Other rules for IOR boats

All IOR boats, whether level rating, time allowance or taking part in any specific series or major course, are obliged to comply with the ORC 'Special regulations governing minimum equipment and accommodations standards'. These in effect give requirements for seaworthiness and features which are essential for sea-going vessels and make sure that no competitor gets a racing advantage by sailing without, for instance, lifelines, bilge pumps, fire extinguishers, stoves and other galley equipment, anchors, life-rafts, emergency steering equipment and much else besides. Like the rating rule itself, these regulations have grown over the years, especially as they have become international. However, after all rules have been applied to a boat, its safety remains dependent on men, not on equipment, and the preamble to 'special regs' states, in words taken from a former RORC rule: 'The safety of the yacht and her crew is the sole and inescapable responsibility of the owner, who must do his best to ensure that the yacht is fully found, thoroughly seaworthy and manned by an experienced crew which is physically fit to face bad weather . . .'. It is not just enough to have equipment that nominally meets the list. Each

piece, in the words of the ORC, 'shall function properly, be readily accessible, be of a type, size and capacity suitable and adequate for the intended use and for the size of the yacht and meet the standards accepted in the country of registry'.

In 1981 a complete new set of rulings was introduced under the name of *scantlings.* This is a term in naval architecture for the strength specification of the hull and structure of any ship. When the IOR was introduced, the existing scantling rule of the RORC disappeared: it had been abused, because heavy scantlings led to reduction in rating and designers had managed to build in some members which were measured, so giving advantage rating without commensurate strength. The 1981 scantling rule did not affect rating. It was not even a rule, but a set of pressure points on the hull to which new construction could voluntarily be designed. Whether such complex regulations would eventually become compulsory remained to be seen. Scantlings, as introduced under the IOR, are a reaction to some losses and accidents to ocean racers from about 1976 onwards: whether these losses were due to the kind of hull strength rule which the ORC introduced as scantlings is somewhat dubious.

Other rules of measurement and time allowances

Cruisers and offshore racers do not have to be raced under IOR, though it is in fact used for most important events. There are numerous local handicapping systems, which, by partial measurement, judgement or recorded or reputed performance, give a time allowance to one boat against others. These are quite satisfactory in clubs or limited areas where the boats are known: their weaknesses only appear if unknown craft join the racing, or if used more widely and coming under pressure of the sort where rigs or arrangements are changed to take advantage of the clauses or conditions. There are, however, several time allowance systems which are more widely known and are mentioned here as alternatives to the International Offshore Rule. Meanwhile, if you are racing under a satisfactory local system, stick with it, but do not try and promulgate it to everyone else!

MHS is *Measurement Handicap System* and is used only in the USA. It is rooted in a project on yacht measurement rating rules at MIT, Boston, which, among other things, developed a way of recording a yacht's hull shape using

an electronic probe. From this information a more accurate picture of the shape can be obtained than the IOR which locates selected points only. A number of measurements are also taken from the IOR certificate, if the yacht has one. The formulae in the rule are geared towards the heavy cruising type of yacht and the whole scheme is a reaction from the fast developing IOR. Built into this rule are certain accommodation needs and penalties loaded against racing yacht features such as low hull surface area, short keels and high rigs. The 1980 Bermuda race used the rule (and had an IOR class as well) which was as a result won by a 16-year-old 36ft (11·0m) ketch, *Holger Danske*, an impossible result under IOR. On the other hand, in what was a reaching race, winning boats in several classes won both IOR and MHS prizes. The popularity of the MHS is uncertain, its launch was much heralded but it seems unlikely to spread from beyond the influence of the Cruising Club of America.

On the west coast of the USA, there is the *PHRF, Pacific Handicap Rating Formula*. This can be applied to almost any type of boat; it is used in the majority of west coast races and has spread elsewhere in the US. A minimum number of factors are examined and a rating somewhat arbitrarily allotted to each boat. As the name implies, the rating can be moved up or down after this, depending on the performance of the yacht. There is a big human judgement factor, but it does away with the complications of measuring and paying for the science of the IOR or MHS. The so-called rating is given in seconds per mile, so is really a straight time allowance. For instance a Morgan 27 class boat is 168 seconds per mile, while a Scampi 30 is 186spm. The bigger boat must gain 18 seconds on average every (nominal) mile of the race. 'Nominal' because the race committee must declare the distance. The organizers in Long Beach California claim that some 18 000 boats race to PHRF. It is clearly impossible to design a yacht to beat this rule, and that is what is intended.

Portsmouth Yardstick might loosely be called a British version of the above because it, too, depends on performance of the class boat. It has been established much longer (over 25 years as opposed to five), but has been used primarily for the dinghy classes. The number of a boat is derived from its results over a period and is defined as the time over a common but unspecified distance (comparable but not

A 1981 maxi - *Kialoa* owned by Jim Kilroy, US, of 81ft, 25m

actually spm). There are various grades of yardsticks and numbers which imply reliability or otherwise of the figure given for the boat. This might be 94 for a Contention 33 and 107 for a Westerly GK24. The higher the number the supposedly slower the boat. In 1980 there were about 250 cruiser classes with numbers issued by the Royal Yachting Association. The Portsmouth Yardstick is not as widespread as it might be because the originators have in many ways hedged about a clever, simple concept with complications and invented technical terms, which discourage many clubs.

MORC is *Midget Ocean Racing Club* and its rule is for fleets in the USA of offshore racers under 30ft LOA. When the IOR was adopted in 1971, the MORC stayed with its own rule based on the old CCA measurement. It has undergone major changes, especially in 1978, and is a 'base boat' rule. In this a theoretical ideal is fixed in proportions and variations are rewarded or penalized. For instance draft for a certain waterline would give higher rating if it went deep and vice versa. Rated length is quite different to the IOR which uses a complex system of girths. It combines length on the actual waterline with length a small height above it and adds a correction for 'transom width'. The rule is keenly raced, but does not come under the great pressures to which the IOR is subjected. Like any measurement rule it needs amendments from year to year.

There are several rules which take information from the IOR certificates and then combine factors in such a way as to give advantage to boats that are not of the latest racing design. Among these is *Scandicap*, used in the Baltic very widely for club and regional racing. For instance, it does give a lower rating if a spinnaker is not carried. For a few races every year there are derivative simple rules used by two American clubs with an informal outlook on their popular events, the *Off Soundings Club rule* and the *Storm Trysail Club rule*. They have no influence on design of yachts.

There are many more. In Ireland some 700 boats have *ECHO* ratings. This is *East Coast Handicap Organization*. Corrected times of yachts are recorded and in the light of results the time factors (using time-on-time as is usual in Ireland) are moderated to increase those on the boats with good results. The system has become centralized and has been well administered, so is popular, but is yet another performance system among many others, usually for smaller fleets, all over the world.

16

Made to withstand the sea

The wide range of methods available by which boats may be built are not all suitable for the ocean racer and one would not today, for instance, see wood clinker or steel ocean racers. A ferro-cement boat won the Sydney to Hobart race once in recent years, but this was exceptional. Ocean racing boats in general will be built of aluminium, reinforced plastics or wood.

Wood

Conventional carvel, that is plank upon plank, is found in older boats: today it is lacking in weight-saving strength. If planking is seen it is likely to be epoxy glued and pinned and supported by an inner diagonal skin. The traditional planking fastened to timbers (frames) and then caulking forced in to keep out the water is just not strong enough for the modern hard driving expected. Nor can the shapes and sharp turns of the keel and stern be obtained. The caption to a picture in 1947 of a yacht being hard driven says 'skippers are wary of this . . . until later in the spring when a hull has had a chance to soak up and swell . . .'. If a modern ocean racer is wood, it may be cold moulded construction. Frames are set and veneers of mahogany strips laid over, first one way, then the other and glued with waterproof resin adhesives (resorcinol). The complete hull is then turned over and laminated frames and stringers glued in together with bulkheads. The result is a lightweight, rigid and strong structure. One minor advantage of wood is that alterations may easily be made and fittings attached.

Aluminium

This is the chosen material for top-rate ocean racers, certainly those over 35ft (10·6m). High grade marine resistant light alloys are used. The result is great rigidity for lightness which the

tensions and loads of an ocean racing rig requires. Fittings have to be riveted or welded to the deck which needs special equipment, but gives tremendous strength. For instance, chain plastic boats as they have to be located and fastened to selected members, but on aluminium they are merely part of the hull. It is interesting to note that 12-metre class boats, which are not ocean racers but are large high performance yachts, have used aluminium since 1974. Note also that light alloy is the standard material for the spars of all yachts. Disadvantages are potential corrosion and electrolysis (salt water and mixed metals are a chemical nightmare), the limited number of builders equipped to construct and maintain the material and finally cost.

Reinforced plastics

The reinforcement is glass fibre (British), fiberglass (American) or carbon fibre; the plastics are polyester resins. It is by far the most popular boat building method and one of the most suitable uses for GRP itself. The most usual system of building involves a female mould and as this takes some time and cost to prepare, builders need to make as many hulls as possible from this same mould. (There are moulds in alloy and wood, but because those materials are rigid when put in place the moulds are comparatively cheap and expendable. Resin flows into position as a liquid!) GRP has many advantages including ease of maintenance and resistance to impact, but these are not paramount with the dedicated racing owner. It has poor strength/weight ratio and is not rigid. The latter is overcome by careful design with frames, bulkheads and longitudinals.

When this is said, the fact remains that at the start of an offshore race, it is likely that most of the boats will be of GRP. There are many minor and some major variations in the construction of GRP boats, but these are the common stages of construction:

1. The designer's lines plan is 'lofted' by being taken off full size on a floor. A table of off sets should have been provided; the builder does not merely scale up the drawing. The designer has a chance to 'flair up' (or alter) at this stage. On these lines wooden frames are mocked up.

2. The wooden frames are set up at the appropriate 'stations' and the shape is built very much like a wooden boat. The emphasis is, however, on fairness and not sea-going strength. The surface has to be very carefully finished with many man-hours exerted in rubbing down and treating with enamel in controlled temperatures, so that there is no local change of shape. The result is the *hull plug*.

3. A similar mock up of the deck which includes all its levels (ie cockpit, coachroof, cabin trunk, hatches) is made and given a finish. This is the deck plug (male).

4. Glass fibre and resin (see below) is laid up round both these structures. When it cures, the hull mould (female) and deck mould (female) have been made. These are suitably set up as rigid moulding before being removed from the plugs.

5. Now a hull can be made (and a deck moulding, but the method is the same). Release agent is applied to the mould to prevent sticking in the later stages. Resin is then applied without glass but with a colour pigment in it (without pigment the hull would be a pale green translucent skin; sometimes this is purposely below the waterline, the theory being that pigments cause soakage and therefore weight increase. But even with pigment one can often see light through the hull in certain conditions). This is the 'gel coat'—the smart outer surface.

6. Layers of resin soaked into glass fibre (which is in various forms of mat and woven patterns) are then applied. Further resin is rolled on by hand to 'wet out' the glass. The resulting thickness is in accordance with the design or building system. Finally a thin layer of resin finishes off this rough side.

7. In sound building practice, bulkheads, frames and longitudinals are now glassed in, *before* the hull is removed. Then the hull, now a rigid structure, is removed.

8. After trimming of the overflow along the edge of the mouldings, the deck moulding is fitted to the hull. This joint is extremely important as it is a potential source of leaking, but must not be permitted to do so.

9. Basically there is now a boat, but the considerable amount of finishing for interior and deck fittings, keel and rudder is not dissimilar to work in other materials. Of course, working in glass has its own requirements, but it is fastening and not moulding which ensues.

Repeats can be made from the same mould for many years, but extra moulds or renewed moulds can be obtained from the same plug. Obviously, plug and mould costs are best recovered by building a large number of boats. Similarly, the somewhat long preparation makes the conventional GRP method unsuitable for 'one-offs' and prototypes.

Other GRP building methods

Sandwich construction involves thin skins of GRP with rigid foam or balsa core between. End grain balsa is frequently used for decks above conventional hulls: it is light, rigid and provides some insulation. Hulls are more usually made of foam, but there are variations of this. It is necessary to build a male plug as above, but this also becomes the mould and foam pieces are laid over this, followed by a skin of GRP. The result is rigid and light, though the complete inner skin and bulkheads cannot be affixed until after removal from the mould. Disadvantages are that in the event of impact the outer skin is weaker than conventional GRP and if water does penetrate it can run between the skins causing permanent damage; the hull requires many man-hours of rubbing down and fairing since there is no smooth outer mould; attachment of fittings is awkward since fastenings cannot be secured as they would merely 'squeeze' the structure; instead pads have to be pre-planned or inserted. *Great Britain II* built of foam sandwich has three times raced around the world, yet the method is less popular for ocean racers than in the past, but is found more frequently on smaller boats.

C-flex is a patent American system, which is supplied to the boat builder in the form of rods of cured GRP, held in rows by loose, uncured glass woven rovings. They are used to build a hull, rather like planks of wood, being laid over a male mould in strips. An advantage is that the mould need not be surface smooth (it must be fair) as the C-flex takes up a fair shape. This first layer is resinated but shows the rods in the surface. Further layers of glass and resin are then applied, the outer skin being

faired up as for sandwich. There is great resistance to impact and weight saving over conventional GRP. This is because the rods have inherent longitudinal strength and only transverse reinforcement need be applied. Because of this uni-directional effect, the material is not suitable for deck structures, where end grain balsa must be used. A further advantage is speed of building; the simple mould and pre-cured basic skin means a one-off design can be made ready for a series very quickly—less than a fortnight has been claimed. *Swampfire*, winner of the 1974 Three-Quarter Ton Cup designed by Gary Mull, was of C-flex.

Vacuum formed thermoplastics and moulded foam, both of which are used for small dinghies and beach boats, are unsuitable for sea-going yachts, but a form of *injection moulding* has been used for ocean racers. A rigid female mould built as for conventional GRP boats is used with a light inner male mould. By means of a vacuum, pre-placed glass is impregnated with resin by a number of injection points. The inner mould is removed and bulkheads inserted. The method can make both hulls and deck structures. The advantage is that there is not a trace of air even in tiny bubbles, which there can well be in ordinary GRP. Then, if hulls need to be exactly alike, there is no possibility of weight variation since a controlled amount of resin is inserted by injection. There is also a health element as resin fumes are not directly absorbed by workers, as occurs in hand lay up. The disadvantages are in the high capital cost of the plant and the difficulty of getting curing without heat build-up and resultant local distortion such as ridging of the gel coat. As far as is known only one builder has used the method for ocean racers, though there is one other builder who made a line of motor cruisers like this. The system is used for cars (the Lotus GRP body) and some industrial components.

As new man-made fibres are invented, so they get used in boat hulls, Kevlar being a case in point. Reinforcement using Kevlar, which is lighter and stronger than glass fibre, enables hulls of plastics to be thinner and of less and less weight, so advantageous, as we have seen, for high performance.

Top left: A wood male plug from which a female GRP deck and coachroof moulding will be made

Centre left: GRP injection moulded hulls await finishing

Bottom left: Production yachts under construction. Note joinery going into position prior to moulded deck being attached

Right: C-flex GRP construction with pre-formed glass panels

Composite construction

Sometimes boats may be built of a mixture of principal materials. For instance there may be a GRP or aluminium hull with wooden deck structure. Some wooden hulls may be sheathed in patent systems such as Cascover, which is a nylon and resin mix. GRP sheathing over wood is now discredited and is unsuitable for an ocean racer. Carbon fibre utilizes the same principle as glass fibre: when mixed with resin it is many times stronger. Being comparatively expensive, it tends to be used for isolated purposes such as strengthening a bow area or for making a complete rudder, combined with a stainless steel stock. At the time of writing carbon fibre is in effect banned from use in spars by the rule of rating (wood, steel, aluminium and GRP are allowed). Substances of greater density than lead are banned from keels.

What method to use for building?

There is no key race winning material. A good standard GRP boat is preferable to a badly designed and built aluminium boat. The owners of the biggest ocean racers certainly seem to go for light alloy, but they were all beaten in the 1975 Fastnet race by *Golden Delicious*, a conventionally moulded GRP production boat. The most successful boat in the 1977 winning British Admiral's Cup team, *Moonshine*, was built by

conventional GRP methods. She was a single design, but entered by the builder knowing that he would be building more boats out of the mould if she did well. He did. The winner of the Fastnet that year was the American *Imp* (David Allen). The hull was balsa sandwich, reinforced with carbon fibre laid along multiple foam stringers. The interior revealed a system of light alloy tubes which took all the main strains including rig and keel, thus permitting the skin to be lighter than usual.

This epitomizes the one-off ocean racer. When further editions were required, the same hull design (by Ron Holland) was produced by conventional means as the Swan 39 class (built by Nautor of Pietarsaari, Finland). It was still a racing boat with only essentials below, but without the tubes and expensive carbon fibre. Was it less effective? How can one say, when different crews sail different races in each boat. Of course, if a one-off repeat was wanted of *Imp*, it could be built all over again like the original. But this would be most unlikely; the designer would be bound to want to make small changes, so the boat would become a different design! Materials have vogues. At the time of writing steel would scarcely be considered a serious proposition for an ocean racer, yet in the late sixties, it was for a time thought to be a requirement for success.

Design and construction obsolescence

It is a common complaint that ocean racing boats rapidly become outdated for the purpose of successful racing. This has been a feature of the world of yacht racing for at least a hundred years, though many people think that it is something new. The real truth is that they do not become unsuitable for racing as quickly as people imagine. Of course, there are badly designed and built boats that are obsolete as soon as they are launched. It is also true that there comes a time in the life of a yacht when she can no longer keep up with whatever the crew do, but even this can vary if new sails and equipment are introduced and alterations made

A male plug being faired for a Swan 371 class in a Finnish boat yard

to save weight. Whether she can keep up or not depends on whom she has to keep up with. In other words, the boat racing in the very top events, such as the SORC, is possibly outdated after three years, but regular regional or club events can extend the time to ten years.

It is far more a matter of attitude of owners and crews. These might be called negative and positive. The negative one is, crudely expressed, that the current boat does not seem to be winning and it would be better to go for a new design. The positive move is by an owner who has been racing a successful boat for say a couple of years, but who would like to keep on top. So he takes steps to have a new boat designed and built. Maybe it is a kind of rat-race, because if owner A does not do this, owner B may do so and find some extra speed. The best crews, too, are attracted to the novelty of the latest yachts and this factor should not be underrated. Also, because the good crews and new yachts go together, it becomes very hard to analyse whether a new design is really better.

Ocean racing design and building as a business

This structure of obsolescence plays an essential part in keeping the specialist design and building, which has just been outlined, in business. Coupled with this is the general, though sometimes intermittent, expansion of the sport as a whole with new owners coming from other types of sailing and boating. To keep designers and builders viable, there is also the tail-back of production boats emanating directly or indirectly from the latest offshore creations. Sooner or later the style of cruising boats follows that of the racers, if not entirely, then in many leading features (rig, keel shapes and equipment like winches, for instance). Changes in the rating rule also encourage new designs, but this can also have a large psychological element. The owner feels he must incorporate the designer's latest idea to maintain potential speed under a fresh rating. Yet boats for unrated races like the single-handed transatlantic swell

A female mould. The boat being laid up in it can be seen with glass ends 'sprouting'! they will later be trimmed off to fit a deck moulding

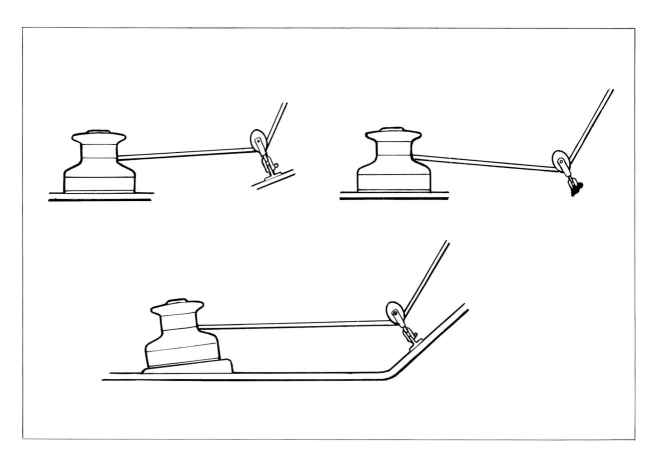

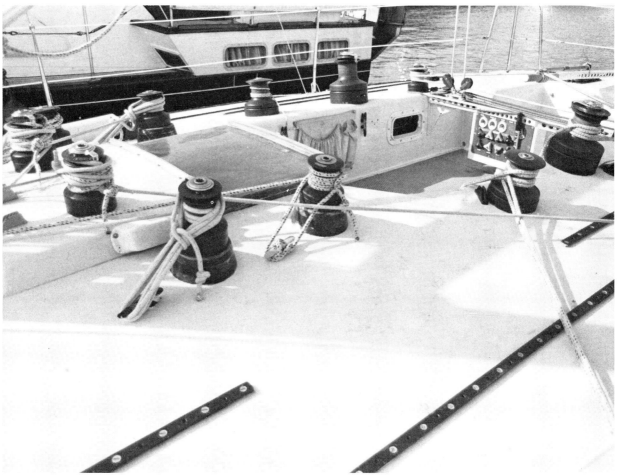

in the new design building stream, so this influence of rating policies is a minor factor. In all new boats there is an element of timelessness and an element of fashion. Adventurous new design and satisfying new construction of ocean racing boats live by both these appeals to sailors.

Deck equipment

Much of the gear on deck when racing varies only in degree from the cruising yacht: it is lighter, quicker to use, has less windage, probably lasts less time and requires more maintenance. Gear which was not considered earlier (in Part II Chapter 4) included winches, electronic equipment, the yacht's life-lines (sometimes known as guardrails), and the structures that go with them for keeping the crew safely on deck.

Winches on the modern ocean racer are the primary method of handling sails, transferring man power into mechanical advantage and speed of hauling. They are applied to sheets, halyards and also to subsidiary sail handling lines like downhauls, foreguys and reefing pendants. Of course, there are many manufacturers but for a decade three big names have dominated the winch market for ocean racers. These are Barient (USA), Barlow (Australia) and Lewmar (Britain). Non-English speakers might argue that Goiot (France) and Barbarossa (Italy) are also widely used. In the English-speaking countries the first three have 95 per cent of the ocean racing market. They are similar in construction, though the manufacturers will claim various minor advantages. Any winch relies on the immense friction available to hold a rope round a drum and then some form of gearing to turn this drum to gain tremendous power ratio, the largest standard Lewmar winch giving 65 times the force exerted by a man. All this elaborate engineering is exclusive to yacht racing (and cruising by derivation), because IYRU rule 62 states that only manual power may be used. For such loads in industry electricity would be applied—in fact electric winches are in use for cruising.

Top left: If a sheet, or other line, approaches winch from above 90 degrees, a riding turn (tight jammed) will result (top left). Line must come from just below (right) or be made to, by blocking up winch at an angle (below)
Bottom left: Flush deck ocean racing layout - note hydraulic control in cockpit
Below: Ocean racing equipped deck on 1979 boat, *Winsome Gold*. Note no toe rail or bulwark, only pieces of track at deck edge

Winches, some of them self tailing, turning blocks, lines and cleats at the base of the mizzen mast of the 1977 *Flyer*

The drums of winches are of chromed bronze or anodized aluminium, but sometimes of stainless steel. Gearing is obtained partly by the leverage of the handles (on the most simple winch this may be the only ratio), but more extensively by inside gear wheels. Two speed winches are common once the power ratio is more than eight to one. This enables the sheet to be brought in quickly and then 'ground' slowly when the load becomes heavy. To change gear the handle is rotated in the opposite direction. The mechanism for achieving this is simple in principle, with a pair of pawls restricting the direction of turn for one set of gear wheels. A three speed winch has three sets of pawls.

Cutting down friction and convenience of use are essential, if the winch is to be fully effective. The first is assisted by precision machining and needle bearings. If a winch is not regularly maintained, it will build up an amalgam of salt, grease and dirt, so it must be stripped frequently. The modern winch is built for this very exercise and only needs a knife blade and

perhaps a medium size screwdriver to get it down; then the crew which does not want winch problems at a vital moment in a race, washes every component in paraffin, rubs a touch of special grease here and there and some thin oil and reassembles.

As for convenience in use, it matters how the sheet (or other line) approaches and leaves the winch and also how the operator can get at it. If the yacht designer has done his job well, the winder will be able to stand or lean over the winch and obtain a rhythmic circular motion. The difficult moment when winding a winch is at 'top dead centre', when the handle is at the furthest point from the winder. It is essential that the movement should carry momentum through this position and this is only possible if the winder is applying his force at steady maximum. There are obviously variations depending on the shape of the deck and cockpit, but the main thing is to get over the top of it, not attack it from the side. He must also have space clear of the tiller and such items as life-lines.

If a sheet (or other line) approaches and meets the winch at an angle of less than 90 degrees, then riding turns will result. For those who have not experienced this, it means the locking of the coils, making it impossible to move the winch or the sheet. The only solution may be to release the tension from the loading end, for instance by lowering a sail altogether to ease the sheet. This is drastic enough, but if it is a halyard that has a riding turn, with wire which will bind worse than fibre, it may be impossible to move anything and dangerous because the sail cannot be dropped. The ultimate solution would be a man aloft to unshackle the head of the sail. At best a riding turn causes a delay and so the line must come into the winch preferably between 95 and 105 degrees. Of course, the sheet lead may not be right for this and that is why a turning block (also called a foot block) is positioned via which every sheet comes. For halyards coming out near the base of the mast, the winch, if on deck, will be canted back on a wedge-shaped block so that the halyard leads up to it. For racing boats winches for halyards are invariably on deck, as opposed to being on the mast near its base. The advantages are keeping the weight lower, more security for the crew using them, adaptability with temporary leads for other purposes, cutting down windage and less chance of fouling sheets when tacking.

The line coming off the winch is less critical. When in use it will be held (not really pulled) by the tailer, who keeps it coming away cleanly. Once the sheet is trimmed, the tail is made up on a cleat. A jammer may be sufficient for a sheet as the load on the tail is only a fraction of that on the loaded part. Halyards, which are more permanent, should be made up on ordinary cleats, where there is no danger of them being dislodged.

Sizes of winch

Lewmar's range goes from the little No. 6 with a drum diameter height of 2·3in (58mm) and a weight of 2½lb (1·2kg) to the No. 98 three-speed grinder of drum diameter 11in (279mm) and of 107lb (48·5kg). The manufacturers and many text books give elaborate tables of the sizes of winch for each job, but such figures are only a guide and experience is the best basis for a specification. Lewmar has no less than 15 different sizes of winch, not counting the variation of type mentioned below. The disadvantages of installing too big a winch are the unnecessary cost and weight, but it is better to go this way than be under-winched. A winch a little bigger than the basic recommendation will mean faster work by the crew and easier handling when racing or cruising. On a typical ocean racing yacht, the biggest winches will be for the genoa sheets (often called the primary winches of the boat), next size down will be the genoa halyards and spinnaker halyards, then almost the same as the latter, the spinnaker sheets and, smaller than any of these, the main halyards. Then smaller winches still (though no winches at all if the boat is less than 33ft (10m)) for the spinnaker topping lift, foreguy and, depending on the layout, the mainsheet.

The bigger the length of winch handle the better the leverage, but such length is determined by ergonomics—the human ability to wind a handle in a circle. The standard size is therefore 10in (254mm) with a variation of 20 per cent less for small winches or where the longer reach would be uncomfortable.

Types of winch on the racing boat

All modern designed models have a slight outward taper on the drum running towards the top in order to increase tension on the part of the line round the drum and make it stick harder. There are numerous secondary variations to operate this simple idea.

(a) *Snubbing winches* have no fitting for a handle. They may be found on the smallest boat (micro-tonners). They help the user hold the line and pull direct.

(b) *Single speed.* A simple handle winding a winch and obtaining power from the handle length only can be used for small jobs. Because the handle only rotates one way, some models have a ratchet so that short strokes are possible. A bottom action handle can be used here, the advantage being that the handle can be permanently shipped while turns are put on or taken off. But there is not the speed and rhythm and where it is not a small size, it will be an obsolescent piece of gear.

(c) *Two speed.* These are common on all modern boats and both speeds will be geared. The No. 30 Lewmar (which one might find on the genoa sheets of a Quarter Tonner) has gear ratios of seven to one and 30 to one. So we have a quick wind until the load becomes too heavy to move; then reverse the direction of the handle and we are 'graunching' in the sheet.

(d) *Three speed.* Merely a development of the above gives a further power ratio and may be found on the genoa sheet of Three Quarter Tonners upwards. A press button puts the winch into first gear, then the handle is reversed; but when reversed yet again, the button pops up on its own and we are in a gear of around 50 to one or more. This is really transmitting manual ability into something quite different. The sheet will feel like a bar of iron.

(e) *Self tailing winches.* These are a most helpful invention and have only been available since the early 70s. Instead of a person tailing, the line runs round a groove in the top of the winch. This grips it so that it is held on the drum in the usual way but comes away under control. Self tailers can be used anywhere. In short handed racers they can be used for sheets, but where there are ample crews they may be restricted to subsidiary use. For the cruising man they are excellent.

(f) *The coffee grinder.* In this the handle is separated from the drum and it is found in large yachts only (over 45ft) (15m). In fact there are two handles operated vertically by two men giving high gearing, yet at high speed. A third man will tail from the big drum. In other words, the two men on the pedestal provide steady power as required manually by the rules, and the crew can apply the sheet to the winch itself a little way from all this powerful

activity. It is used for rapid handling of sheets only.

(g) *Reel winches* are used for halyards only and the wire halyard simply winds round them. This means no loose tails, single-handed use and stowage, but they have a history of accidents, mainly caused by running away under load with a handle in and breaking wrists and arms. An essential control is therefore a fool proof brake. They invariably have two gears for quick winding at first and then the final tightening.

Stanchions and life-lines

In the 1981 safety regulations of the international Offshore Racing Council, which controls ocean racing conduct around the world, no less than two and a half pages are taken up with the rules about life-lines, stanchions and pulpits. These are the main guard against crew falling overboard: the basic requirement is that a line, wire or rail extends all round the yacht at a height of not less than 2ft (610mm) above the working deck. A second line has to be placed about half way between this line and the deck. There are rules about the intervals of stanchions (not greater than 7ft) and the fixing of the stanchions which must be bolted through the structure or welded to it. The stanchion bases must not be outside the deck nor more than a prescribed distance inside it. They must not be angled at more than ten degrees from the vertical. Why all these rules? Well, all sorts of variations have been tried in the past for various reasons to give supposed racing advantages. These are often to do with setting sails, or with getting the crew, especially on smaller boats, further outboard for weight distribution. This is because an IYRU rule says that crew may not be stationed outside the life-lines. Life-lines have long been adopted by cruising yachts, though Gary Hoyt the idiosyncratic American

Left: Self tailing winches: manual 'tailing' is not required

A coffee grinder pedestal and the two winches which, alternately, it can turn

Offshore! Sun and spinnaker

promotor of cat rigged cruising ketches has said 'Hobies don't have life-lines. Windsurfers don't have life-lines: why should this boat (his 25-ft cruiser) have life-lines? Because the rule says it should? You'll never move the state of the art (of yacht design) if you worry about the rule.'

Life-lines were seen long before pulpits; then bow pulpits came before what the author is happy to call pushpits, but some prefer to remain with stern pulpits. Austin Farrar, designer and sailmaker, of Ipswich, England, claims to have invented the pulpit early in 1937. When the Robert Clark designed ocean racer *Ortac* was being built he suggested two tubular half hoops on stanchions at the bow outside the forestay, and terminating the life-lines on their arms instead of leading them down to the stem as was then normal. The builder Morgan Giles of Teignmouth, duly fabricated the steel tubes, and other boats subsequently followed. The same arrangement spread to the stern. Today the pulpit and pushpit are institutionalized as continuations of the upper life-line. A lower bar is not compulsory forward because of anchor handling and safety because of the narrowing geometry. Many are the variations in design, which still all comply with the rule, a rule which has been in force many years and seems unlikely to vary other than in detail in the future. Since the 1979 Fastnet race, a toe rail forward of the mast has also become compulsory of height not less than 1in (25mm). Many yachts have toe rails, often all round the deck as standard.

Pulpits have developed auxiliary uses. These include the siting of the navigation lights, because the latter are then outside the sails. The stern light carried by all vessels goes on the pushpit. Metal beckets welded in corners of the pulpit are invaluable for clipping on halyard shackles when changing headsails or when in harbour. The pushpit makes a useful site for emergency life-buoys and man overboard lights, and a holder for the ensign staff can be fitted as well.

At sea, with crew relaxed but using their weight on the weather deck

Electronic equipment

Many types of print out and electronically fed instruments are common on ocean racing yachts and indeed on cruisers too. Certain instruments are virtually essential for racing, including boat speed, wind speed, wind direction, distance run and depth of water. In the 1980s all such readings are now available on digital print outs which can be watched by the helmsman and then repeated in other parts of the boats, for the crew, sail trimming forward and for the navigator at the chart table below. The control boxes for such print outs are now not much bigger than the size of a nautical almanac and can be used in the smallest boat. Data originate in the water from very small impellers on the yacht's hull which give boat speed (not speed over the ground of course) and in the air from a light weight anemometer and direction indicator at the masthead. If a magnetic compass is fed into the system, it is possible to compute the dead reckoning position since its variation from a chosen course can be combined with distance run. For deciding when to change to which sails, wind velocity readings are invaluable. Maybe our fathers could do this by their

A helmsman's instrument panel. This one includes wind direction, depth of water, remote compass, quartz clock wind speed and optional digital displays (for many items of information such as distance run, speed to windward, wind angle on next leg of course)

own observations, but every ocean racing skipper knows that, especially at night, the wind speed given is a major aid to the always difficult decision of when to change up or down. For instance the crew can say to the skipper 'the wind is now down to 14 knots, would you like us to go to the No. 1 genoa?' As for wind direction, which can be digital, but is possibly best seen on a 360 degree dial with an arrow pointing at an angle to the ship's head, it is an invaluable aid to steering closehauled at a certain angle, or off the wind to avoid gybing and keep the wind angle at so many degrees on the quarter.

The reliability and low electricity consumption of modern electronics, leaves the only major problem as siting. It must be possible for the helmsman to see the vital dials and such siting has to be considered at design stage with all the other many demands of the cockpit and steering area in the after part of the yacht.

17

Courses in the ocean

Offshore racing events are now so numerous and varied around the world that it is not possible to list them all; besides they expand in one place and contract in another from year to year. There are some that stand out for reasons of historical importance or international support and here are some of them.

The Bermuda race

This is the father of them all and the course is now every even year (1980, 1982 etc) from Newport, Rhode Island, to Bermuda, 635 miles. Like many events in sailing, it was a yachting magazine that started it. Thomas Fleming Day, editor of *The Rudder,* believed that small yachts manned largely by amateurs could race as a sport across open water. Three yachts took part in the first race from Gravesend Bay, Brooklyn to Bermuda. Subsequent races were from Marblehead, New London and finally in 1936 Newport became the point of departure. St David's Head is the finish. Since 1923 the race has been organized by the Cruising Club of America.

Though sometimes a largely reaching race, some experienced skippers reckon that a gale is more likely than during the Fastnet. The landfall is tricky, the low lying islands being 22 miles across and surrounded by coral reefs. The race course crosses the Gulf Stream whose line is never quite predictable, and hitting this off so that its meandering course gives a shove in the right direction is essential for success. Thermometers hung over the side are a big aid here as there is an 8–10°F difference between the Stream and surrounding ocean. The rules allow the navigator to use hyperbolic aids, such as Omni and Loran C. This helps considerably in the featureless approach in the final stages. The Onion Patch trophy is for three boat teams of countries within the race and combined with

some shorter events before it, but has never had more than five teams entering.

Southern Ocean Racing Conference

This is the series which runs every year during February, off the coast of Florida, and represents the most advanced boats to the IOR each season. It especially attracts crews with sailmakers, builders and designers on board to prove their latest products. In Admiral's Cup years it is also the trials for the always formidable US team of three. Since 1978, when the Cruising Club of America began to dilute the IOR in the Bermuda, introducing rules to curb the flat-out racer and subsequently a different rating rule (MHS), the SORC could be said to have replaced the older premier event as the big international ocean racing series in American waters. Numbers of starters reached a peak in 1973 with 706; since then numbers have declined, partly because of the world economic changes and partly because the very high standard has driven out the more relaxed crews. The name Conference comes from the grouping of clubs which organize the different races in the SORC (the 'C' standing for 'conference' and not, as some would think, for circuit). Since the series began in 1941, the courses have been changed from time to time, but they are now (see chart):

St Petersburg triangle, 50 miles
St Petersburg—Fort Lauderdale
The Ocean Triangle
The Lipton Cup
Miami—Nassau
Nassau Cup

In the whole series and in each race there are overall placings and class placings. The classes run from A to F and divide the fleet into approximate parts. This is the usual system of classes in North America; in Europe classes are more usually divided by rating or TMF figures

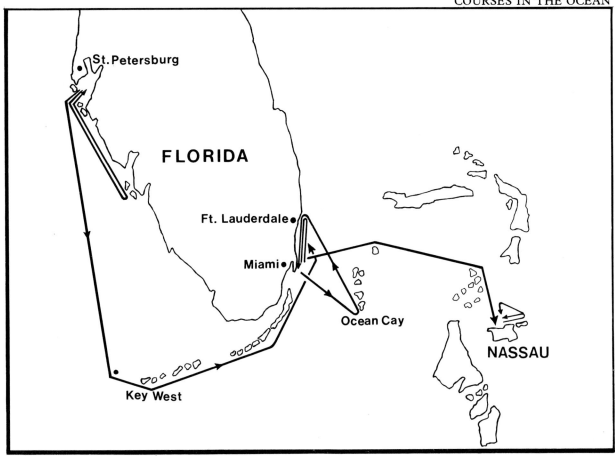

Courses of the Southern Ocean Racing Conference, held every February and March

which are announced well before entries are accepted.

Among other numerous US races are long-standing events including Annapolis to Newport, Marblehead to Halifax, Block Island week and feeder races, Chicago to Mackinac and many others on the Great Lakes; on the west coast as many races take place as in all Europe with the trans-Pacific (see below) and Newport (California) to Ensenada which attracts the biggest numerical entry for offshore racing in the USA.

Trans-Pacific race

This is actually from Los Angeles to Honolulu, a distance of 2225 miles. Like the Bermuda race it has early origins, the first one being in 1906 (it does not claim to be the mother of modern ocean racing in the same way because it was for very large vessels with professional crews). Since 1936 the race has been held to alternate with the Bermuda race, so it is on each odd numbered year starting on 4 July; organizers are the Transpacific Yacht Club, whose sole

function is the handling of the event, and therefore has no club house. The course gives a relatively short beat to Catalina and then there is invariably a down wind sail in the north-east trade wind to the finish at Diamond Head buoy off Honolulu, Hawaii. Eight to 12 days of spinnaker work means that owners are tempted to design boats which are for running with no pretentions to windward ability. The IOR and its time scales are meant for all round sailing and cannot expect to cope with one point only, and winning designs have often been ultra light displacement (ULDBs, a term coined for this race). The race committee has to modify the measurement rules and time allowances almost from year to year.

Cowes Week, Fastnet and the Admiral's Cup

From the sun of the tropics, top yacht racing is, every second year, seen in the totally unpredictable weather of the English Channel and western approaches. The first club-organized racing at Cowes was in 1826, the first Fastnet race in 1925 and the first Admiral's Cup was

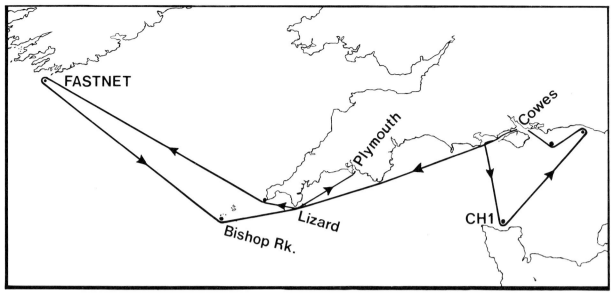

Admiral's Cup courses, held in August on every odd year
(1983, 85 etc). Channel triangle round buoys off Cherbourg
and Brighton and Fastnet race (Cowes-Fastnet
Rock-Plymouth) of 605 miles

in 1957, but on odd numbered years they combine into a major yachting festival. On even numbered years Cowes Week continues for all its usual classes, but without the Fastnet and AC.

The Fastnet was established as a direct result of the participation of English yachtsmen in the Bermuda race of 1923 and 1924. The Ocean Racing Club (later Royal) was formed immediately after the first race from Ryde, round the Isle of Wight to Fastnet Rock, around it and back to Plymouth, in 1925. The course is now established as Cowes, westward along the Solent past the Needles, round Land's End,

Gale conditions. Taken just after the worst of the storm
in the 1979 Fastnet race

around the Fastnet Rock off the south-west tip of Ireland, then back outside the Isles of Scilly to the finish at Plymouth; this totals 605 miles. The Royal Ocean Racing Club, the organizers, allow all IOR boats to enter down to a rating of 21·0ft. Depressions are common to the August weather and the race has traditionally been one for gales and dirty weather, this combined with the prevailing westerly winds can mean a long beat to windward. The course is therefore one of the most testing in the world. Tidal difficulties along the headlands of the English coast add to the necessity for skill by the navigator.

During the seventies, several of the races belied the Fastnet reputation and gave moderate

weather with much reaching and running. The year 1977 was particularly smitten by calms and the race was thought by some to have become in recent years a rather unremarkable one. All that changed in 1979, when the fleet of more than 300 (thus had it grown from the seven that started in 1925) was hit by storm force winds, when spread out between Land's End and Fastnet Rock. The particular local intensity of the storm and the fearsome seas created, coupled with the sheer numbers of boats and crews of all standards of ability, caused the worst disaster in offshore racing, if not in yacht racing. Twenty-four yachts were abandoned, 19 of which were later recovered, but five sank. Fifteen men were lost all from yachts smaller than about 38ft LOA

Left: Rounding the Fastnet in summer's afternoon conditions in the 1977 Fastnet race

Below: Fastnet Rock. The seas foam white around it in the famous gale of August 1979

(11·6m): they were swept overboard, washed out of life-rafts, died of hypothermia in life-rafts or, in one case, lost when trying to board a rescuing ship from a life-raft. Of the 303 boats which started, 85 boats actually completed the course and 194 retired safely by putting into ports along the Irish, English or Welsh coasts. A major inquiry was conducted by the RORC and RYA, which resulted in increased attention to and rulings on many aspects of crewing, equipment and yacht design as well as construction. There was to be no change to the Fastnet course, its traditional date or the size and general type of yacht permitted to compete. It was not only racing boats which suffered. In the same waters a higher percentage of people were drowned from non-participating boats at sea—four from a multihull which capsized and two from cruising yachts on passage.

Cowes Week has, since 1946, been predominantly for the ocean racing and cruiser classes, although many inshore keel boats take part in daily racing. Ten days of courses in the confined waters of the Solent give the IOR boats opportunities for close sailing that they would not get offshore. They are divided into four classes and there are also offshore one-designs (see below). Hundreds of boats start at five-minute intervals from the line off the Royal Yacht Squadron castle and under the organization of the Cowes Combined Clubs. With the courses so close to the shore it is a rare spectacle. This is frequently enhanced by the strong tidal streams which force yachts to go really close to find advantageous slack water and counter currents. At least half the appeal of Cowes Week is that racing finises in mid or late afternoon; a packed Cowes with its clubs and pubs means the most social of weeks for sailors.

The Admiral's Cup often makes more news than Cowes and the Fastnet. In 1957, the Admiral of the RORC and some other senior members gave a cup to be raced for by visiting American boats to 'add some interest'. Each country would put up a three-boat team and there would be points for two of the existing races in Cowes Week, the RORC Channel race which preceded it and the Fastnet results. The idea has been so successful that it would be hardly recognizable by the originators. Now any nation can enter and on several years there have been a maximum (so far) of 19 teams, meaning an impressive 54 ocean racers at each start. Boats are specially designed and built to the IOR limits for the series. There are rules on points systems, accommodation, radio reporting and, since 1981, Fastnet race qualifications for crew. Fourteen other cups are given for such subsidiary success as best individual yacht in the series, best European team, second team overall and even Australia versus Great Britain. The inshore races are no longer ordinary Cowes Week events. There are two inshore races prior to Cowes Week, when the team boats will not be crowded out by so many other competitors, and one race for cup boats only during Cowes Week. The RORC Channel race is sailed in the first week-end of the Week. The course is Portsmouth–buoy off Poole–buoy off Cherbourg–buoy off Brighton–Owers light float–Nab Tower–Portsmouth, a distance of 220 miles and the Fastnet starts on the last Saturday of the

Mini-transatlantic boats (maximum length 6·5m, 21ft) at Antigua at the end of a race from England

The French *Muscadet* **and Polish** *Spanielek* **(with twin rudders)**

Week. The three inshore races each count points, the Channel race counts double points and the Fastnet treble points. The winning yacht scores points equal to the number of entries in the AC, the second one less and so on. The team with the most points at the end is the winner.

The AC was the first of the combined inshore-offshore series which are now a common format. Before its creation, ocean racers sailed offshore and day boats went 'round the cans'. Ocean racers may have sailed on short races in Cowes and elsewhere, but the series combination was not known. The concept was adopted for the Ton Cups, Southern Cross and events run by clubs (for instance in South America there is a comparable Rio circuit). It has had a vast influence in the design of yachts and crewing techniques that are seen in offshore boats today.

The Royal Ocean Racing Club programme

The RORC from its headquarters and club house in London is unique in that it runs a season of offshore races. In other parts of the world, ocean races are run by individual clubs, each club running perhaps one or two long races in its own locality. There are associations of clubs that run events during the season, but these are not of RORC length which is over 200 miles (with one or two exceptions). In a non-Fastnet year the RORC will always have a race of some 600 miles in August, usually to Spain. From time to time it organizes a transatlantic race (for fully crewed IOR boats) and is also responsible in conjunction with clubs at the start and finish for the courses Hong Kong–Manilla, Middle Sea (from Malta to Malta round various marks and islands) and the Skaw race in the Baltic. Every year it runs some fourteen events, the remaining being 200-mile courses in the English Channel, North Sea and Irish Sea. Sometimes they are down into the Bay of Biscay, such as the regular Plymouth to La Rochelle, just after the Fastnet. All the races use the IOR, as before 1971 they used the RORC rating rule.

Sydney Hobart and Southern Cross

Every year since 1945, the Cruising Club of Australia has started on Boxing Day, 26

Right: Admiral's Cup boats crowd the mark at the south-east Ryde Middle buoy in the Solent

December, the 630 mile course inside the huge Sydney Harbour. The course takes the boats down the Australian coast and across the Bass Strait, with its notorious reputation for gales, on to Hobart, Tasmania. The course usually meets heavy weather at some stage. The final leg up the Derwent River to the finish is often beset with calms. The Southern Cross Cup is modelled on the Admiral's Cup, though for geographical reasons does not get so large an entry and there is less limitation on size. American, British and New Zealand teams participate, as well as several teams representing different Australian states.

Across the oceans and round the world

From time to time there are very long races indeed—trans-ocean events. Transatlantic races are held most years with a variety of start and finish points. They may start from one of the

Below: Ocean racers massed in a lock at the conclusion of the RORC Cowes to St Malo race

yachting ports in the US north-east, Marble-head, Newport, Gloucester or sometimes from Bermuda (after a Bermuda race) and finish in Norway, Sweden, England, Ireland or Spain. Such races are sometimes 'feeders' for Cowes Week and the Fastnet. Races back against the prevailing westerly winds are not so common, but in 1981 the RORC scheduled a Solent–Canaries–Antigua race in the trade winds. The east going races are organized by various clubs, usually including the Cruising Club of America. Although greater feats than the 600-mile tradi-tional they attract little publicity—perhaps a two line result in a quality daily.

The single-handed races every fourth year are west going, because they are European ori-ginated and until recent years had few American entries. (This was decidedly reversed when, in 1980, the winner was an American and the US entry was the largest, with class wins as well.) There is considerable publicity, for the races began in an era of sponsorship with the backing for the most famous race from *The Observer*. Many entries are sponsored by large and small firms and the idea of sailing alone seems to cap-ture public imagination. Famous names immediately come to the public mind in a way not found in other sorts of racing—Francis Chichester, Clare Francis, Naomi James, Eric

Clare Francis in *ADC Accutrac* **(a Swan 65 class) gets a welcome in her home port after completing the 1977–78 race around the world**

Tabarly, Phil Weld, Jerry Cartwright, Jean Yves Terlain, Jean Lacombe, Alec Rose, Michael Richey, Tom Follet, Mike Birch, Nick Keig, March Pajot. No doubt some of these names mean more to their own countrymen and it is mildly invidious with many names omitted. One should not forget Blondie Hasler who founded the race and enlisted the support of *The Observer*. The race is now known as OSTAR.

Now there are other great short-handed races including the two-man round Britain (again with publicity, so that when the author sailed his own boat a few years ago in a fully manned RORC race round the British Isles, casual acquaintances invariably assumed that he had taken part in the two-man race: his own event had little press notice). The two-man race round Britain has also grown in popularity over the years and in 1978 it mustered 74 starters. Once again it is international and in some ways a training ground for the Atlantic event. There are compulsory 48-hour stops, after the start at Plymouth, in south west Ireland, the Shetland Isles, and Lowestoft before the final leg back to Plymouth. A single-handed race so close to the potential dangers of the shore and some-times among shipping and oil rigs was never thought appropriate. Since the first race in 1966 with its 16 starters on this 1700-mile course the speeds have increased. In 1974 Robin Knox-Johnston in *British Oxygen* scored his second

win in a row by taking in this large catamaran (later to sink without loss of life in the 1976 transatlantic race) 18 days 4 hours 26 minutes. In 1978 Chay Blyth and crew Rob James in the 54ft (16·5m) *Great Britain IV* won in 13 days 1 hour 24 minutes.

A race of potentially warmer and easier sailing is the AZAB, which means Azores and back (to Falmouth). It is 1200 miles from Falmouth, Cornwall to Ponta Delgada, Island of São Miguel. Boats can be single-handed or two-handed and there is an upper size limit of 38ft (11·6m), the object being to exclude the sponsored giants. The event has been held in 1975 and 1979, and was due again in 1983 and has been well supported. It can, incidentally, act as a qualifier for the single-handed transatlantic (for which skippers must have sailed 1000 miles offshore in their entered boats).

Even more of a revolt against size and commercialism is the Mini-transat. This, unlike the single-handed race with its northerly courses, is routed in the trade winds which are warm and fair, leaving late in the year from Penzance; there is a stop off at the Canaries and then a crossing to Antigua in the Caribbean. The important aspect of the race is that the maximum overall length is 21ft 4in (6·5m) and there is an international entry mainly from France and Britain, but also Germany, Switzerland, Italy, USA and others. This single-handed race for such small boats has been often criticized, especially after two lone sailors and their boats were lost in the first race in 1977 though 20 completed the course. In 1979 the event was held again and all 25 entries (out of 31) completed the course. Four of the entrants were women. In 1981 there were 50 entries.

Turning point in races round the British Isles. Muckle Flugga (the most northerly piece of land in Britain)

From France the amazing Transat en Double has been organized—from Lorient round Bermuda without stopping and to Lorient! The Route de Rhum from St Malo to Martinique followed the reduction by the OSTAR authorities on maximum size, having no such rule for sailors (especially from France) in big single-handers. On the first of these races in 1979, the famous French single-hander Alain Colas disappeared without trace with his trimaran *Manureva*, holder of the record for the fastest sailing vessel around the world and previously winner of many races as *Pen Duick IV*, under skipper Eric Tabarly.

In 1968–69 there was a single-handed race around the world; the only yacht to complete the course according to the rules was Robin Knox-Johnston in *Suhaili*. Another such race is planned to start from Newport, Rhode Island in 1982. No other such short-handed races have been planned or held.

Ocean racing round the world is a development of the seventies, but this is in fully crewed IOR class yachts of minimum 30ft rating, complying with ORC special regulations and other stringent equipment rules for such an arduous race. The Whitbread Round the World race, run by the Royal Naval Sailing Association, could be said to have become the world's longest regular sailing event having been held in 1973–74, 1977–78 and 1981–82. The intention is to have it every four years. The first race had 17 starters and 14 completed all four legs of the nominal 26 950 miles (Portsmouth–Cape Town–Sydney–Rio de Janeiro–Portsmouth). The second race had 15 starters, all of whom finished. The third race had more than 25 starters. In this third time round the second and third stopping ports were changed to Auckland and Mar del Plata (Argentina). A race round the world for IOR boats without handicap was

Below: The Whitbread Trophy for the winner of the round-the-world ocean race every fourth year (1973–74, 1977–78, 1981–82, etc.)

Bottom: About to win the second Whitbread race around the world in 1978, Flyer (first of the name) finishes in gale conditions

held in 1975–76 from England with a single stop at Sydney, but only four yachts competed and it is unlikely to be repeated.

Local organizations

An offshore race can be 27 miles just as well as 27 000 and it would be impossible to list the races starting every week-end and many week-days and at holiday times throughout the world, or at least in the nations in which offshore racing is a sport. In Britain alone there are some twelve major associations, mainly combinations of clubs which give racing for offshore boats. The table shows both the similarity and differences, as they are listed clockwise from the Thames Estuary. Some of the bodies shown are actually clubs, which are primarily for giving races to all comers, others are geographical groupings so that owners along a coast can get together for best competition. It is evident that most use both IOR and then some form of handicapping for the balance of the fleet. In addition to them there are numerous clubs giving racing for cruisers, which could hardly be classed as off-shore racing.

Offshore round the coasts

The twelve major associations or organizations round the coasts of Britain which give offshore racing to yachts, whether to the International Offshore Rule class or other forms of time allowance. The number of starters whether average or maximum will always be much lower than the total number of boats which take one or more starts in a season, as many yachts compete in just a few of the available races.

Organization	Area covered	Classes eligible	Safety rules used	Type of programme	Main event	Longest event	Any special prizes or divisions	Number of starters Av	Number of starters Max
Royal Ocean Racing Club	Britain and Overseas	IOR rated ORC classes	ORC and additions	18 ocean races each over 200 miles		Round British Isles	Numerous overall, classes, level and other classification	90	300
East Anglian Offshore Racing Association	Norfolk to Folkestone and North Sea	IOR Rated. Minimum 18ft LWL. Class 1 25·5–70·07 Class 2 21·8–25·4 Class 3 19·5–21·7 Class 4 below 19·5	ORC modified	13 offshore races each about 60 miles		Harwich–Ostend	Overall, class and level rating	40	80
Solent Cruising and Racing Association	Solent outwards and cross channel	IOR rated and local club systems	ORC modified	More than 50 events including Solent points championship of 13	Solent points championship series of 13	Hamble–Roscoff	Class, level rating, OOD and many traditional club trophies	100 (for SPC races)	Over 700 (annual ISC round the island)
West Solent Cruiser Racing Association	West Solent and offshore	One IOR class. One west Solent class	ORC category 4	20 events		Round the Isle of Wight	Contessa 32 and J24 class prizes	20	30
Junior Offshore Group	English Channel	IOR rated 28·9ft and below. ORC classes	ORC category 3	14 events		Morgan Cup (channel triangle)	Level rating and some OODs	30	45
Poole Yacht Racing Association	Solent to Weymouth and cross channel	IOR classes 1. 19·5ft and over 2. 16·0–19·4 Two non-IOR classes	ORC, local and OOD rules	Every weekend in season		To Jersey	Level rating and J24	45	105
West Channel Offshore Racing Association	From the Exe to Lands End	One IOR class One Portsmouth Yardstick class	ORC categories 2 & 3	30 events by 15 clubs		Wolf Rock	Tapol Trophy for different race each year	Big variation	50
Bristol Channel Yachting Conference	From Lydbury and Thornbury on the Severn to Milford Haven and Bideford Bay	Portsmouth Yardstick	ORC modified	Club and open events	BBC TV Race	Mumbles to Cork	Overall and class	16	200
Irish Sea Offshore Racing Association	North-west England, Wales, Isle of Man and Ireland east and south	IOR rated classes A1. 24·6–70·0 A2. 22·1–24·5 B1. 20·0–22·0 B2. 16·0–19·9 Class C local handicap	ORC category 3	12 races including 5 with CCC and 2 with RORC	ISORA race week	Holyhead–Dun Laoghaire (with RORC)	Overall and class	40	60
Clyde Cruising Club	Clyde, west of Scotland and north Irish Sea	IOR rated classes A. 23·0–70·0 B. 16·0–22·9 CCC handicap class	ORC modified	10 races including one with RORC	Tomatin trophy	Blue water trophy	Scottish level rating, mini ton and Sonata class	100	200
Forth Yacht Clubs Association	Forth Estuary from Tay to Farne Islands	Two divisions of local handicap IOR rated and NECRA handicap. Each two divisions above and below 19·5ft rating	ORC categories 3 & 4	One offshore race per month in season 9 offshore and 2 short series		Farne Islands race		15	25
North East Cruiser Racing Association	Amble to Bridlington		NECRA rules			North Sea race to Holland	Some level rating awards	25	45

193

Offshore one-designs

As already remarked, racing boat for boat offshore came late for the historical reason that ocean racing began in assorted cruisers with handicap rules that were ultimately refined into the IOR, giving IOR class yachts. But to gain success in level racing in the Ton Cup events it is necessary to have a very new boat of the latest design, such is the progress in hulls, rigs and techniques. The almost annual amendments to the rating rule cause actual ratings to change and expensive alterations may be needed to bring the boat back into class. All boats which are raced, in due course suffer from the march of design progress. This is accentuated by the fact that the best crews drift towards the latest boats, so making older designs even less likely to win. Early in this century there were important inshore racing classes built to rating rules, but this continuous process of outdating killed them off and now all inshore classes and racing

dinghies are either one-designs or closely restricted classes. Offshore there was a delay in such an evolution as the vagaries of weather and fortune on long events tend to even out the results over a season or longer period. In the late seventies, after nearly ten years of IOR racing, several one-design classes of genuine offshore yacht were formed. In them crews are able to enjoy the same kind of racing as IOR boats, yet with the knowledge that their boats will not be outdated. Nor will it be necessary to have a 'stripped out' machine, because one-design rules invariably ensure that the yacht has a standard of moderate cruising comfort.

Offshore one-designs can be defined as follows:

(a) They are under rules which ensure that the boats are alike enough to give potentially equal speed in racing.

(b) They must race reasonably regularly as a class in one or more places.

(c) They must take part as a class in offshore events.

(d) They must be under control of a class owners' association and not be merely a commercial creation.

Left: The Sonata one-design (21m) has a small cabin. The class is for coastal cruising and one-design racing
Below: Three different one-design class boats: OOD34, 101 and Impala classes.

(e) They must comply with most of the ORC special regulations (safety and equipment).

If a group of boats falls down on any one of these they cannot be called an offshore one-design. For instance if they do not fit (c) and (e) they are probably a one-design class, but an inshore one. If (b) is not fulfilled, it probably means that they are similar boats, but just another production class spread around and happen to be exactly the same when they leave the builder's yard. If (a) and (d) are missing, then it is certain they are under no control which will prevent them having alterations so that they are not fairly the same for long.

One-design classes can really only form effectively in major yachting areas (there is less need for them where competition in measured or handicap boats is relaxed) and are bound to be few in number. Indeed, if there are too many jostling for loyalties then we are only a little better off than having a variety of rated boats. There is no means of official recognition of an offshore one-design (the author recommends recognition by (a) to (e) above) but there is a

system of IOR one-design ratings. These are only allocated when the boats are so alike that the ORC is quite certain that a check on the one-design characteristics showing compliance with class rules must mean that the boat so checked has a rating the same as all the others in the class.

On this basis the offshore one-design classes are the following:

Class	LOA	Where Sailed	Number of boats
North American	40ft	Great Lakes	45
Offshore One-Design 34	33ft 8in	South coast England	50
Sigma 33	32ft 6in	South coast England	110
J 30	29ft 11in	North east USA	70
Ballad	28ft 6in	Sweden, Germany (elsewhere not an OOD)	375
Sprinta Sport	24ft 9in	Germany	280
Sonata	22ft 7in	Great Britain	315

Other classes which race as one-designs and have enough accommodation to be called cruiser-racers are the Impala 28 OOD, the J24 and the Sonata.

J 24 class one-designs race under lowering skies

18

A race

A sample race

No ocean race is typical, for the sea and weather are ever changing. Yet scenes do repeat themselves in different guises: weathering a headland, struggling across a finishing line in light air, just carrying a spinnaker with a strong wind abeam. In this section we go aboard an ocean racer for a comparatively short race—one lasting about 48 hours. Yet this means two nights at sea and the necessity to sail the boat around the clock.

In a 35ft (10·7m) long boat, in this case in 'normal' conditions, the distance covered might be around 270 miles—an average of 5·75 knots. Let us say that one third of this was dead to windward, so for the remaining time the boat speed would be greater than the average. This is not difficult in a wind that is anything more than light with the spinnaker set. If there is light air for much of the time, it could take 76 hours to cover the distance: on the other hand if it is a fast down hill ride, 40 hours would not be impossible. Such a speed is more likely on courses which are in roughly a straight line (along the coast or from port to port), where the wind is blowing steadily from one direction. In 'closed' courses a patch of windward work is likely to be met, which lowers average speed. However, like other offshore sailors, the author has been on closed courses where the wind has changed near each mark to give a fair wind right round—and also to give a contrary wind right round the course!

275 nautical miles—typical times for a 35ft offshore racer:

Speed	Time	Comment, as an average
3 knots	91¼ hours	Slow
4·5 knots	61 hours	Expected
5·75 knots	48 hours	Fast, not exceptional
6·75 knots	40½ hours	Unusually fast

In sketching in the activities on a '48-hour race', many of the same incidents apply to both longer and shorter races. On longer races the crew seem to settle down more. It takes a day or so to get over the habit of sleeping at night and working by day, but once this is done it is possible to snatch an hour or less of sleep at any time and remain alert in the night hours. One can perhaps exist for 48 hours quite comfortably without substantial meals, but after this period crew morale and fitness suffers without proper and varied diet. It is better to eat adequately even for a two-day race and this will be assumed here. As a race is expected to be longer, so those on board must be more self-reliant and able to make repairs which last a long time; again, a shorter event means harbour facilities are not so far away in time and distance. But even on the shorter race, the necessity may arise to improvise or prevent some hazard developing.

Another variation on our sample event is possibly a major climatic one. Outward appearances are certainly different. In cold conditions, boats may have charcoal stoves going and short watches so that the crew can get below to warm up frequently. Emphasis will be on ease of handling to obviate the necessity to get cold and wet with much sail changing. In tropical or semi-tropical areas, it will be adequate ventilation that is required, clothing will be minimal and the precautions will be against the sun's rays and heat exhaustion. In general, of course, yachts, including ocean racers, are inclined to be built for hot ('holiday') climates rather than cold.

A normal crew is assumed in the sample race. On the 35ft boat, say, six or seven. For the single-handed or two-handed races, gear and equipment may need to be laid out differently, the work schedule rearranged and slightly less driving of the boat expected—though the winners of these events would seem to give the lie to the latter assumption. The type of boat need not be different for short handed races. Though many varied types do enter these special races, there are also a proportion of 'conventional' ocean racers which turn in good results. The reason that they normally require many more crew is that the full crew can execute manoeuvres quicker. At other times they will certainly not all be sailing the boat. They will be off watch resting and anyway it is more pleasant if there are plenty of hands to work at sea.

Preparations

In cruising and sailing generally it is a precept that preparation before going to sea is as important as competent sailing and sound navigation. Difficulties, when they occur at sea, are frequently due to not checking gear and equipment before leaving. The same applies when racing, but it is magnified because not only is seamanship at fault, due to lack of preparation, but race winning capability suffers.

For instance, if the bottom surface is not completely clean and smooth, the yacht will come to no harm, but you can forget any prospect of doing well in the race. The ideal way to keep a boat is out of the water, sometimes known as 'dry-sailing'. Launching her when required ensures without question that the bottom is smooth. There is more tendency to 'rub down' between races. As the boat becomes bigger, so this is less practical and in any case it is expensive because of continual hauling and launching. An advantage is that anti-fouling (see below) is not necessary and the surface can be rubbed for hour after hour until there is an utterly smooth surface. Something that feels like smoothed bone is best.

Most ocean racers are kept afloat in marinas or at moorings and the bottoms treated with one of the several bottom finishes, suitable for racing boats. New products are produced not infrequently, but the anti-fouling will be purpose produced for racing bottoms, possibly with a copper or mercury base. Unlike some anti-foulings which leach out, this will dry hard and respond to hard scrubbing without damage. It will also be of a type that does not deteriorate when exposed to air for any period. Whatever the claims of the makers it is advisable to have a hauling programme for the season to add that extra smoothness and check that all is well with the bottom surface. The boat will almost certainly come out before any long and important event. Every part of the bottom must be smooth, but extra attention should be paid to

surfaces forward, as here laminar flow is most likely. Fouling which slows a boat down may not even be visible: transparent slime can be equally harmful.

As most ocean racers are based in well equipped yachting centres they will invariably be hauled out by a 'travel-lift'. The boat can be suspended in air long enough to deal with the bottom of the keel—or even left in the slings for a quick check and rub down. If left for any time on shore the boat is best rested in its own steel cradle which will support it fairly and safely; this applies to today's short keels.

Preparation aloft

After the bottom comes the rig where access during the race, though not impossible when sailing, is extremely inconvenient. Everything above deck must be inspected by a man hoisted in a bosun's chair: condition of fastenings, clevis and split (cotter) pins at the masthead and where spreaders and standing rigging attach to the mast. The spreader ends and roots are looked at, too, as well as halyard sheaves. Signs of wear should be cured by replacement or repair, since once sailing, faults can progress aloft without anyone seeing them. The bosun's chair is an important piece of equipment at sea: without it, there is no means of dealing with work on the mast—unless the crew contains some of those young men, who think nothing of shinning up the mast. The modern mast has few lines to grasp, all its halyards being internal to save wind resistance. (This may not apply to single and short handed boats on long voyages which are equipped with built-in mast steps.)

Loss of mast

If the mast collapses under compression strains, then it must be inadequate and should have been designed with a more substantial section. It is possible to hold some small section masts in the boat with multiple staying. but then, if an error is made in releasing a runner, the mast can be lost. If an adequate section mast is lost, it will be due to failure of a stay or much more likely, its fitting. Hence the reason for frequent close inspections.

Pre-race checks on deck

These are comparatively simple. Winches are stripped and oiled and the same treatment will make spinnaker track and poles easily usable. Worn sheets are replaced. Stanchion bases and rigging screw with split pins are rebound with tape to prevent tearing oilskins (foul weather clothing) or cutting hands.

Replenishment

Fuel tanks should have adequate fuel for possible distance under power (eg to the start), but not too much because of weight increase. Water must be put aboard, but, again, not too much. Food and drink for the period of the race has to be stowed. If the boat is racing regularly during the season, there are bound to be minor repairs from the previous outing. Most likely these are small nicks in the sails, but a locker door may be jamming, a seacock may be stiff to turn, the cabin sole may have a cracked board.

Night equipment

As this category concerns small electric components which are never happy near salt water, they must be checked in harbour. It will be difficult to wrestle with the tiny screw in a navigation light terminal after dusk out at sea. Most important is the compass light(s), then the navigation lights (running lights), chart table and other internal lights. There must be spare, dry batteries for torches (flashlights). Navigational instruments and the engine also use electricity, but these are on by day and any failure would be noticed as soon as the yacht leaves harbour; but such electrics would also be part of the pre-race check.

Navigation and tactics

It will pay for the skipper and navigator to make as much preparation as possible. Courses, possible tactics in different circumstances, summaries of the lights and radio beacons likely to be met—all these can save time and muddle when later in the race conditions on board are not conducive to navigation.

The race cannot quite be won by preparation before the start, but it can certainly be lost without thorough preparation; large and small things will go wrong on the race; this will cause at the best distraction, at the worst serious delay or be the cause of retirement.

The engine

Ocean racing boats are distinguished from other racing yachts by having an engine. In a racing context this is required in order to reach the start line from the harbour in time, and as a matter of convenience for returning there after the race. It is of course more than this, being

virtually necessary for docking and manoeuvring in harbour. There are few boats that do not have motors now, though twenty years ago there were a number of engine-less ocean racers. Waters have become more crowded, moorings tighter, motors more reliable and lighter and propellers less resistant under sail. Boats under 25ft (7·62m) may well have outboard motors, hung on the transom when motoring and stowed away when not in use.

The start line

The most common form of start line is that between two marks on boats, with possibly distance marks inside them to limit the length of the line. More and more on offshore races there is a tendency to arrange a start to windward, as is done with ordinary racing yachts on an Olympic course. This may well mean a leg of a couple of miles to a specially laid buoy before carrying on with the ocean course. Once ocean racing skippers, realizing that they had many miles to go, took a casual attitude to the start, but those days are gone and the start for the 600-mile Fastnet, for instance, is contested as closely as any short dinghy race.

Since ocean races are on fixed courses regardless of the wind at the time, starts are frequently not to windward. Reaching and running starts, which are seldom seen in inshore racing, are therefore likely. Some races are also started from shore based lines, in which case there may be a transit, with an inner and outer distance mark. (A finishing line is never a transit: if the finishing station is on shore, which is quite likely so that long watches can be kept, the line is between a post on shore and a floating mark. It can be in a narrow channel between two shore marks.)

It is exciting and sometimes not a little perilous when a crowd of ocean racing boats are sailing around fast in all directions before the start, but near the start line. Assuming a wind of 15 knots and a windward start, the yachts will be under full mains and genoas. The crew will be stationed as follows: the helmsman (with eyes all round him), one man on mainsheet, two on genoa sheets, one on the stop watch (navigator), one in the pulpit keeping a look out as the genoa will obscure the view to leeward forward.

Until the five-minute gun of the class, the national ensign should be worn to indicate that the yacht is not racing. On the five-minute gun it is brought in and the yacht becomes subject

A low cut genoa blots out the helmsman's view to leeward

to the racing rules of the International Yacht Racing Union, which apply to the racing of all yachts. In Part IV of these lengthy rules which are revised every four years (1981, 1985 etc) among the right-of-way rules are rules particularly applying to the start. Even experienced spectators of yacht racing, arriving at a start line with yachts milling in all directions, have difficulty in discovering just what stage the starting preparations are at. If the yachts are just all beginning to turn in the same direction then there is less than a minute to go. Otherwise it is essential to see the signals on the committee boat (start control boat). A major aid to start control is the use of VHF by broadcasting the timings and subsequently any recalls for boats over the line. Back to flags, if a single one is up, then there is more than five minutes to go: if the single flag and the 'blue peter' is up, then there is less than five minutes to go. At the starting gun, both flags come spinning down. A different system, more common in America than Europe, is to use flags or shapes of distinct colours:

white shape—ten to six minutes to go

blue shape—five minutes to one minute to go

A red shape hoisted—'go'.

If the starting gun is followed by two guns, it means a general recall: all boats return. The 'first substitute' signal of the international code of signals is hoisted. If one gun fires after the start, it recalls only those yachts which are over and they are responsible for returning: a code flag is hoisted. If they fail to return they are disqualified or have a time penalty. Under IYRU racing rule 44, a yacht which is returning to cross the line after starting prematurely, or a yacht working her way to the start line from the wrong side after the start gun, has to give way to all yachts which have started correctly. A number of ocean racers moving fast in the same direction just after the start are a formidable obstruction. There is every incentive to be behind the line when the gun goes.

Ocean racers do not accelerate like dinghies, so with one and a half minutes to go we begin our turn for the line. The pulpit man calls 'See the blue boat two-seven-nine-four?' The helmsman has. 'Lee-oh'. We are getting on to starboard tack, so we have right of way (over port tack boats) as we cross the line. Only the helmsman speaks now, except for the navigator calling the seconds from his stop watch. 'One . . . minute . . .' 'Not too hard on the genoa—let it flap'. Evidently he does not want too much speed yet or we will be over too soon. 'Forty . . . five . . . seconds' 'In with the main'. Yachts crowd round us nearly touching, somebody's pulpit seems almost into our cockpit. To weather there is a big fellow. 'Watch it—it's our right of way'. Yes, we are to leeward of him and he must keep clear under IYRU rule 37.1 and 40. 'Thirty . . . seconds' 'Right. In with the genoa'. Now we gather speed, those around us heel and the sounds are of mingling bow waves and ratcheting winches. The navigator keeps calling, but the helmsman is going for it and there is little he can do but slow by easing sheets. But that does not seem necessary. 'Eight . . . seven . . . six . . . five . . .' The weight of the man in the pulpit is bad for speed and he comes aft since we are all going in the same direction; spare crew members climb to the weather deck and put their weight where it is most effective. 'Two . . . one—GUN'. Somewhere, a few seconds later, comes the sound of a cannon over the water: it took time to reach us. Damn it, there is one boat to windward taking our clean air, but apart from that we are clear and sailing fast to windward on starboard tack. These first minutes are important since, if we fall to leeward, it can affect our position for a long time. Can we tack to clear our wind? No, because there is another boat on our weather quarter and we cannot tack in front of him (IYRU rule 41). Meanwhile the boat to windward, which has a rating half a foot greater than us, draws ahead and we are now getting clear air, even though he did get away. Now we just sail. The helmsman concentrates, the rest of the crew is on the weather deck: except for one hand who stays near the helmsman to adjust either the main or genoa sheets.

Three hours later

On the horizon is a light tower which is the first mark in the race, say, three and a half miles off. We will be there in another thirty-five minutes. We are on port tack now, having made several tacks since the start. The last of these was after a slight shift of wind made this the best tack for the mark. However, we shall not lay it without one more tack and it has to be left to port. What is each member of the crew doing now? Skipper. He was on the helm at the start and after two hours handed over to the other helmsman in his watch. Navigator. He listened to a weather forecast which predicts a change of wind. Navigation has been simple so far in broad daylight along the coast to the tower, but from here it will be offshore and night coming on. With the skipper he discusses tactics for the next leg. He lays off a course, checking it against pre-race figures. The skipper warns the crew that at the mark a spinnaker will be required and it will be starboard gybe (spinnaker pole on starboard side). He selects which spinnaker to use. In winds of any strength, all or most of the crew will be involved in this typical ocean racing operation. Indeed, without spinnakers 45 per cent of deck activity on board ocean racers would be eliminated. So it gives the crew scope for their skills, or a great amount of extra work!

Here is an idea of the activity (the crew numbered one to six apart from helmsman and navigator). The helmsman keeps his concentration and allows the crew to thunder round the deck (very often he is distracted and loses out). The navigator makes sure he is ready to check the new course (it may be that they cannot quite lay it—we will see). No. 1 and 2 drag the spinnaker bag forward, from the main hatch where it has been passed up. No. 2 stays by the mast leaving only 1 to secure the bag, because undue weight forward will slow the boat. No. 2 moves the inner end of the spinnaker pole up the mast track and when 1 has connected the spinnaker pole topping lift, 2 hauls away on it by the mast so the pole becomes nearly horizontal; meanwhile 1 has threaded the spinnaker guy through its end. No. 3 right aft lets slack the spinnaker sheets and guys on both port and starboard and 4 eases the foreguy without which the far end of the spinnaker pole could not be lifted up by its topping lift. No. 5 is at the halyard winch, ready with a winch handle. No. 1 connects the halyard to the head of the spinnaker. No. 6 is by the genoa sheet winch and has also ensured that the spinnaker sheet is ready round its winch, probably just aft of the genoa winch. Now 3 moves to the windward side where the spinnaker guy is round the windward genoa winch (not in use).

They are at the mark. 'Bearing away' says the helmsman; the yacht turns. No. 3 moves

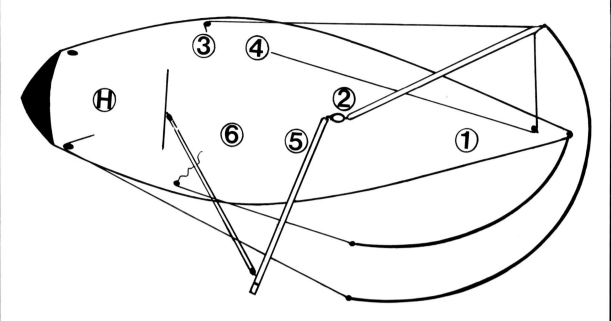

Helmsman (H) and six crew hoist the spinnaker (see text
for duties of 1 to 6)

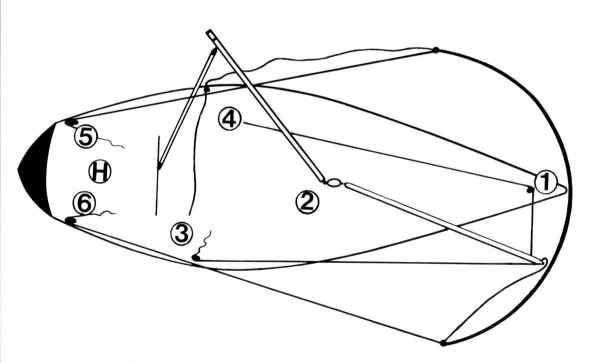

Helmsman (H) and six crew gybe the spinnaker. Here
main boom has moved across. Spinnaker pole is on its
way across to new (starboard) tack of spinnaker

across to the main sheet and eases it. No. 6 eases the genoa sheet quickly and then turns it up, getting back on to the spinnaker sheet which in a few seconds is going to be much more important. 'Up spinnaker.' Hand over hand 2 hauls the halyard, while 5 swiftly pulls slack in around the winch. Once the load comes on the halyard 5 takes the strain on the winch. No. 2 comes aft to help him wind it in the last part. Meanwhile the most vital man in all this, 6, has hauled in the spinnaker sheet and is already trimming it with one or more turns on the winch, depending on wind strength. No. 3 has also wound in his winch, so the pole is brought aft and trimmed to the correct angle to the wind. No. 4 at the foreguy eases it as 3 winches in and vice versa.

So the spinnaker is up and pulling, the yacht has gained several knots, the crew are in new positions. No. 1 clears up forward by retrieving the spinnaker bag lashed to the deck or pulpit and assists in lowering the genoa and lashing it down on deck. No. 5 clears up the spinnaker halyard and makes up the end of the genoa halyard. No. 4 can get the mainsheet trimmed exactly. Nos. 1, 2, 4 and 5 have for the moment finished, and that leaves 6 continuing to trim the sheet; for any shift of wind or course 3 and 4 will need to trim the pole. But the helmsman and No. 6 must work together to speed the boat. There is hardly a dull moment for the others if the pole height is to be changed, but there may be some time with this rig until the wind increases or decreases, or changes direction.

Enough has been said to indicate the great amount of activity for even one operation in sailing an ocean racer (in this case about the size of a One Tonner). On the race there will be hours when sail changing follows in different patterns and other occasions when steady conditions mean keeping watch, sail trimming and little else. Once that One Tonner is on her way under spinnaker, the navigator will recalculate the likely time of arrival at the next mark and allow for tidal streams, if any; therefore, he is

Team work on deck with coffee grinder winches

going to order a change of course however slight, with its subsequent trimming of spinnaker and pole and mainsail. Let us say, this course means the boat comes closer to the wind, so the spinnaker is shy with the pole hard against the forestay (or rather not quite touching, so a reaching strut must be rigged to windward to hold the spinnaker guy away from shrouds and life-lines and to keep control of the end of the pole). 'It is touch and go' says the navigator, 'we do not want to go below this course. If you have to go off to carry the spinnaker, it won't suit me'. Shy spinnaker reaches like this are an uncomfortable point of sailing. The boat is heeled, if the wind strengthens she may broach by rounding up into the wind momentarily out of control. And as the navigator says, it may not be possible to hold the course and better to drop the spinnaker, hoist the genoa and sail closer to the wind. This will certainly lower the speed, so the skipper may

Running fast under spinnaker - and with a necessarily alert crew

turn to the navigator and say 'Yes, I know, but the wind may well free us in this sort of weather. I am going to carry the 'chute for 20 minutes. Then we will decide again'. Sure enough the wind frees them and they find that soon they can lay the chosen course and ease the spinnaker sheet, while the yacht comes a little more upright and gets easier to steer. Had they lowered the spinnaker, it would have been premature and they would have been busy hoisting it all over again with certain loss of time in the race. But you can never tell and this is what keeps it a sport despite all the modern aids.

The scene below

There is a great delight in being conveyed as swiftly as possible through the sea with an entirely silent source of power. One never fails to thrill to the satisfaction of living at sea and under sail. Sometimes, of course, there is much noise when beating to windward, crashing and banging into the seas. On the other hand, if off the wind, in reasonably smooth water, the

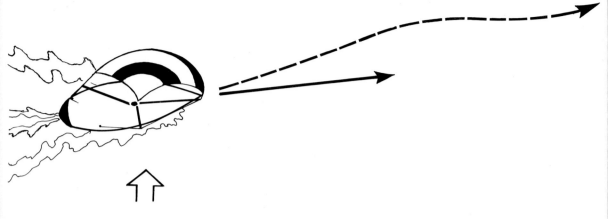

Shy spinnaker reach is easier along dotted line. Solid line
is course required, but difficult to hold

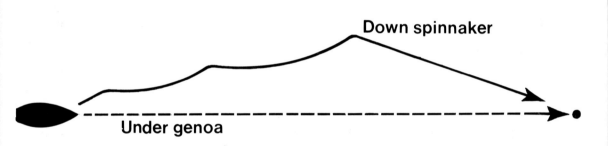

Down spinnaker

Under genoa

Using genoa instead gives better, shorter course. Solid line
is longer, erratic and means lowering spinnaker before
long

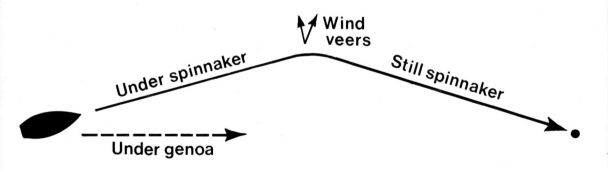

Wind
veers

Under spinnaker

Still spinnaker

Under genoa

Skipper decides to hold spinnaker, anticipating wind shift.
So he carries it on solid line course. Genoa was slower,
though initially 'correct'

Stark bunks keep off watch crew to windward depending on which tack boat is on

motion is barely perceptible, bar that delicious hiss of water an inch or two from the bunk in which one lies.

Returning now to the sample race, where the spinnaker is up and some sort of course settled, the cook is preparing a meal before darkness falls. The galley can operate at night, but for anything else than quick hot drinks, it is better to eat and then clear up in the last of the daylight. It is seldom easy to cook at sea, though it may be rewarding in terms of satisfying a hungry crew and coping with difficulties. Generally the cook is keeping components of the meal in saucepans or in the oven until it is time to serve each plate; these are left in the heel proof locker until the last moment. Ventilation is always a problem and except in the worst weather, if the galley is near the hatch, leaving it open provides an escape for heat and steam from cooking food. The cook, and perhaps one man helping with holding plates, tells the watch below to be ready for their food. When racing, it is not practicable to send food up to the cockpit; at least it is distracting and at worst it is in jeopardy when some inevitable move is made on deck. So the watch on deck come down one by one and eventually one of them assists in clearing and cleaning the galley. Ready use supplies are left available for the night. Tea, cocoa, soup; hard tack biscuits; sweets including barley sugars; all these are drawn on at the change of watch or at a quiet moment in the small hours of the morning.

Clothing

As darkness comes the new watch are pulling on more clothing. The best equipped of them have a remarkable choice of garments specially made for conditions in small craft at sea. In fine, warm weather there is no problem, but in northern waters or bad weather except in the tropics, protective clothing is essential to keep warmth and energy in the body. Rain and spray can quickly bring discomfort, loss of body heat and approaching hypothermia. These things are better understood today, so we can stay warm and dry (most of the time) and more people are physically able to complete long distance races. This can be compared on advice given about ocean racing a generation ago, which was 'bring a change of clothing for every hundred miles of the course'.

Outer layers can be waterproof and a great variety of foul weather clothing is on the market. The heavier gear used for offshore racing is some form of woven, man-made fibre on a layer of PVC, Nylon or other synthetic sheet which is totally water impervious. It is not quite as simple as this, because seams immediately mean potential holes (hundreds of needle size); therefore seams must be overcoated, or welded so that machine holes do not show. Then come the vital design points for cuffs, neck, pockets and front. Zips, buttons, poppers, Velcro and tapes all have their part to play. Trousers are more simple. The legs outside the boots, of at least upper calf length, keep that end dry (unless you are kneeling on the foredeck the moment a sea sweeps it) while the upper part should come almost to the arm pits and the garment is held on by braces. Such properly designed offshore trousers are a major comfort and are frequently worn without a top in moderate conditions and still keep the midriff and small of the back protected.

Much progress has been made in recent years on insulated clothing to be worn under the foul weather gear. Selling under such names as Polarwear, Body warmers, Warmwear, or simply described as fibre pile, there are trousers and tops with varied combinations of cellular construction and synthetic pile to trap the heat

of the body and maintain an even temperature. In other words there is a high level of insulation which the old fashioned sweater could never retain, while the new garments are shaped to cling and fit for best effect. On the head there is nothing to beat a woollen hat, for a high percentage of body heat loss is potentially from the head. Over it, in foul weather, will be pulled the hood of the outer jacket. So the water cannot find a way down the neck and back of the head. Goodbye to the old sou'wester of tradition. Even the lifeboat men are seen in hoods now. As for footwear there are two kinds: in fine dry weather, sailing shoes with non-slip soles, should be worn of which the mocassin type are best, and the finest qualities have a very long life indeed (canvas shoes quickly rot). When it is wet however, boots should be high enough not to scoop heavy water on deck. There are other auxiliary bits of clothing. Sailing gloves of various designs

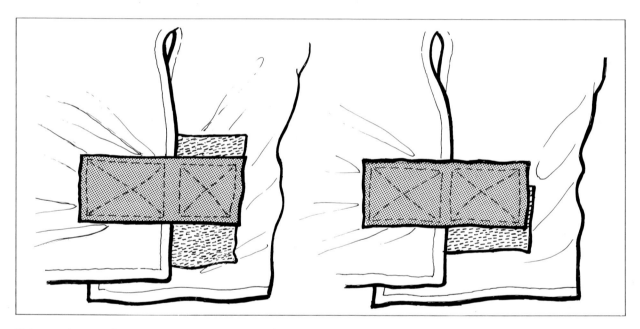

Velcro on foul weather gear. It should have one surface extra large to ensure full area contact

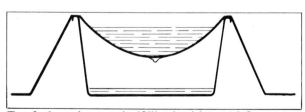

Test foul weather gear by 'filling it with water'. Spray proof is not enough at sea

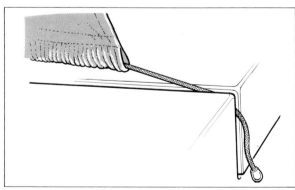

Draw strings can foul equipment

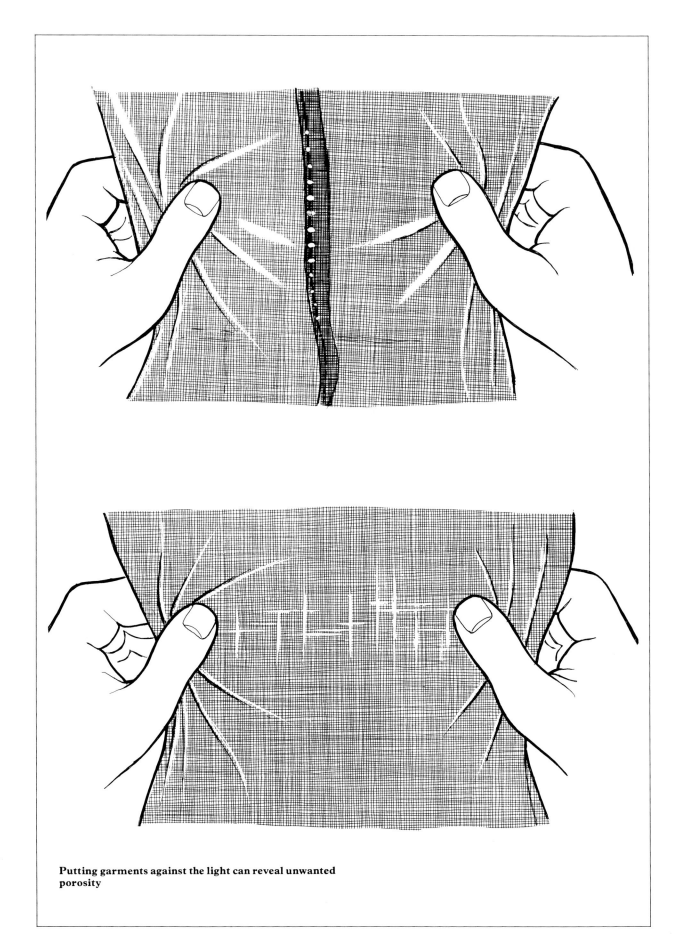

Putting garments against the light can reveal unwanted porosity

are obtainable. Towelling for the neck is standard with most sailors; underwear of insulated types for sporting use is a further possibility.

So time is taken by the crew about to go on watch to don their gear for the night, the foul weather clothes ideally stored in a designed area, where they can drip and air. They should not be dumped in the saloon. Each piece is marked with a name and can be found, the named harness also added. If the weather is starting to turn nasty, there is feeling of remarkable confidence if properly equipped (knife in pocket, readily available) and clad.

The navigator and his place

A full time navigator is favoured on boats of more than about 34ft (10·4m). As he is not distracted by other duties, he can warn of change of course, and identify shore or marks being approached, which unnoticed would result in loss of time and the loss of the race. When cruising, the same urgency and accuracy does not apply and navigating an ocean racer is a much higher and more demanding art than navigating a cruiser, even though the latter may well be brought safely and without undue delay to her destination.

Night brings no great rest for the navigator. Apart from anything else he keeps the race instructions and documentation and is the person to say when the navigation lights are to be switched on (as laid down). He checks his night equipment, chart table light, compass lights, torches. Before darkness he can take a radio fix because after dark reception is poor with considerable interference. Once again he reminds the man in charge of the watch on deck to enter the log every half hour with distance run, read off the instrument at the chart table, and the course, as reported by the helmsman. These readings are vital for the dead reckoning plot which the navigator 'works up' from time to time. Some time in the night there will be at least one weather forecast on the radio and the navigator will tune in on time and take it down. Because the navigator knows the position and future predictions of tidal stream, estimated time of arrival at mark and so on, he must be able to advise the skipper, as conditions and the boat's position change. His decision after a joint discussion will be final. How often is there no clear-cut solution (from the race advantage view point) and the right or wrong are only known after the results of the race are known.

The chart table is more than just a single horizontal surface—it is the part of the boat with navigational facilities. This applies to cruisers, which make any open water passages. The table is the basic requirement so that a chart can be spread out and worked on. Sometimes it is said that dimensions should match certain standard charts, but this is exaggerated because the chart can be folded (not allowed in the Navy!) for convenience of use. A deep fiddle must prevent the chart slipping athwartships when the yacht heels. The navigator's seat must be stopped from slipping as well, by means of a belt to hold him to windward, or a deep leeboard or cloth. Chart stowage must be flat as rolled charts are impossible to handle. Usually the table lifts to reveal a corresponding box. Immediately and literally *at hand* must be pencils, dividers, erasers, pencil sharpener and protractor or parallel rule. These will have to be on rack and in holders from which they cannot fall. A pencil rolling around the table is annoying and impracticable: after using it, it should be dropped back into its holder.

A book case is also needed. If it is athwartships, so much the better and the books have little tendency to tip out. If fore and aft they must be behind a screen (Perspex is a neat way) or secured by bars or shock cord. Tide tables, almanacs, note books, tidal stream atlases, pilots for areas of sailing waters will all be there and astro-navigation tables for longer events. On the bulkhead and alongside will be the instrumentation that is standard today, as mentioned earlier. Control boxes and read outs are there with radios, both receivers and VHF or SSB medium wave. Several small lockers are essential, full of spare dry batteries, bulbs, little pieces of wire and myriad spares for instruments and parts of the boat with small but vital components. For all this valuable gear, a prime site has to be chosen. It is part of the overall design, but it is more important that the chart area is kept dry than even the galley (what is a bit of spray over a sink and sideboard or even on boiled potatoes?). Wet charts disintegrate and electrical equipment can be threatened. In boats over about 40ft (12m) it is often possible to find a centreline position well aft under a bridge deck with a window to communicate with the cockpit. In smaller vessels the chart table has to be to one side, often nearly opposite the galley; too far forward means too much movement and lack of ventilation; too much under the hatch means it will get wet, but some form of screen is anyway an additional protection against spray,

Left: J 24 class originating in the US. A popular one-design world wide, with cabin accommodation

Above: Yachts of many nations jostle in the Solent in Admiral's Cup competition

Right: Ocean racers at the start of one of the Sardinia Cup series races—the Mediterranean version of the Admiral's Cup

Below: Start of the long single-handed haul from Plymouth across the Atlantic—OSTAR

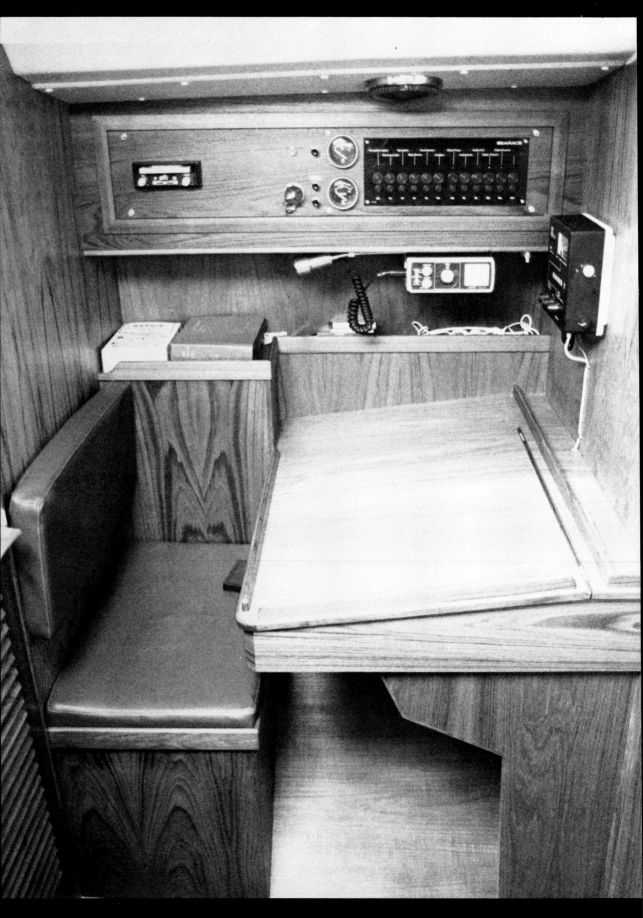

Standard navigation area in production boat Atlantic 43

Above: Navigators chart table and instruments in a large cruiser racer

Below: Typical chart table and instruments on a modern 40ft ocean racer

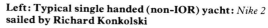

Left: Typical single handed (non-IOR) yacht: *Nike 2* sailed by Richard Konkolski

Centre left: *Paul Ricard,* **Eric Tabarly's high speed hydrofoil trimaran which held for a short time the transatlantic record for speed under sail from Sandy Hook (New York) to the Lizard (Cornwall) in 10 days 5 hours 14 minutes 20 seconds, gained in 1980 from a record standing since 1905. In July 1981,** *Elf Aquitaine* **sailed by Marc Pajot crossed in 9 days 10 hours 6 minutes 34 seconds**

Below: The 76ft (23m) *Flyer* **designed by German Frers and launched in 1981 for the Whitbread round the world race (1981–82) represented the latest in big ocean racers**

Bottom: Racing in big one-designs. Offshore One-design 34s slog it out in close competition

Right: The Sigma 33 class is well supported in Britain

crew moving around in wet outer clothing and sails being carried through the accommodation. It is fun to navigate and even more fun when the chart area has been meticulously planned.

The finish

So the team—helmsmen, watch leaders, crew, cook, navigator, perhaps a sporting sailmaker (also a crew man) who has put in a few stitches around the course—head their boat within miles of the finish. If keenness flagged during the race, now with the line not far away it returns. If the boat has been out of touch with the others in the fleet, now they begin to converge from remarkably different directions, depending on tactics in recent hours. On some occasions it has been a close race around the course and never more so than at the finish. The finish line has to be identified with unseen officials in a committee boat or concealed in a building on shore. As in all racing the most advantageous part of the line is selected to cross and if our sample boat is in the first three in her class, a gun booms out. Already the crew will have a close idea of how they have fared in the race order. If she is a level rater or a one-design, then the sail ahead and astern give an immediate answer. If the whole fleet is on time allowances, then a rough calculation is possible; but if racing has been close the finishing order will have to wait until race officials have multiplied

Above: The ultimate yacht chart table on *Flyer* **(76ft, 23m) built 1981. Radio receivers, weather facsimile receiver, Hercules computerized sailing data, satellite navigation, precision barometer, pilot book shelf**

Right: The finish. An Italian ocean racer about to cross the Cowes finish line of the Royal Yacht Squadron

factors by elapsed times or subtracted time allowances (in minutes) from elapsed times to give a corrected time for each boat and therefore a finishing order.

Seconds after crossing the line, unless there is a long way to harbour with a fair wind, the skipper will be ordering the spinnaker or headsail down and the motor, banned for all these hours or days, except to charge the batteries with the propeller shaft firmly clamped, springs to life. The boat is upright, the crew alert only enough to sail and motor safely into harbour, which needs only a few of them. Within minutes of coming ashore, it is most emphatically a different world. The little things that were so important, the strange time scale of watches and sometimes covering ground for hour after hour at a quick walking pace, the elimination of most thoughts except those that affected the world of aluminium or glass fibre with the circle of the horizon around: all these things change back to the places of streets, houses and rooms and floors and chairs and beds that stay still and horizontal, making it hard to concentrate the mind that there they were, racing under sail at sea.

Above: This 60ft American Ocean racer, *Running Tide* built
in 1970 to Sparkman and Stephens design has been
continuously succesful for ten years. Many other boats
have come and gone. *Tide* has been steadily up-dated in
gear and sails, prevented from accumulating heavy gear
and been sailed with devotion

Below: The successful IOR racer *Imp*, (built 1977) designed
by Ron Holland to take every advantage of modern light
weight construction

Above: Up spinnaker! Halyard man pulls and it climbs out of the bag

Right: What yacht crews must contend with. A heavily reefed ocean racer beats to windward in a Mistral of 40 to 55 knots wind

Below: Down spinnaker! Spinnakers are handed under the newly set genoas as leaders in race alter course. The green spinnaker astern will have to come down soon if the user is not to steer a course to leeward

19

Power from the wind

Sails! At the end of this *Guide to Sailing*, we come back to the centre of it all. Sails are what differentiate the boats which use the wind instead of mechanical power. Sails are what the enthusiasts go aboard to heave and pull and set and stow. It is harnessing that wind power which is at the heart of it all. The systems on ocean racers which turn wind from (almost) every direction into forward motion are the most highly developed of all. For some the modern offshore rig may not be the ideal, but it is the forcing house for advancement in design and materials and risk-taking. Every year one or more of the latest designs in rigs collapse

into the sea, for there are few other ways in the sport of sailing to find out whether the latest ideas have gone too far or not. Indeed the rig on a boat is an undeniable nuisance and handicap, but it is there to hold those creamy sails to the wind and control them for best performance. Thus there is a constant effort to reduce the weight and windage of the rig without sacrifice of control and reliability.

The modern rig is partly a development of the IOR and other and previous rating rules, but since cruising yachts carry something very like it it cannot be that rule-orientated. To be fair, the rule makes restrictions and only a

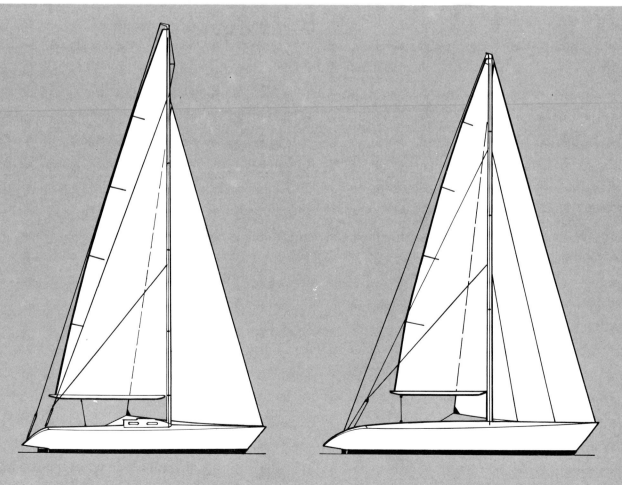

minority of cruising yachts ever bother to go outside them. How the offshore sailing rig would develop without any rules is a matter of conjecture and largely pointless, because the influence is there and would continue even if the IOR, other offshore rules, the 12-metre rule and one-design were abolished tomorrow. Racing rules and cruising conventions, to some extent arising from them, should be accepted as one of the influences besides the basic requirements of the rig which are: to be possible to handle, to stay up and to drive the boat.

In theory there is no limit to the number of masts that may be used, but most ocean racers have a single stick. Until recently it was usual in the larger sizes, say over 55ft (16·8m), to go for two masts in order to break up the sail plan into easily-handled segments, but this

is no longer the case and maxi yachts today (for instance on the 1981–82 round the world race) tend to carry everything on one tall mast. A single mast is more efficient per square foot with one huge headsail giving immense drive. As for three masts, such a configuration is not rated under IOR and occurs only in large non-IOR yachts.

Outside the IOR there are for instance all-headsail rigs, first widely seen on the 128ft (39m) *Vendredi Treize* in the 1972 single-handed transatlantic race. It is quite clear that this rig, now spread to at least one line of cruisers, is intended to be easy to handle and secure, but lacks great drive and the sail area exposed per amount of spars required is rather miserly. The IOR insists on a mainsail, or rather measures it whether it is there or not. Then

Three rigs of the 80s (to equal scales). The IOR fractional rig of *New Wave,* **designed by Bill Trip (LOA 40ft, 12·2m) and the masthead rig of** *Scaramouche,* **1981 American Admiral's Cup team boat, designed by German Frers (LOA 45ft, 13·7m). Both the latter have triple spreaders and** *New Wave* **has small jumper struts near masthead. Then the 2160ft², 200m², of the 65ft 7in (20m) trimaran** *Brittany Ferries,* **winner of the 1981 two-handed transatlantic race, has a big jumper strut lower down her mast. Unrestricted by rules, she has six battens in the mainsail leech (the others are confined to four)**

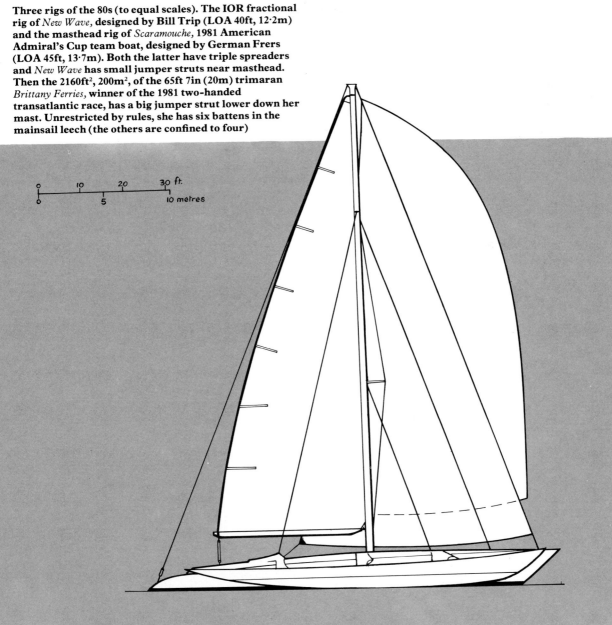

1

1: Junk rig for short handed sailing and easy control, but it lacks area and power

2: Close reaching under spinnaker. Too much wind and the boat will round up, temporarily out of control, (from left to right here)

3: Ready to gybe. Bow man has lazy guy in right hand and fore guy to pull pole end to himself in left. Man at mast is about to release pole end by remote control

4: Bloopers or big-boys, an additional running sail allowed by the IOR

5: A spinnaker on the large ocean racer *Bumblebee* splits as it is lowered

6: Freedom rigs eliminate headsails

7: Just before gybing *Irish Mist* rolls heavily to windward

8: A vicious roll to windward. The main boom could crash across and both the mainsail and spinnaker pin the yacht down out of control

3

2

4

5

6

7

8

there are various examples of all-mainsail rigs and these are allowed under the rating rule, though only seen in recent years on very small yachts. If such a sail lacks drive it is because of the interference of the mast ahead of it, a fate not suffered by headsails; therefore the next logical step is to incorporate the mast inside some effective aerofoil and this is done on C-class cats (see Part I) but 'wrap around luffs' are not permitted under IOR. The 'Freedom' design range employs wrap-round luffs and two or three unstayed masts with mainsails set only. The junk rig which has been used to cross oceans sets only one sail per mast (it can be a single mast or two), but a defect of these rigs is the lack of ability to increase area off the wind and it is fair to say that they do not sail close and fast to windward in the same way as single masted boats with conventional headsails.

Masts and spars

Back to the Bermudian sloop rig as most commonly seen and today's mast which is light alloy and held by a variety of staying. The light alloy mast is an extrusion, drawn out in the section of a die from molten aluminium alloy. The most used shapes are pear, oval and delta, the oval being used for the biggest yachts. Mast makers will have a range of sizes in stock and it is their task to turn these plain tubes into the complexity of a yacht mast. One immediate application is to taper the section towards the top where there is less compression and weight and windage can be reduced. The mast maker slits the tube along to a certain point, cuts out a narrow wedge and welds it up again. There is a certain minimum point below which the spar is going to collapse once any strain comes upon it, but frequently the choice lies between a thin-walled mast of large cross-section or a thick-walled mast of small cross-section (the terms are relative). The second will be heavier but create less windage. The rating rule gives a bonus for weight aloft, but not for windage, so the choice would appear to be the small section. However, it is not quite like this because the rating may already carry minimum CGF (the rating factor for weight aloft) and designers increase the amount of wire rigging to hold a mast of minimum scantlings aloft. They get thinner and thinner, year by year, with little increase of wall thickness. It may be thought that the extra rigging itself causes windage, but a wide mast is more damaging to air flow over the mainsail.

Light alloy is not the only material for masts, but it remains the most useful. It ousted wood in the early fifties, before which beautiful pale spruce was glued to make hollow masts, but heavier than metal, difficult to affix fittings and liable in due course to rot. Glass fibre has been tried, but is quickly ruled out because of heavy weight and lack of stiffness. Carbon fibre has been tried and a huge mast of this material was rigged on the round the world yacht *Heath's Condor* in 1977, but broke after a few thousand miles' sailing. She was re-rigged with light alloy. Soon after this a penalty was inserted into the IOR if materials other than alloy, wood, steel or glass fibre were used in spars and this has ruled out experiments in carbon fibre and other exotic material.

All sorts of gear is attached to the mast, the most obvious being the spreaders and standing rigging which hold the mast straight or at least to the desired degree of bend. Modern spreaders have aerofoil section and are heavily reinforced where they join the mast. Gone are the heavy and conspicuous tangs for attaching the wire rigging; instead it disappears into the mast through a slot with the attachment internal, or simply locks into the mast wall which has been found effective. Running rigging—halyards and lifts for sails and spinnaker gear—is invariably internal. It must exit near the bottom to go to winches on deck, but such exits must be well staggered. In the early days when such exits were placed at the same level, it was not long before such a designed mast tore off at the perforation. Exits for genoa and spinnaker halyards have become more and more refined, so the modern mast is remarkably clean and uncluttered. For instance the spinnaker halyard can exit from a groove, subject to fairing either side of it. Until recently it was considered that the halyard must pass through a free suspended block to avoid chafe. The latter arrangement is still best for cruisers and for long distance racers where undue chafe on the halyard is not acceptable. Up inside the mast as well as halyards goes wiring for the lighting as described below and this must not be chafed, so should be in its own conduit. More wire is needed for the radio aerial, wind speed and direction indicator. Some older masts, or ocean cruisers, may have a mast track running right up for the mainsail which carries sliders. The great advantage of this arrangement is that the

Fittings drilled at the same level around this mast were the main cause of dismasting

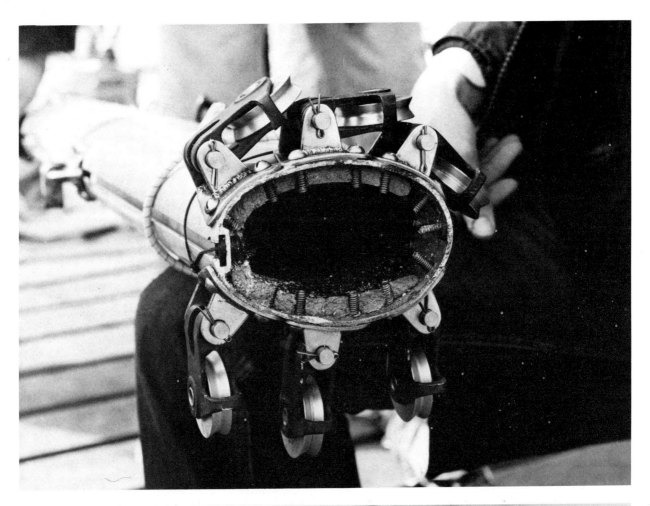

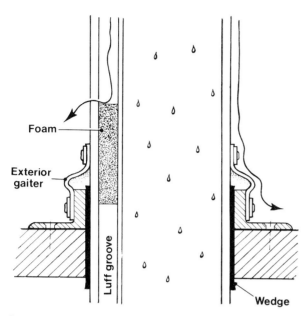

A mast must be watertight at deck. This is achieved by an exterior gaiter and plugging luff groove. Solid arrows indicate exterior water flow. Some drips are inevitable via sheaves and rigging, but will drain to foot of mast and thence direct to bilge

mainsail remains attached to the mast when it is lowered and thus easy to control. On all modern racing boats, the mainsail groove merely passes up a slot in the extrusion. When the mainsail is lowered, the whole thing can blow away and needs grabbing and lashing by the crew. The groove is fairly fool proof, whereas slides can break off and track be damaged. Certainly by closing the gap it is better aerodynamically and it is cheaper. When reefing, the slides do not have to be fed off and back when making sail and generally the groove has it.

On the forward side of the mast, at least as high up as the rating rule allows, is the spinnaker track and gear to hoist and lower the heel. If the mast is keel stepped which is preferable, the bottom part will be quite smooth and this runs down into the accommodation: only wiring emerges from it. An effective mast coat and flange is needed to prevent leaks down the mast into the cabin and any mainsail groove must be blocked right off at and above deck level to stop water pouring in. Some drips are bound to enter halyard exits and run down inside the mast and thence to the cabin sole or bilge.

Most mastheads have an array of equipment. There will be an electronic wind strength and direction indicator and an additional wind vane (such as a Windex), there is a VHF aerial and most boats now have a tricolour navigation

light allowed by the international collision regulations since 1976. When motoring, a white steaming light has to be shown on the forward side of the mast and this can be fitted a short way above the spinnaker track. Other fittings on the mast will be the gooseneck where the main boom is connected and the anchorage for the kicking strap. This must be vertically below the point at which the boom swings, otherwise as the mainsheet is let off, the kicking strap pulls tighter and tighter. Cleats may be needed on the mast (for the spinnaker topping lift for example), but they are better together with winches on deck so that they do not foul lines passing by the mast, particularly the genoa sheets when tacking. On short handed boats, masts may be seen rigged with mast climbing steps all the way up. On fully crewed boats, they are unnecessary (a bosun's chair will be used with at least two men to heave a third up) and are extra weight/windage and can even foul halyards at times.

The main boom is more humble, simple and easily got at by the crew! It needs to be efficiently arranged, however, so that the mainsheet controls the sail, for pulling out the clew to flatten the sail and with reefing gear to reduce sail. If the sail is reefed by rolling it round the boom, then the latter must be circular, but roller reefing is less popular than it was in the sixties and indeed has not been seen in new ocean racers for many years. Rather than extol the merits of slab or jiffy reefing (as pulling pre-arranged areas of the mainsail out of use is termed), which can be a struggle to use in heavy weather (and you are not going to do reefing in light), it is worth looking at the disadvantages of roller reefing. It is an example of how yachts are primitive compared with modern life, and purposely so because yachting is a sport and calls, as we have mentioned before, for manual power only. A roller boom has to be clear of all fittings, so a kicking strap is not possible, the mainsheet can only be on the end of a swivel (both can use a device called a claw ring which allows the sail to roll up inside it, but it is a poor fitting and chafes the sail. The boom may bend because the sheet is at one end. When the sail is reefed it tends to become baggy with folds, whereas as the wind increases a flattening of the sail is required. Additionally the boom tends to droop.

Slab reefing works well if the leads for the reef pennants have been carefully sited, winches are easily available to wind down the reef and the crew can work easily at the foot of the mast to pull the luff cringle down to a simple hook at the tack. The problem arises with the third reef, which is going to be in use in severe conditions (on a 35ft yacht going to windward, say, first reef at 22 knots, second at 30 knots of wind, third at 36 knots (force 8)). The boom only has two pennants and the tack has two hooks. It therefore becomes necessary to clear the first reef pennant (the second already being in use) and re-reeve it up the leech. This is a bad job in such conditions. One tip is to have a messenger line already through the leech cringle and this is used to haul the third reef pennant up through it and down back to the boom. Better systems for reducing sail will no doubt be devised in the future (the mast furling mainsail has been mentioned already).

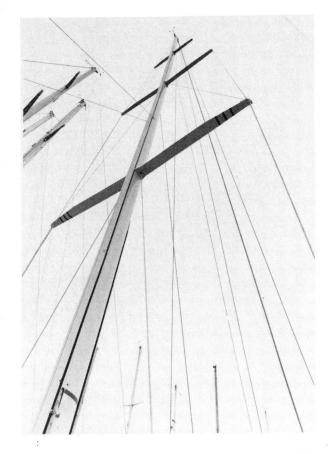

The slender mast head three-spreader rig of a modern ocean racer

Mast head fittings can include wind indicators (electronic and visual), tricolour navigation light and VHF aerial

Standing rigging varies in arrangement with the design of rig and is commonly made of 1 × 19 stainless steel wire or rods which stretch less, but which must be treated with great care when stepping and taking down. Several reliable end fitting terminals are used and these lock to rigging screws at deck for tightening down or the correct type of fitting for attachment to the mast itself near the root of the spreader or near the masthead. The big choice of rig is whether it should be masthead or fractional. In very general terms fractional rig is favoured for boats of less than Admiral's Cup size where it gives more area for the rating, but above this size masthead rig is most common. The big boats cannot pull the rig about, a technique which is required to gain best advantage of fractional rig; the heavy sail cloth of the mainsail will not respond to shape controls and the stresses on the rig mean it has to be largely left set up. Big boats are less often at maximum speed than small ones, which reach their maximum in lower wind speeds, and it is less advantageous for

Half Tonner (rating 22ft) (Roller Coaster design) showing standing rigging: forestay, adjustable backstay, running backstays, upper, intermediate and lower shrouds. (LOA 31ft 3in, 9·5m. Displacement 5750lb, 2613kg)

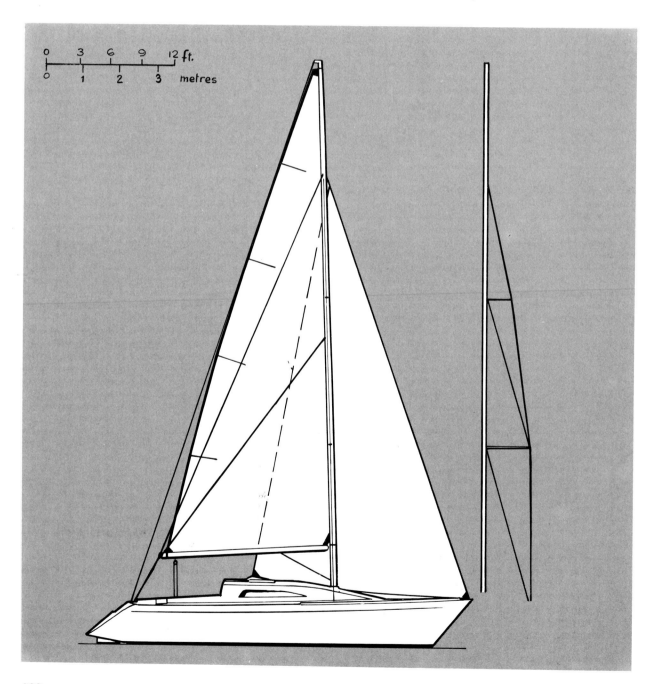

them to be of light displacement, where fractional rig pays off. Fractional rig requires running backstays to support the forestay and additional runners are usually fitted lower down to regulate mast bend. A skilled crew is needed to let these off and set them up again to windward, when tacking and gybing. There is a history of lost masts, when a runner has fouled and released in some way. So the fractional rig of the eighties has a rating gain and a thin mast and demands close control for maximum performance and safety.

1981 fractional rig to IOR rating. Note very thin mast section and multiplicity of rigging

The masthead rig simply means that the forestay goes to the head of the mast. Runners are only required on yachts over 40ft with certain types of rig. A simple single spreader rig is commonly seen on small racing boats and cruisers. It was very much in favour until about 1975. Forestay, backstay, upper shroud, lower shroud and inner forestay are enough to hold it. On some boats a second lower shroud gives support aft against the inner forestay forward.

The inner forestay can be removed and forward lower shrouds fitted. This makes the spar more rigid (they cannot be adjusted like an inner forestay) and is not seen on racing boats. It

means more anchorage points below decks and extra weight/windage. Another variation on the masthead single spreader rig is spreaders swept distinctly aft, say to at least 15 degrees. This prevents the mast bowing aft, and no aft lowers or inner forestay are therefore required. A disadvantage is that the shrouds come far enough aft to stop the main boom being squared-off on a run and there is considerable loading at the spreader roots. The tendency now is to go to double or even treble spreaders for masthead rig allowing a smaller mast section and short spreaders, which in turn means the genoa can be sheeted in close when sailing to windward. On a two spreader rig there will be upper, intermediate and lower shrouds and these can all come to the same securing point at deck (the top of a massive chain plate going down into the hull). An inner forestay meets the mast in the panel between the two spreaders and the runners at the same place. In boats up to about 36ft, if a mast section with adequate fore and aft strength is chosen, such running backstays are not needed. There will be a backstay. Such are the masting systems readily available for the 'simple sloop' masthead rig; small variations and inventive designs are also seen every season.

Hydraulics are frequently used to control tension in the rigging of ocean racing boats. The backstay is the rigging most commonly adjusted, and tensioning it when on the wind takes up some of the load in the forestay caused by the genoa. The kicking strap may also be fitted with a hydraulic ram which holds the boom exactly at the desired angle. An IOR clause prevents any hydraulic adjustment to the forestay, and before this was introduced the entire rig could be swivelled fore and aft. Hydraulic systems are used because they allow manual application combined with speed, whereas previous simple screw mechanisms were insufficient. Hydraulics are neat, allow remote control with a short stroke and applying a high load without further locking. An inner forestay hydraulic can apply mast bend. Unfortunately, hydraulics introduce expense and an additional possibility of rig failure into racing for dubious extra enjoyment. Although the IOR allows them, except on forestays, they are banned in one-design classes and never seen on cruising yachts.

Hydraulic rigging tensioner

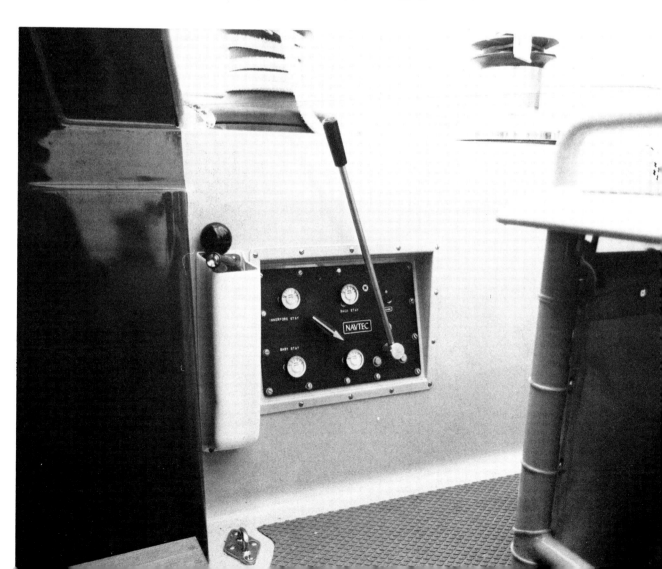

Sails and material

By the end of the eighties, sails will be made of unwoven film with no stretch, with easy folding properties, extreme lightness (making the boat heel less with less weight aloft) and the ability to suit a wide range of wind speeds for any one weight of material. Meanwhile sailmakers continue to experiment with cloth to achieve this ideal which has come since the last century via flax, then Egyptian cotton for many years until man-made fibres brought Terylene (Dacron) and Nylon, the latter for spinnakers and the former for every other sail. Special Dacron weaves have given soft and smooth sails; and the life expectancy and convenience when compared with natural fibres has been immense. The more recent Mylar and Kevlar film are laminated to old style Dacron to give a very lightweight two ply sail. As yet the film cannot be used on its own as it would not be tear resistant. The Mylar/Dacron still has to be made in panels and cut with skill like a conventional sail, but it keeps its shape in a greater range of wind speeds and is lighter in weight. Kevlar, a more expensive synthetic, makes a stiffer sail which can keep a more exact shape. Both these materials are hard film and do not fold well. They show thousands of minute creases when they have been stowed away a number of times but, apparently this makes no difference to the performance and longevity of the sail.

Sail cloth weights using terylene (dacron) or, in the case of spinnakers, nylon. The American ounce weight is the most frequently quoted, as much of the most sought after quality cloth for racing is imported from the USA into Europe for making into sails. The synthetic fibres are specially woven for yacht sail making.

Type of sail	USA ounces	UK ounces
Spinnakers of nylon		
Floater (very light)	0·5	0·63
All purpose	0·85	1·1
	1·00	1·3
Heavy reaching	1·5	1·9
'Storm'	2·2	2·8
	2·6	3·3
Headsails of dacron		
Light Genoa	3·5	4·3
Heavy Genoa (small yacht)	5·5	6·7
Heavy Genoa (big yacht)	6·0	7·6
For heavier winds	7·0	9·1
	8·0	10·3
	10·0	12·6
Mainsails of dacron		
Small yachts	5·5	6·7
Medium yachts	6·5	8·3
(30–45ft)	8·5	11·0
Big yachts	9·0	11·5
	10·0	12·3
	12·0	15·1

Typical sail cloth weights are shown in the table for conventional Dacron and Nylon. A range of weights is set aside for mainsails, genoas (and jibs) and spinnakers respectively.

The design of sails

The mainsail is the one sail that is in use at all times, except in a severe gale, when a storm trysail may be hoisted instead. Under the IOR a yacht is rated for a mainsail of a minimum area and so inevitably carries one. In any case, besides its actual addition to the total driving sail area it has two other functions in an ocean racer beating to windward. It acts as a rudder in the air, not exactly to steer to either side, but to be trimmed to have a major effect on the feel in the yacht's own rudder. Easing the mainsheet relieves weather helm, in other words a strong pull on wheel or tiller with a tendency for the yacht to try and head into the wind. Secondly, it acts as a support for the mast, which could tend to pant and flex under the influence of a big masthead genoa alone. The mainsail is less efficient than a genoa and in masthead rig it is not really the *main* sail, as the genoa will be larger and give more power per square foot, because the mainsail has the mast ahead breaking up the air flow over it. It can, however, be adjusted much more exactly by using the following controls:

(a) The mainsheet on a traveller. In light airs this traveller is hauled up to windward to help give the sail plenty of curve and strapped down to leeward in strong winds. Once reaching or running, the traveller is no longer effective as the mainsheet is not pulling vertically down.

(b) The kicking strap then comes into its own stopping the boom from lifting when the mainsheet no longer has a downward component. Pictures of old yachts (before 1960) show no kicking strap and huge booms lifting, causing the sail to be an uncontrollable, full shape. Dinghies were using kicking straps for thirty years before that.

(c) The main halyard tension has the same effect as on any other sail. Tightening it flattens the sail and when the wind eases or the yacht comes off the wind, the sail will be seen with vertical creases near the luff. As the halyard is eased, so the sail assumes a smooth shape.

(d) The clew outhaul is another flattener or easer. It needs a really powerful tackle or winch so that the sail can be pulled out against all the friction in the boom groove as the breeze gets up. A black band limits the amount under the rating rule to which it may be extended (maximum foot dimension).

(e) The leech line, a thin cord running up the seam at the leech, adjusts the 'pucker' of the edge between the sail battens (which are themselves another form of control) allowing the curve of the sail, the roach, to be extended. In general terms, the leech line will be tightened off the wind and slacked when beating, or when there appears to be excess tension between the ends of the batten pockets.

(f) The flattener or leech cunningham is a cringle about a foot above the clew (depending on the size of sail and boat) through which a reef pennant is rove. As the wind increases to around 20 knots, this is hauled down by winch, which lifts the boom and flattens the whole sail. Before this system was in general use, there was a luff cunningham (named after the helmsman) who invented a simple hole in the sail) which tightened the luff, also flattening the sail. In earlier times the gooseneck could be hauled down on a slider, but this was limited by the rating black bands on the sail. The leech cunningham means there is maximum area for the sail under the rating in light weather, but that it can be tightened and tautened without going outside the limits as the wind strengthens.

Headsails

Headsail development has caused many complaints as the IOR progressed. Modern sails are large and need huge winches and big crews to hoist them, trim them and claw them back down below when the wind pipes up. There are too many of them and the sailmakers encourage the 'arms race' of the foretriangle, suggesting every size and type of sail to be hung in it for different conditions. There is much truth in all this, but the modern genoa is a great driver with its synthetic materials and sheets, and controlled by powerful winches. In earlier times, it was just not possible to hang on to such sails; wooden masts and stretching cotton sails would not have stood it. So they are fun and after all, if there is a large crew, it gives them plenty to do to change headsails for different wind

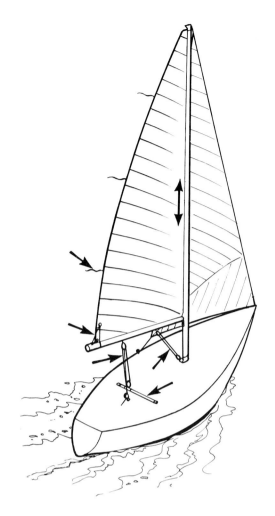

Mainsail controls consist of halyard tension, leech cunningham (near clew), kicking strap (vang), mainsheet, mainsheet track and leech tell tales to assist correct trim

strengths and direction and gain maximum performance by being in the 'right gear'. The IOR limits the number of headsails (and spinnakers) for respective sizes of yacht, but not very stringently. The rules are the result of compromises, with a strong sailmakers' lobby, and changes for several years until they were finalized (in 1978); since when there have been small adjustments. A boat between 29 and 33ft rating (small Admiral's Cup size) can carry nine genoas or jibs and four spinnakers: with a mainsail and trysail on board, this means 15 sails on board, not to mention spares on shore on which there is no restriction. In yachts over 45ft rating there are no sail restrictions. The rule makers felt that cost was little account in this size and the owners preferred to plan their own complex sail plans. A large ocean racer (say 50ft LOA) might well carry four *full size* genoas. These are apparently all the same size and shape, but are of different weights and cut

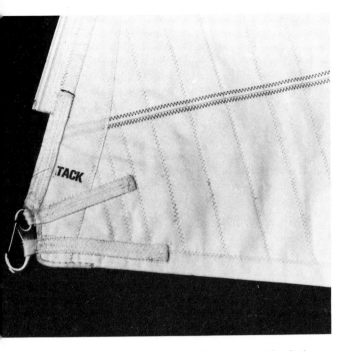

Genoa tack reinforcement with Wichard hook for fitting to loop on deck

(fuller or flatter). For instance a drifter (very light, maybe Nylon), light No. 1 of 2·5oz Mylar, regular No. 1 of 6oz Dracon and heavy No. 1 of 8·2oz Dracon. Only when some or all of these have been used in a theoretical wind increasing slowly from calm to fresh breeze, would there be a change to a smaller area No. 2 genoa of 9oz. The silhouettes of headsails show many of the variations (one boat would not have all of these) in fore and aft headsails. There are sails to go to windward, for reaching and for carrying under spinnakers when reaching or running. Genoas and jibs adjust less than mainsails because they are each for a limited set of conditions. Adjustments are by halyard tension (powerful winches are needed to increase luff tension when the sail is in use), obviously sheeting (in or out) and sheet lead position, using a fairlead on a track or selection of tracks, and by leech line. There are several restrictions on headsails under the IOR. Stiffening in the form of head and clew boards or extra cloth is forbidden, battens are not allowed except in small jibs. Big boys or bloopers are genoas set flying and used with the spinnaker and to windward of it; these are limited in luff length and fulness.

Spinnakers give the most exhilarating rides and some most frightening situations; they give the finest photographs and the most unwelcome sights to crews on occasions. Under the IOR they have developed into specialized racing sails and races are won and lost on selecting the right spinnaker, hoisting and lowering it at the right moment and without mishap and sailing the boat to her optimum under it. The attraction of the spinnaker under the IOR is that it gives much more area than is shown on the rating certificate, though its dimensions are strictly related to the height of mast and length of base of foretriangle. Off the wind more sail is needed and the hoisting of the spinnaker to increase the area vastly is logical. What has been developed is the ability to carry these sails with the wind abeam or even forward of the beam with all the extra, area given. The IOR limits the characteristics of the spinnaker: it must be symmetrical (no bogus genoas) it can only have a sheet at one corner and one pole at the other, it is not allowed leech lines, the distance between the points at the centre of each edge (luff/leech interchangeable) must not be less than 75 per cent of foot length (this keeps them distinct from genoas again).

Within these restrictions the sailmaker is able to cut sails for different wind strengths and for reaching or running with the wind nearly aft. An all-round sail today is the tri-radial spinnaker, very commonly seen, with vertical panels at the top and horizontal ones in the middle. Radial seams extend from the corners. This sail emerged after the 1974 America's Cup trials and the construction of panels has eliminated distortion which used to occur with earlier cross cut sails. A yacht allowed to carry four spinnakers might have two of these, one simply a spare because spinnakers are prone to damage. Then a heavy spinnaker might be carried somewhat less than maximum size and cut flat allowing for strong winds and reaching where it is sheeted in as far as possible. For light weather a floater is carried. This is a spinnaker of 0·5oz nylon, probably cut as a radial head. This is a close cousin to the tri-radial, with the vertical panels near the head, but horizontal all the way to the foot, giving less seams which add weight because no great strain is expected on the corners. If strain comes, then it is time to change to the all round tri-radial which is probably 0·75oz on a vast range of boats from 25 to 60ft LOA.

Spinnakers work on the same principle as any other sail with a luff and leech: the sail is sheeted in the closer the boat is to the wind. The difference is that it is only suspended at each corner. Thus control problems follow with, dramatic results. One of the ultimate skills in racing a big boat is to sail her down wind in

Typical headsails on a masthead rig

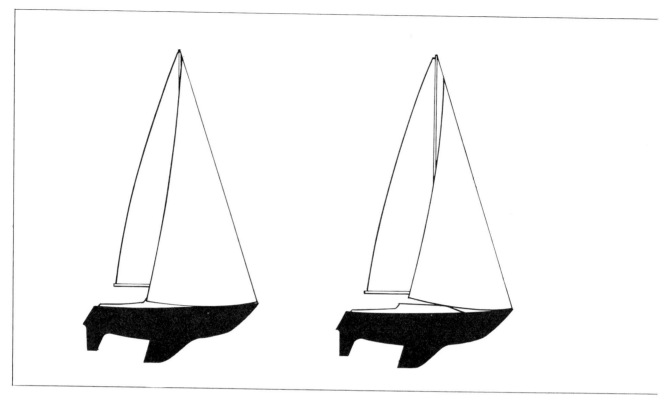

a   Full size genoa, there may be two or three sails this size, light, heavy etc

b   No. 2 genoa for 20 to 30 knot winds

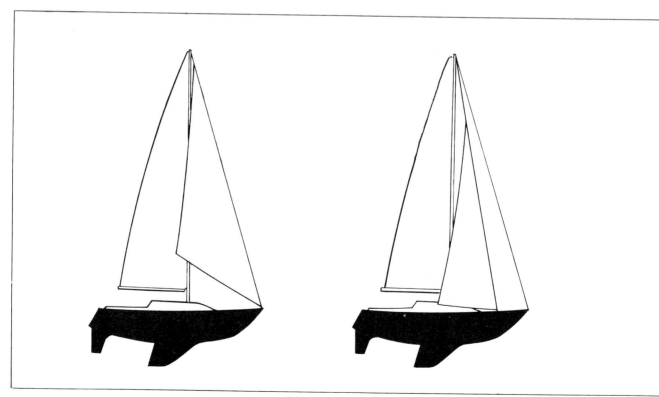

e   Blast reacher. Small high cut sail for reaching in heavy weather

f   Tall spinnaker staysail. A sail for setting in addition to a spinnaker or another headsail

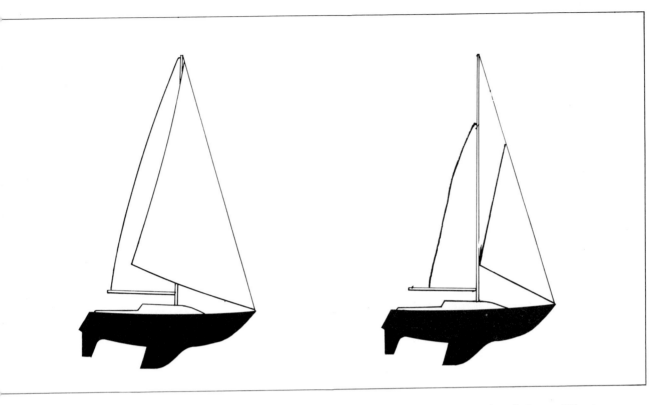

c   **Reacher, high cut but full size under the rule**

d   **No. 4 jib (working jib), for winds over 35 knots**

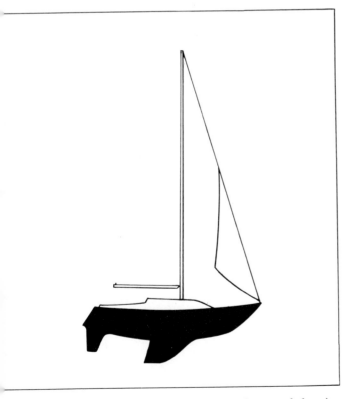

g   **Storm jib. For severe conditions (45 knots and above). Compulsory safety equipment of regulated maximum size**

a breeze. Only experience can ensure this is done in a way to be admired, but here is what ought to be done to get it right.

The spinnaker pole is adjusted parallel to the water (not the deck, if the boat is heeling) using the topping lift and at right angles (or up to 15 degrees less when reaching) to the wind. The foreguy on the end of the pole is kept taut at all times, it stabilizes the sail and prevents it suddenly blowing aloft. The spinnaker sheet is eased as much as possible so there is just a curl in the luff of the spinnaker: it is hand held, but taken round a winch all the time. As the wind strengthens, a second person can be available to wind the winch. The pole is moved up and down (both ends) so that the centre seam of the spinnaker is vertical at all times. The halyard is eased off a few feet or so in dead running or heavy weather, otherwise it can be tight up to the spinnaker halyard block. As for the helmsman he must work closely with the spinnaker (sheet) trimmer, bearing away slightly as the wind increases, luffing a little as it eases. In this way he follows the wind round, because change of strength means change of apparent direction. In strong winds this prevents that broach and in light winds it keeps the boat going when she would run away from the wind with her own speed.

And what of a spinnaker broach? It can be amusing, eventually tiring, sometimes dangerous. The yacht rounds up under her press of sail, the helmsman no longer able to keep her on course. The most common occasion for this is with the wind on the beam and pole nearly on the forestay and the spinnaker sheeted in hard: any closer to the wind and it would be time to drop the spinnaker. Suddenly the helmsman finds he can hold the boat no longer. She rounds up into the wind, the main boom trailing the water, the hull heeling acutely, the spinnaker flogging with reports like a cannon. The helmsman with the tiller round his neck or the wheel hard over can only wait while the main spinnaker sheets have been let go, the strain comes off and the boat begins to bear away again. Then it is in on the sheets and sail away, hoping such a windward broach will not

happen again, though it probably will on the next puff.

More dangerous and frightening is the broach to leeward. This occurs when running nearly dead down wind. It all starts when the boat begins a rhythmic roll, first heavily so the main boom touches, or nearly touches, the water, then the other way so it is the turn of the spinnaker pole. Trouble begins on one of the rolls towards the spinnaker ('windward', though windward is really astern), the main boom now high in the air gybes itself; now both sails are on the same side and the boat rounds

Nicholson 30 in near gale conditions rounds up in a broach under spinnaker despite easing sheet . . .

up with them trailing to leeward; this time releasing the spinnaker sheet does little to help, because the spinnaker is already pinned by the breeze almost on the water. The boat may come up, gybe back and hurtle on her way, or she may remain pinned down. In the latter case the only course may be to release the spinnaker halyard—then all is quickly quiet, though the race is no doubt lost as the competitors stream away at speed.

Using a boom vang to prevent gybing does not help and can make matters worse, because the main is subsequently pinned down by the vang. Cures for this sort of incident include carrying a small flat spinnaker, overtrimming sheet and pole to flatten the spinnaker further, trying to steer so as not to add to the tendency to roll by heavy rudder changes, concentrating crew weight aft to keep the rudder well into the water even when rolling and taking the spinnaker sheet well forward through a snatch block at the rail. Some say hoisting a big-boy (blooper) helps by balancing the sail on each side, but it is advice of desperation for, if the yacht broaches with that up as well, the mess aloft will be that much worse. The weight of men on the foredeck trying to set the extra sail may unbalance the boat and cause the broach.

Such incidents occur only in the cause of getting the maximum speed out of an ocean racing yacht under the rules as they exist. They are one extreme of a sport and a life whose existence depends on the wind across the seas, rivers and lakes. What a wealth of ways we have found to enjoy it.

. . . she is out of control with sails flogging and slamming

Index

238